"If I had
  it to do over again . . . "

"If I had
it to do over again..."

AMERICA'S ADULT DROPOUTS

by Robert S. Gallagher

E. P. Dutton & Co., Inc. *New York 1969*

6-78-21

Published simultaneously in Canada by
Clarke, Irwin & Company Limited, Toronto and Vancouver

Library of Congress Catalog Card Number: 69–10297

A16235 [01]

REQUIESCANT IN PACE

Robert Sylvester Sertell
1878–1968

Anna Handschy Sertell
1882–1968

Acquainted with the Night

I have been one acquainted with the night.
I have walked out in rain—and back in rain.
I have outwalked the furthest city light.

I have looked down the saddest city lane.
I have passed by the watchman on his beat
And dropped my eyes, unwilling to explain.

I have stood still and stopped the sound of feet
When far away an interrupted cry
Came over houses from another street,

But not to call me back or say goodbye;
And further still at an unearthly height,
One luminary clock against the sky

Proclaimed the time was neither wrong nor right.
I have been one acquainted with the night.

—ROBERT FROST

Contents

"If I had it to do over again . . . "

I

An Open Gate

> Lewis H. Come home or contact us.
> Everything will be alright.
> Children crying. Your loving wife.

Someone is missing. His family does not know where he is or how to reach him or why he left. Outwardly he was a doting father, a dutiful husband, an enterprising business-man, with a house in the suburbs. Weekday mornings he went to work; weekday evenings he returned from work.

One night, instead of coming home, he disappeared.

Instinct, logic, necessity, and the investigators all tell us that this sort of thing could not happen today in our well-structured society. Yet it does. It happens at any hour of every day. With bewildering regularity, people, men and women, just go away. They abandon families and property and lucrative jobs and credit ratings and friends. They are never seen or heard from again, and their relatives do not know whether they are still alive.

But they are.

One of them, as a matter of fact, is sitting over there at the narrow end of the bar, where it corners before the unwashed front window. That man, the one with the untouched glass of draft beer by his elbow. He has ordered a sandwich. While he waits, he casually studies the sports pages.

Every city is pockmarked with such gathering spots. In New York, these bars remain open twenty hours a day in those areas where workingmen live and seek employ. Indirect lighting softens their harsh interiors and camouflages much of the dirt. The food is hot and plentiful, the conversation muted and pedestrian. The toilets reek of perfumed disinfectant, and there are wire traps in the urinals.

For us, what distinguishes this particular East Side Manhattan tavern is its unusual patron. He is the night foreman at a nearby service establishment. He has worked there, regularly and dependably, for approximately five years. He was described by his employer not long ago on a questionnaire for group insurance as an "easygoing man who makes sure the work gets done on his shift."

That shift begins at 3 P.M. There is a thirty-minute meal break at seven o'clock. The plant workers customarily take a quarter-hour "slide" at the end of the shift, which deposits them back on the sidewalk before eleven. Sometimes this man will stop by this tavern for a nightcap before returning to the privacy of his furnished room a few blocks away. But he invariably lunches here, arriving between 2:20 and 2:35 P.M. His presence is an unspoken signal to the bartender, who draws him a beer and then scrounges around for an extra copy of the New York *Post*. Meanwhile, he studies the menu, chalked on a blackboard near the grill. The fare changes slightly from day to day, mainly in the consistency of the gravy. He gives the bartender his order and immediately turns the tabloid over to the sports section on the back. His luncheon habits have become a minor routine that approaches ritual.

The man is almost bald. He is of medium height and weight. His features—their blandness accentuated by his continuous forehead—are rather ordinary. His clothes, neat and subdued, do not set him apart from his fellow workers. His expression is generally placid. He is not what you might call a conversationalist. Whenever someone does speak to him, he has a way of smiling slightly and instinctively. His answers, if indeed he does answer and not merely nod his head, are perfunctory and do not encourage further discourse. Even in a crowded tavern, he gives the impression of being somehow separate, although he does not appear to brood about it. Most of the other regular patrons know him only by one of those incongruous nicknames that strike the listener as funny so long as one does not think about them too much.

He has a name, obviously. It is not, however, the name that appears on his employment records, that his landlord knows him by, that the bartender calls him when he cashes his paycheck on Tuesday nights. This other name, his real name, is typed on his birth certificate. It has been embossed on several diplomas and one honorable discharge from the United States Army. He wrote it himself on his marriage license. He used this other name faithfully during the first forty-one years of his life.

It also appears on his death certificate.

A dead man sitting in a bar, reading a newspaper?

The contradiction is not easily resolved, but it can be simply explained. His demise was the logical assumption of a judge, not the conclusive verdict of a coroner. Certainly he is alive; legally he is presumed dead. The evidence of his passing consisted primarily of a lack of proof that he did not die, which is not, on reflection, an especially comforting proposition.

In the summer of 1954, this man—let us call him Wakefield*—was working in the accounting department of his

---

* Named after the central character in "Wakefield," a short story by Nathaniel Hawthorne, published in 1835. His Wakefield, a London businessman of Means and Intellect, capriciously abandoned his wife and, for the next twenty years, lived in disguise a few blocks away. Hawthorne considered his subject an Outcast of the Universe, because, he wrote, Wakefield "had contrived, or rather he had happened, to dissever himself from the world—to vanish—to give up his place and privilege with living men, without being admitted among the dead."

father-in-law's factory in a city some twelve hundred miles from this tavern. His wife and three children were vacationing at her parents' summer cottage at a lake fifty miles from the plant. He did not return to the office after lunch that final Friday, but he frequently left early to join his family for long weekends at the lake. This weekend, by prearrangement, he did not. Four days passed before anyone realized that he had disappeared. There was little publicity about the incident. The police declined to disclose the contents of the note his wife found when she hurried home.

Unsuccessful searches were conducted by, among others, two private detective agencies. No one seemed to have any idea where he could have gone or, more importantly, why. A brother did tell the investigators that Wakefield had expressed a vague dissatisfaction with his life, but insisted that he had not heard from him and did not know where he was. For several years, quiet inquiries were pressed by the wife's family, mostly among relatives and former acquaintances.

Then, in 1963, Mrs. Wakefield petitioned the county Superior Court for a legal declaration of death. Attached were the negative reports of the detective agencies, a photostatic copy of the note her husband had left, and sworn statements from members of the family and several friends to the effect that the missing man had not been heard from or of since the day he had vanished. No dissenting testimony was introduced. After a brief discussion in private with the wife and her attorneys, the judge issued the declaration in October 1963.

As far as the law was concerned, Wakefield, if not dead, was no longer living.

His widow, as an extra precaution and at the urging of her fiancé, flew to Alabama for a divorce. She had been remarried seven months when she learned that her first husband was alive. On the basis of the legal decision, as Wakefield's beneficiary, she had filed for death benefits on his two life-insurance policies. One of the companies quickly responded by announcing its determination to rebut her claim. After a conference between lawyers for the family and the company, she withdrew both of her requests for benefits, and the matter was dropped. Even four years later, however, no effort had been made to reverse the court edict.

How had the company located the missing man? The investigator, who on that first spring afternoon in the tavern had pointed Wakefield out to me, would not say, beyond the broad hint that the man had maintained contact with his brother. The company's investigative procedures, he emphasized, were subordinate to its defense of the privacy of its missing policyholder. The evidence submitted to the wife's attorneys had simply demonstrated the absentee's continuing existence, not disclosed his current whereabouts, he said. As far as the investigator knew, Wakefield himself was unaware that he had been located by anyone.

"Bastard" and "idiot" are two epithets that come quickly to mind. After all, who but an idiotic bastard would voluntarily walk away from a wife, three children, a comfortable home, and a well-paying position with social tenure? And for what? A menial job under near-sweatshop conditions in a strange city, without friends and with an unfamiliar name; a cramped and lonely room full of secondhand furniture.

This is one reaction. Other people, with equal justification, might characterize him as irresponsible, neurotic, immature, cowardly, weak, insensitive, demented, even misanthropic. The defense waives right to rebuttal. Legally he has committed the crime of desertion; morally he is guilty of self-indulgence far exceeding the permissible limits of pride; the spiritual depravity of his act would shock his minister or priest or rabbi; he would be considered an incomprehensible failure by anyone who values his attendance record at Rotary. Depending upon the perspective, Wakefield is probably all of these things—and more.

But invective mainly declaims; it seldom defines. The same abuse may be leveled—in some cases with greater accuracy—at many persons who have not abandoned family, position, and identity. No mitigation is intended here. Appearances are not deceiving, but neither are they always self-explanatory. Particularly in this extreme circumstance. There is a deeper, more essential significance to this man, and it lies not so much in the nature as in the direction of his example.

Wakefield is an adult dropout from the middle class. He has flouted the fundamental assumption of our society: improvement. By so doing, he has denied the root function of each father's son to ensure the outdistancing of the previous generation. He has exercised an individual option to reverse the thrust of our national success ethic. He has made personal, if private, witness of his renunciation of the American Dream—or at least the portion that had become for him an empty cliché.

The qualification is necessary and important. Wakefield is, in a word, apolitical. He is motivated by no conscious philosophical malaise; he seeks neither to convert nor to influence nor to malign. Unlike today's flower children who rebel en masse from what they sincerely view as repugnant but have not experienced, he has rejected that which has failed to fulfill him. This valid distinction endows him with an authority lacking in our recent collective dissent, the so-called hippie movement.

The generation gap is inevitable, natural, and frequently healthy. It has ever existed; it always will. Each next generation will continue to have a great deal to say, one way or another; and each older generation will have much to learn from this unequal dialogue—and vice versa. But the fact remains that basically youth has only two choices: to revolt or not to revolt. The painful reality of age, in this context, is the heaping on of inconclusive alternatives that eventually diminish for adults the possibility of simple, meaningful confrontation.

Confrontation—visible and dramatic and direct, but most of all visible—is the *raison d'être* of the hippie movement. And this is why its affected followers are merely rebels and not bona fide dropouts. Their uniforms and manners and mores, programmed for angry contrast, are thus proscribed by the loyal opposition. And this is the principal reason that the movement will evaporate, if indeed it has not already begun to, the minute it ceases to concern anyone, as the saying goes, over thirty.

In contrast, Wakefield's voluntary retreat to less complicated circumstances was a private decision. His systematic and symbolic identity conversion contained no vibrant message for the rest of humanity. When he vanished, he was not protesting the fact of middle-class existence; rather—by refusing society's proffered alternatives to an unsuccessful marriage, an unproductive job, an uncomfortable status—he was discarding the very notion. This essential difference is precisely why there must ultimately be more meaning for the rest of us in the measured act of one desperate adult than in the instinctive, undisciplined gyrations of a thousand or a hundred thousand teen-agers.

One adult? Hardly. If Wakefield were alone, if his extreme deed were only the callous calculated performance of a disenchanted *isolato,* we should be compelled by his numerical irrelevance to ignore him, to pity him, to forget him. But he is not alone, as we shall see. There are others, many, many others, some of whom we shall meet, glimpse at strategic moments, hear their scattered and cloaked utterances, share vicariously a degree of their anguish, and never really know. Except perhaps intuitively.

There is no point in pretending otherwise. What is involved is the difference between knowing a person and knowing a lot about a person. The information, the data, the dates, the surface symptoms of darker inner turmoil—this is all the matter of record, but it is hardly an open gate to understanding. The most charitable thing that can be said of most of these people is that they are nonconformists, and the most accurate generalization that can be made of nonconformists is that they prefer not to conform even to other nonconformists.

In this special syndrome, however, their activities pass through a number of common reference points, where they will be introduced for purposes of illustration. Separately, each has his or her own necessity. Collectively, in assemblage, they have the capacity to answer, even though inadequately, some of the important unasked questions about the content and quality of the daily routine in the United States today. They speak primarily to the inner ear, however. Publicly, they are mute, and the factual frameworks from which they disappear will serve mainly as impersonal orientation, much as familiar shore lights position the midnight swimmer.

Consider, for example, that uninformative item which appeared in the daily Public Notices column on page 62 of *The New York Times* for Tuesday, February 28, 1956:

> Lewis H. Come home or contact us.
> Everything will be alright.
> Children crying. Your loving wife.

Some of these cryptic messages, despite the vigilance of that newspaper's classified staff, are coded signals for purposes quite different than the tone and content would indicate; but most are just what they seem—open, unaddressed telegrams of anxiety.

This particular one was intended for Lewis Bertrand Hano, the thirty-eight-year-old owner of the Island TV Service Corporation, a string of television repair shops in the New York metropolitan area. Six weeks before, on January 16, he had failed to return for supper at his $40,000 home at 63 Wildwood Road, in the fashionable Long Island suburb of East Hills. At first his absence doubly puzzled his wife, Marianne: during their twelve-year marriage, her husband had never stayed out at night, and that special Monday was the sixth birthday of their son, Stephen.

The mystery soon became more involved, when the New York City police notified her that his car, a 1950 Oldsmobile coupé equipped with a mobile amateur-radio transmitter (call letters W2NFT), had been found locked and abandoned aboard the Staten Island ferry that had docked at South Ferry in Manhattan at 6 P.M. From the start, the investigators strongly suspected that Hano had voluntarily absented himself. There was no suicide note, and the ferry had been jammed with hundreds of rush-hour commuters, none of whom reported seeing anyone jump into the water.

The day he vanished, Hano was supposed to have been visiting his repair shop in Jersey City. The detectives found it empty, with the rent not paid for four months. Subsequent visits to Hano's shops in Long Island City, Floral Park, Manhasset, and New Hyde Park uncovered a tale of business reverses that the missing man had managed to keep a closely guarded secret. But the investigators, even with the aid of a post-office "mail cover" and a special tap of Mrs. Hano's telephone by the New York Telephone Company's intelligence unit, turned up no clues to his whereabouts.

His last name at birth had been Tobias. He changed it to Hano when his mother remarried during the Second World War, while he was in the Navy aboard the destroyer *Biddle*. Chief Radioman Hano was discharged in September 1945. For the next two years, he owned and operated the Gotham Radio Shop at 956 First Avenue in Manhattan. He was highly skilled and he worked hard. His income increased. It was only natural that with the spectacular advent of commercial television his business would expand. And expand. And expand.

About the only promising information gleaned by the investigators was that Hano suffered from arthritic rheumatism and had once mentioned to a business associate that the Southwest would be a much healthier climate for him. But before the detectives could start pursuing this geographical possibility, Hano himself terminated the search by contacting his wife from Fort Worth, Texas, in response to her advertisement in the *Times*.*

Wakefield's tangible "life facts" are not much more revealing. The reason should be apparent by now. A complete biographical outline of him would tell us quite a bit about his life, very little about him. His actions, the unimportant ones, are recorded; his voice, his thoughts, his intentions are not. His accomplishments and failures are listed, but nowhere is there more than a hint of his goals and aspirations, much less of his dreams.

Wakefield was born on August 17, 1913, and graduated through the public-school systems in his home town, after what must be assumed from the available evidence was an uneventful childhood. The first obviously traumatic incident in his life occurred during his sophomore year at college, when his father, an assembly-line worker, was seriously injured in an industrial accident. Wakefield left school and went to work in the same factory to supplement the family income, ostensibly until his two younger brothers finished high school. He was married at twenty-six, but the childless union was dissolved in 1944, while he was stationed in the South Pacific.

By the end of the war, Wakefield had been commissioned and promoted to first lieutenant. There is some indication

---

* Why illustrate the potential for successful flight by publicized cases involving persons who disappeared and later returned or were located? In brief, the difficulties inherent in researching a phenomenon that has been ignored by the social scientists mandate such a procedure, since more information has been published about those absentees who have been recovered than about those who have not been. Moreover, many absentees are known by the police and insurance companies to be alive, although, like Wakefield, they are still "missing" as far as their relatives are concerned. As for Lewis B. Hano, he was reunited with his family. His wife and children joined him in Texas. For the next three years he worked as a real-estate developer in Dallas. On February 5, 1959, while on a business trip to Phoenix, he telephoned his wife, then pregnant with their third child. After they had talked for a while, he hung up. And disappeared again.

that at one stage he considered making the Army Corps of Engineers a career. What changed his mind, it would seem from the sequence of events, was a woman.

On January 23, 1946, Wakefield married again. A few weeks after the ceremony, he enrolled at a large state university. It was his second wife and his second attempt at a college education. His new wife bore him two children before his graduation at the end of the 1948 summer session. Three days later he joined his father-in-law's firm as a junior accountant. This association was abruptly terminated on July 16, 1954. The note he left on the kitchen table was described by the police as "suicidal in tone."

Just what are we permitted to infer from such meager knowledge? Not much, beyond a fragile empathy at those intersections where his experience touches our own. There has been no mention of the proverbial other woman, and his current unattached status would appear to confirm her absence. Working for one's in-laws is hardly a guarantee of financial security, yet the investigators found no evidence of money problems. To his associates in the accounting department, he seemed content.

Wakefield's biographical sketch does contain one inconsequential hint. His first college classified him as a student of mechanical engineering. When he left the Army and matriculated at the state university, he changed his major to business administration. This may not mean anything at all. Many people switch the direction of their formal educations before, during, and after college; later, more wish that they had. The shift, in his case, tends to be writ larger because, six years after receiving his diploma, he changed not his academic major but his entire way of life.

As a gesture, Wakefield's collegiate detour serves also to emphasize the whimsical quirks and twists of happenstance that have so often determined—if we honestly consider it—the shape and direction of our own lives. Fateful accidents have brought most of us to our current stations, as much as we might prefer to believe that our routes were blazed with thoughtful personal decisions. So it probably, more than likely, was with Wakefield.

And with Lewis Hano.

And with Lawrence Bader and with Norman Briggs and with Thomas Buntin and with Barbara Follett and with Ted Robinson and with John Symes and with William Waldron and with Orja Corns and with Vernon Holmberg and with James Barber and with Bernard Bueche and, well, with all the rest. Most of these singularly impulsive people have little in common. But then, like the rest of us, they are not really dissimilar. To understand them and the necessity of their desperate acts, we must examine ourselves, the way we live, the goals we pursue, the values we assign to things and ideas and ideals. To comprehend what they have done, we must voice that most disquieting self-query: "If I had it to do over again . . . ?"

II

"Call Me Fritz"

Take a name. Any name that comes to mind. Your own, for instance. Write it on a piece of paper. Stare at it for a while, then erase it. Do this late at night, in the echoing silence that anticipates the false dawn. A curious sense of disembodiment is evoked. The name is gone, vanished, yet the personality is still in force, the body unchanged.

Extend the presumption.

Remove that name, your name, from hundreds and thousands of pieces of paper: birth certificate, church records, school reports and diplomas, employment files, insurance questionnaires, deeds, canceled checks, notes, letters, medical records, encumbrances, memorandums, membership rolls, summonses and subpoenas, credit applications, direct-mail lists, publishers' circulation files, directories, and all government documents, in a sort of Reichstag fire of the mind.

Next, penetrate the privacy of the Federal Bureau of Investigation (a distinct role reversal) and remove your fingerprint card and political dossier. Arrange with the personnel department to abolish the job attached to your name; have it blotted from the table of organization, with the thin line of obligation continued down to the next hollow rectangle. Tear up your commutation ticket and leave the pieces on your customary seat aboard the 8:27.

The telephone company will be delighted to intercept all

incoming calls to your residence with an insulting taped message to the effect that the caller is in some way incompetent. Instruct the post office to deliver all of your mail to its dead-letter section. Cancel your subscription to *Life*.

Such documents and records and procedures are, of course, mere prods to society's aggregate memory. After your name has been obliterated, all recollections of person and personality must somehow be expunged from the consciousness of everyone you have ever known—family, relations, friends, neighbors, colleagues, associates, acquaintances, servants, salesmen, service workers, tradesmen, and creditors (debtors have an annoying habit of forgetting even before one disappears). Your associative memories of places, persons, experiences, objects, and situations are the next to go. And finally, you must relieve yourself of such distinctive characteristics as skills, habits, hobbies, tastes, and preferences—in other words, all the identifying peculiarities of personality that at once set one apart from others and provide one with a sustaining sense of past-present.

Obviously, like all Herculean tasks, this is demonstrably impossible. It would be far easier, in that hackneyed metaphor, to clean the Augean stables than to try and retrace the bureaucratic footsteps of a single man or woman through the labyrinthine social structure. Nor is it given to man to survive his own records; life is more tenuous than paper.

But suppose we reverse the presumption.

Instead of trying to erase one's own name, suppose one were to simply abandon it in favor of another name. Any name. The name of some other person. The name of, say, John F. Johnson. . . .

Normally the employees of television station KETV in Omaha are not permitted to take their vacations early in the year. But in January 1965, Station Manager James Tetrick was asked by one of his most popular on-camera personalities, John "Fritz" Johnson, to make an exception to the rule. Johnson was a sportscaster who, only three months after surgeons had removed his left eye, had successfully defended his Nebraska archery championship. As a result, he had been hired by the Sanders Archery Company of Columbus, Neb., to represent it at a sporting-goods show in Chicago. Since his wife Nancy's parents lived there, he wanted to combine the trip with a homecoming. Tetrick hesitated for only a minute before giving his approval. "You don't know how much this means to me," Johnson told him. Neither, as it turned out, did Johnson, who was about to embark on a shattering odyssey into the past that would test the credulity of practically everyone involved.

Fritz, as he preferred to be called, had arrived in Omaha by bus one May afternoon in 1957. He had taken a taxi to the Roundtable Bar and promptly asked a barmaid for a date. She turned him down, but almost everyone else found him irresistible. It was hard not to like this well-dressed, easygoing man. He spoke quietly and without rancor about his early life in a Brookline, Mass., orphanage. The tales of his experiences during his thirteen-year Navy career were exciting and believable. Discharged at thirty, he had plenty of mustering-out pay and a strong appetite for pleasure; life, he announced, was meant to be sweet and uncomplicated. Had anyone asked for identification, he would have shown them a Navy driver's license with John Johnson on it. But the only question a prospective bartender is asked is whether he can mix drinks and with people. Fritz watched the other bartenders at work, bought himself a bar guide, and was soon installed behind the mahogany shelf at Ross's Steakhouse. His working uniform was invariably plaid Bermuda shorts, and he had an engaging way with the customers, some of whom worked for local radio station KBON.

His roommate for the next three years was a fellow bartender, Tom Haley. "That book that Fritz got with the drink instructions in it," Haley remembered, "also listed three-hundred sixty-five reasons for having a party every night. We tried most of them." It was a lark. For dates, the two men purchased an old hearse, had it licensed as a "hunting vehicle," and fitted it out with cushions, a coffee table, and an incense burner. Their apartment was just as unconventionally appointed, with pillows on the floor in lieu of furniture and four large bathtubs to accommodate Fritz's extensive collection of tropical fish. Outside was Johnson's red MG sports car. He affected a leather beret, and dated a number of Omaha beauties. Searching once for a secluded cottage to rent, he described himself in an advertisement as a "nocturnal bachelor with a loud stereo and a large dog."

One item that stands out in Haley's recollections of Fritz was his roommate's uncanny memory for details about his Navy career, which spanned the Second World War and the Korean War and included three Purple Heart decorations. Fritz could rattle off the various carriers and destroyers he had served on, as well as the names of many of his shipmates and commanding officers. In graphic detail, he could relate how he had been swept off a ship in the "stormy North Atlantic," an experience that resulted in his being paralyzed for three years and eventually discharged. To strengthen his back muscles, he took up archery soon after he reached Omaha. He proved so proficient at the sport that he won his first state title only five weeks after shooting his "first" arrow. Haley was properly impressed, the more so because there seemed to be some striking gaps in Fritz's memory. For instance, he could describe the Brookline orphanage in considerable detail, but he could not seem to remember the name of it. There was, if one thought about it, something slightly mysterious about John F. Johnson.

Perhaps it was Johnson himself. He was vague about a number of things that seemed harmless eccentricities. He always dated his checks by the season; he even had one of the girls at his bank trained to call a few days before the season changed ("It'll be winter in three days, Fritz," she would announce). While he was still a bartender, he would often take his tips to the bank and deposit them with a slip marked "One Quart—Money"; he would frequently enter a restaurant and order "a couple of dollars' worth of food," leaving it to the waitress to make the selection for him. He was almost fanatical about the use of his nickname. "Fritz what?" a reporter once inquired. "Just Fritz," he replied. All the boys at the orphanage had been named John Johnson, he told Haley; he had earned his nickname by constantly fighting with another boy, until someone likened them to the Katzenjammer Kids, Hans and Fritz. He wanted to be called simply Fritz. He signed his checks Fritz. For a while, he even waged an unsuccessful battle with the telephone company to be listed in the directory as just plain Fritz (he compromised on "Fritz Johnson").

Not that this sort of behavior bothered anyone. His employers were delighted with him. His many friends considered most of these peculiar obsessions as the amusing affectations of a warmhearted exhibitionist. If there were information gaps in his biography, they did not disturb the clerks at the local Social Security office when he approached them for a new card; and the official at the motor-vehicle office never noticed that Fritz had hesitated over certain questions on the application. None of this was considered out of the ordinary for a man raised in an orphanage and hardened by thirteen years of military service. He once explained that whatever personal papers he had accumulated, he had left inadvertently in a Navy hospital. These papers, he maintained, included his birth certificate and documents attesting to his Naval service.

In any case, Michael Chiodo, the manager of Ross's Steakhouse, did not need a dossier on Johnson to make up his mind. His swank establishment was known for its popular bar, soft music, and attractive waitresses. His workers had to be friendly, good-natured, and competent. As far as Chiodo was concerned, Fritz was "an ideal employee." In some respects, he was too ideal. Chiodo eventually lost him to one of his customers, Joe Halcom, then program manager of radio station KBON, who was attracted by Johnson's smooth voice and manner. He suggested several times that Fritz try out for a position as an announcer, which he did successfully.

Fritz soon became a local celebrity. He seemed to have an instinct, a friend recalled later, "for just the right gesture— the one that gets remembered." This flair for the unusual meshed perfectly with the promotional aspects of the music-and-news industry. As a personable disk jockey, Fritz was always ready to participate in the offbeat stunt, whether it meant dressing up in a white wig and colonial clothes to hand out candy for a Washington's Birthday promotion or perching on a flagpole for two weeks in front of the Douglas County Courthouse to publicize the station's polio-fund drive. Anyone else camped on a fifty-foot pole, hoisting up a milk bottle full of martinis twice a day, might have been considered a show-off; somehow it just seemed natural when Fritz did it. He had a ready explanation for his flamboyance: "All my life I have had people tell me what to do—in the Navy, in the orphanage. Well, now I'm going to do what *I* like to do." And the first thing he did when he returned to earth was to hop into an open convertible filled with gorgeous women to lead a parade.

If his friends were used to seeing him with attractive girls, they were equally accustomed to listening to his tirades against marriage. "Oh, you fool! You fool!" he would exclaim whenever a friend announced his intention of getting married. Fritz laughingly accepted the inevitable ribbing he took in 1962 when he married a lovely Chicago divorcée, Nancy Zimmer, whose father, a former mayor of Falls City, Neb., was the grand secretary of the national headquarters of Elks Clubs. She had a daughter by her first marriage. In 1963 she bore a son to Fritz, who that year switched from the radio station to television station KETV. His broadcasting career prospered, despite his unshakable aversion to "bad news," a distaste that for a long time kept him from reading newspapers or watching newscasts on television.

As sports director of KETV, Fritz was on camera frequently. Exposure was part of his eclectic personality, and he did not shy from it. The contacts and friendships he made among reporters and sports writers in Omaha led to a number of illustrated news feature stories and Sunday-supplement articles. He even converted his dislike for "bad news" into publicity by agreeing to subscribe to the Omaha *World-Herald* on the condition that his friends on that paper would have a custodian mount a ladder and increase by one the circulation figure over the building's main entrance. Many of these stories were related to his unusual background, and although the biographical "facts" were sometimes altered slightly or embellished, no one seemed the least bit suspicious. Fritz was good copy, and he seldom let an interviewer go away empty-handed.

One particularly fascinating tale that Fritz spun for a writer from the Omaha *Sun* involved his tropical fish, which, after his marriage, he continued to breed in the four bathtubs and several glass tanks. Fritz related how he had become interested in tropical fish during one of his convalescences in a Navy hospital. "The guy beside me had received several books on tropical fish from his dad," Fritz explained. "And I used to read them to him." Then, during a tour of duty in Panama, the word was passed that the admiral's pet tropicals were dying from some mysterious ailment. "I was the only person around with a familiarity with tropical fish. But I didn't know much. I put Mercurochrome and salt in the water and raised the temperature. The next day they had perked up. From then on, I was the base fish expert."

Fritz's escapades had a habit of multiplying almost as fast as his Emerald Tiara guppies, which he conservatively estimated he had parlayed from a pair to about 2,500. In the retelling, of course, Fritz kept altering his life story. His arrival at the Massachusetts foundling home gradually evolved into a Biblical anecdote in which he was abandoned on the doorstep in a wicker basket. As for his back injury, well, he had more versions of that than he had vertebrae. First he was washed off a storm-tossed ship in the North Atlantic; then he was thrown out of a careening jeep at the end of a pier; later he told *Sun* reporter Don Kemp that "A five-inch gun exploded and blew me off a ship, breaking my back. It healed properly and I was doing fine until three years later I fell, hurting it again." To this version, Fritz apparently could not resist adding a final fillip of convincing detail: his back trouble not only shortened his naval career but it actually had taken a half inch off his before-enlistment height!

Whenever Fritz was called upon to explain a particular interest or aptitude, he frequently returned to the tale of his extended hospitalization ("three and a half years paralyzed from the waist down"). Books had introduced him to the underwater world of tropical fish; when Navy doctors informed him that special exercises would be needed to strengthen his back, he forthwith "spent most of my hospital stay reading articles on archery." At least, that's what he told a writer for the Sunday *World-Herald Magazine,* which devoted its cover to Fritz on August 11, 1963 (by this time, the five-inch gun that had exploded was on a ship "under submarine attack just outside the English Channel"). In this account, Fritz had not rushed to the nearest sporting-goods store upon his discharge from Bethesda Naval Hospital and the Navy. Instead, he had decided to use the money he had saved "to see the country." It proved to be marvelous therapy: in Florida he had discarded "his braces"; in New Orleans, which he obviously mistook for Lourdes, he threw away his crutches; by the time he reached Omaha, all that remained was his yen for archery. He even had an explanation for how he came to win his first tournament five weeks after he took up the sport. "I want to emphasize," said Fritz, then moonlighting for a Nebraska manufacturer of grass targets, "that purchase of the right kind of equipment is the secret of success in archery. I might have quit had I been misled on equipment."

Four months after his magazine-cover story, Fritz decided to pit his bow against the "white ghosts" of Boone County—an elusive herd of European white fallow deer. Naturally, he invited a reporter-photographer along to cover the trip for the *World-Herald.* From a hunting standpoint, the trip was a failure, although it started well enough, with a quick sighting of a fallow doe. As writer James Denney summed it up in a magazine piece published on December 8: " 'Luck is with us,' declared Fritz. Little did he know what lay ahead." The words were more prophetic than anyone realized at the time.

Fritz had cancer. Specifically, a malignant melanoma had developed on the back wall of his left eye. An Omaha oculist removed it, along with the left eye itself, on March 17, 1964. Typically, Fritz shrugged off this affliction and was soon making daily rounds of the hospital to cheer up his fellow patients. Three months later, he successfully defended his Nebraska archery championship. It was his thirteenth title, a testimonial to the skill and fortitude of a man who in 1961 had placed ninth in the National Field Archery Tournament at Crystal Springs, Ark.

The black eye patch (which he wore when damp weather irritated his glass eye) and pencil mustache, moreover, added a debonair look to this well-spoken, muscular man; just the person, decided the officials of the Sanders Archery Company, to represent the firm at the 1965 sports show in Chicago. They had no way of knowing that their representative—a man so obviously dedicated to enjoying life—had been declared "dead" five years before in Akron, Ohio.

But one spectator at the show did. On February 2, 1965, in Chicago's McCormick Place, he stood staring incredulously at Fritz Johnson. He had been a schoolmate of Johnson's in Akron. Only the man he had known was not named Johnson; his name had been Lawrence Joseph Bader, the youngest son of a prominent Akron dentist.

The spectator's shock was only natural, since the man he was staring at had supposedly drowned eight years before in Lake Erie.

The man who recognized Johnson as the missing Bader later told newsmen, who respected his precondition of anonymity, that he had been in Chicago on business. Before the mysterious tangle was unraveled, there would be many others who would wish he had concentrated on his own business and thus protected the actual identity of Bader-Johnson.

Instead, he got in touch with the Bader family upon his return to Akron. The family, having pursued numerous false leads in the past eight years, was openly skeptical until they heard that Johnson had been spotted in an archery booth at the sporting-goods show. Since Larry Bader had also been an archery buff and former Ohio champion, this clue was too strong to ignore. Bader's brother John, unconvinced but intrigued, telephoned his twenty-one-year-old niece, Susanne Peika, in Chicago, and asked her to drop by the Sanders Archery Company booth for another look at Fritz Johnson.

"Pardon me," she asked, "but aren't you my uncle, Larry Bader, who disappeared seven years ago?"

Fritz laughed; Mrs. Peika did not. She convinced him that he should at least talk with John Bader on the phone. In Akron, John listened incredulously. "If I thought my brother was alive," said John Bader to the man called Fritz Johnson, "I would say you are him."

The brother that John Bader was now convinced was dead had been born in Akron on December 2, 1926, the third son (there were two daughters) in the well-known and respected family of Dr. Stephen A. and Charlotte Bader. "Though the family is strict Roman Catholic and bound together by strong family loyalties, in other ways it was loose and easy-going," *Life* reported in March 1965. "Larry and his two brothers and two sisters were encouraged to get as much fun out of life as possible. Their big house in Akron's fashionable west side was a regular neighborhood hangout. In this carefree atmosphere the children apparently did not develop much appreciation for money or other kinds of responsibility. 'All the kids used to go to Daddy whenever they wanted money,' a family friend remembers. 'They were really terribly spoiled. Larry, especially. He never had a penny in his pocket. He was always a happy-go-lucky kid, looking for a pot of gold somewhere.' "

Larry liked to learn but hated to be taught. Although he was an avid reader and a good talker, he disliked school; he even flunked one year at Saint Sebastian Grade School. His marks at Buchtel High School were not much better, and he assiduously avoided extracurricular activities, preferring the more individual pursuits of the outdoorsman. He fished and hunted, and he was a very strong swimmer. He demonstrated an early skill as an archer, and, while still in high school, he won a tristate archery contest.

His hobby was raising tropical fish.

On December 9, 1944, Larry Bader dropped out of his junior year in high school and joined the Navy. For the next nineteen months he served as a pharmacist's mate. Prior to his honorable discharge on July 4, 1946, he was stationed at the San Diego Naval Hospital. His service medical record contains no mention of any kind of injury. He saw no combat and was not even stationed outside the United States.

Bader returned to Akron and managed to complete enough high-school credits to graduate with the class of 1947. He then entered the University of Akron, only to flunk out after the first semester. One of the reasons given for this failure was the inordinate amount of time he spent working in the campus restaurant owned by his father. "Larry really ran that restaurant," a friend recalled. "He was the chef and everything. He loved eating and he really knew how to cook."

That venture ended, however, when his father sold the place. Larry next joined his brother John in operating a drive-in eatery, only to leave this for a job as a driver-salesman with the Pearl Coffee Company. Meanwhile, since October 1949, he had been dating Mary Lou Knapp. They had been childhood friends, had lived within ten blocks of each other, had attended the same schools and the same church. At the University of Akron, where she received a bachelor's degree in 1950, Mary Lou had been a finalist in several beauty contests. On April 19, 1952, the couple were married. The ceremony was treated by the local press as one of the top social events in Akron that year. Three children were born during the first five years of the marriage.

By then Larry had become a kitchenware salesman for the stainless-steel division of the Reynolds Metals Corporation in Cleveland. Like most commission-type sales work, it was an arduous assignment that placed a premium on aggressiveness. The job required a winning personality, a touch of the Blarney, and a tremendous amount of unflagging energy; overly sensitive people need not apply. But the work had certain compensations, one of the most attractive of which was the opportunity to schedule one's working hours to include free time for outside sports activities.

By the spring of 1957, Bader was earning an estimated $10,000 a year in commissions. He needed every single cent of it—and more. There was a $17,000 mortgage on his suburban Akron home at 145 Goodhue Drive. His wife was expecting their fourth child in August. Larry Bader was in financial trouble. His current debts totaled some $2,400, the milkman was threatening to stop deliveries, and he had neglected to file any income-tax returns since 1952.

Lawrence Joseph Bader disappeared on Wednesday, May 15, 1957.

It happened with a casual attention to routine. He spent the morning playing with his children, Mary Elizabeth, four; Lawrence Joseph, Jr., three; and Stephen Frederick, two. About noon, he announced that he had to drive into Cleveland on business, after which he might try to get in some fishing on Lake Erie. Dressed in slacks and a sports jacket, he loaded his fishing gear and a small suitcase into his pink 1956 Pontiac and told his wife he would be home "late." Mary Lou would afterwards insist that she suggested he forget about the fishing and come straight back from Cleveland; the last thing she remembers him saying was, "Maybe I will and maybe I won't." He didn't.

Before leaving Akron, Bader cashed a $400 check and paid a few bills, including one quarterly insurance premium that was due. He also paid fifteen dollars to Lawrence Cotleur, the owner of a boathouse on the banks of the Rocky River near its confluence with Lake Erie. It was the deposit on a fourteen-foot boat. Bader insisted on having running lights installed on the craft, even though he promised to return before dark. Cotleur pointed to the ominous cloud bank gathered on the horizon and told Bader that storm warnings had already been posted. But Bader disregarded the warnings and pushed off from the dock in the green-and-white boat with a small outboard motor. The last people to talk with Bader that night were the crew of a Coast Guard launch that spotted him just offshore after sunset; he refused their traditional offer of assistance.

The boat, slightly damaged, was found the next morning on a beach about five miles from the boatyard; all it contained was an empty gasoline can, two life preservers, and his fishing gear. One oar, the suitcase, and Bader were missing. His car was still parked at the boathouse. The Akron *Beacon-Journal* headlined its story on the case "LITTLE HOPE FOR SURVIVAL," and quoted Chief Petty Officer Robert Edwards of the Coast Guard to the effect that even a good swimmer could not stay afloat very long in that part of the lake under the conditions that prevailed. Edwards also insisted that it was not uncommon for Lake Erie to refuse to yield its victims.

Despite such observations, the circumstances of his disappearance aroused the suspicions of a number of people, including his own father. "I can't put my finger on it," the dentist told police, "but there's something about this that stinks." In an effort to puzzle it out, Dr. Bader often returned to the spot where the boat was found beached and would sit for hours staring at the water and reconstructing the events; he gradually became convinced that his son had been the victim of foul play. The mystery was still unsolved when he died, at the age of seventy-one, in May of 1964.

The testimony of the Coast Guard chief to the contrary, many people could not understand how a tested swimmer like Bader could have become separated from his boat—with the suitcase. A few investigators surmised that Bader might have been beaten and robbed for the "large roll of bills" he had flashed while renting the boat. But it was an unsatisfying theory for many reasons, some of which became apparent after Bader's financial predicament was revealed. Police Chief F. E. Stephens of Lakewood, Ohio, was more emphatic. His report stated frankly that, in his opinion, Bader's "death" was either a suicide or made to seem accidental. Chief Stephens said his investigators had received "several hints from co-workers that Bader had family problems."

An eight-week investigation by police, however, failed to turn up any evidence to support the theory that Bader might have staged his death; neither did the private investigators hired by the Bader family. Eventually, doubt gave way to resignation and—after grief had run its natural course—belief.

Now, after all these years, John Bader sat talking on the telephone with a man who sounded exactly like his missing brother Larry and who, according to two witnesses, bore a remarkable resemblance to him. John Bader moved quickly. With his other brother, Richard, he gathered up a plaster cast of Larry's teeth made by their dentist father and chartered a plane for the flight to Meigs Field, an airport located across the lagoon from McCormick Place. The fact that both Fritz and their brother had been Navy pharmacist's mates was merely one more startling coincidence. For Richard and John Bader, however, this additional information was quite unnecessary; one look at Fritz Johnson had convinced them that he was their brother.

The only trouble was that Fritz, resplendent in a blue blazer, pin-striped shirt, and eye patch, insisted he did not have the slightest idea what they were talking about. He knew nothing about any Lawrence Bader, had never been in Akron, and, as far as he knew, had no brothers. Instead, he detailed for the Baders his background in the orphanage, the

Navy, and his subsequent discharge before arriving in Omaha.

At 4:30 that afternoon, February 4, Johnson, the Baders, and their niece entered Chicago's police headquarters and patiently related their bizarre story to an uncomprehending desk sergeant. It required considerable explanation before the group was finally directed to the fourth floor, where the Bureau of Identification is located.

There the entire procedure was repeated, this time across a long counter, behind which stood Lieutenant Emil Giese, the bureau chief during the four-to-midnight shift. Giese was told that the group had come for the purpose of finding out whether or not Fritz Johnson was really another man who had allegedly drowned in Lake Erie eight years before. Since Johnson insisted he was not, would the police run a fingerprint comparison and establish the truth, once and for all?

Giese studied the group carefully before asking Fritz to accompany him into a glass-enclosed cubicle. He closed the door. Carefully, the lieutenant explained to Fritz that he was under no legal obligation to have his fingerprints taken. He even asked Fritz if the Baders were in any way forcing him to submit to fingerprinting. Giese remembers that Fritz only smiled at this suggestion. No, said Fritz, the fingerprints had been his own idea. The lieutenant shrugged, then instructed his secretary to type out an affidavit for Johnson to the effect that he was consenting voluntarily to be fingerprinted. Fritz signed it without hesitation.

After the prints were taken, Giese brought the rest of the group into the office and showed them a brown envelope that, he said, would be sent special delivery to the FBI's Fingerprint Division in Washington. At the request of the Chicago police, the federal experts would be asked to compare Johnson's fingerprints with those taken from Bader during his Navy service. The system, he assured them, was foolproof.

"In twenty-four hours," said Giese, "you'll have your answer."

"I don't need to wait, lieutenant," John Bader replied. "I know this is my brother."

Fritz, calmly puffing on his slim pipe all the while, appeared relaxed and unperturbed. Before he left Giese's office, he gave the Baders his Nebraska address and warmly invited them to drop by if they ever were in the area. The Baders flew back to Akron that night; Johnson, his wife, and her two toy poodles returned to Omaha the next day.

The news reached Richard Bader around noon on Saturday. Lieutenant Giese called to inform him that the FBI had decided Fritz and Larry were, on the basis of the fingerprint comparison, one and the same. In Omaha, Fritz got the news from inquiring reporters. About 6 P.M., he telephoned Giese, who read the FBI report to him.

"What should I do?" Fritz asked him.

"Better get a lawyer," answered the lieutenant.

III

The Shared Impulse

When a man from one city turns up in a second as someone else from still another city, three city editors have an obligation to get terribly excited about it. Which is precisely what happened in Akron, Chicago, and Omaha. This local coverage varied directly with the degree of involvement. Chicago, inured to fire, violence, and visitors, treated the Bader-Johnson affair with the detached amusement of a spectator at someone else's séance. Omaha reacted with disbelieving shock. Akron handled the event like the Second Coming, dispatching reporters in every direction and inundating the inhabitants of Ohio's rubber town with every conceivable kind of news, feature, and sidebar story, including a long copyrighted interview with Mrs. Mary Lou Bader.

Such treatment is both customary and understandable. But, as it rapidly turned out, the story of Lawrence Bader, his presumed death in Lake Erie, and his proved "resurrection" in Omaha as a popular television personality was of considerably more than local interest. From the beginning, the Bader-Johnson saga moved out on the "A" wires of the national press associations to the front pages of a thousand newspapers across the United States. Ample accounts of the story were broadcast over the radio and television networks; late-hour talkathons were convened on local radio stations in many cities, and a host of "experts" were asked their profound opinions on missing persons in general and Bader-Johnson in particular.

Next came the special-feature writers from the large-circulation metropolitan tabloids—perceptive "in-depth" reporters like Christine Kirk of the New York *Daily News*—to prepare lengthy articles that probed Bader's background, described Fritz's Omaha activities, and attempted to analyze just how everything might have occurred. Finally the national news-magazines moved in with their coteries of photographers, researchers, stringers, and rewrite men to sum up the coverage under such provocative headlines as "MAN WITH TWO WIVES—AMNESIA OR HOAX?"

This initial flurry of reportage lasted more than a month, an inordinate amount of time by the normal yardsticks the media use to measure reader interest. Thereafter the press settled down to report sporadically the subsequent developments. Such coverage at the local level is simply the standard attention a newspaper devotes to a running story; nationally, it was additional evidence of the power the story exercised on the fickle imaginations of city editors around the country.

What was the source of this enduring appeal?

The basic elements of the story are easily isolated: missing person, presumed death, bigamy, and amnesia. Each is considered newsworthy. But unless the person involved has some pretensions to prominence, unless he or she is, for instance, a New York Supreme Court judge, a former debutante, a West Point cadet, or a famous writer, the news interest is generally limited. Thousands upon thousands are reported "missing" annually, yet most of these are not mentioned in the newspapers, even when they return or are located. The same applies to staged deaths and to bigamy; both stories are normally assigned to the staff's crime reporter, especially if the possibility of fraud exists. Amnesia is generally considered a medical problem, with the press becoming involved when the police are trying to establish identity.

What captured the nation's attention, then, was not so much what Bader-Johnson did as it was the manner in which he did it. The contrast between the lives of Bader and Johnson was quickly apparent. Larry Bader sold kitchenware; his suburban home was heavily mortgaged; his wife was pregnant with their fourth child in five years of marriage; the circumstances of his social position placed a premium on visible conformity. Fritz Johnson was the sports director of a television station, a job that provided maximum interplay between vocation and avocation; his flamboyant inclinations and eccentricities became assets, bounded only by public taste; he lived in a modest bungalow with his ex-model wife, who had borne him one child during their three-year marriage. Bader was a Roman Catholic, Johnson a Unitarian.

Yet it was precisely the similarities and not the differences in these two situations that so fascinated the American public. Bader and Johnson were both gainfully employed, they had married attractive women, they enjoyed comfortable living accommodations. In short, both existed in substantially middle-class milieux. The fantasy possibilities that all this suggested were infinite, a fact that did not escape the attention of an editorial writer for the Akron *Beacon Journal*. "It's an old plot for storytellers," he wrote two weeks after Bader's existence had been confirmed; "also, it probably represents a secret dream that many of us have had at one time or another—to leave the past behind and start life all over as a new person. Usually, it is done purposefully—sometimes successfully; more often, not."

More often, not. With just three words the anonymous *Beacon Journal* scribe defined the nation's momentary absorption with Bader-Johnson. The public was intrigued because "many" people have a shared impulse to discard the past in favor of a new (and, by implication, better) life; but it remains a "secret dream" for the simple reason that it cannot be done: that our society, despite its diversity and mobility and number, is actually a very tight organism; that even after a period of years a "missing person" may still be spotted at a sporting-goods show in Chicago.

More often, not!

The phrase rings of conclusive judgment. It slams the door on impulse more effectively than overwhelming statistics. With contrapuntal force, it slays the daydreams of escape, stunts the self-generated wish. In context, it is a well-wrought phrase turned by a professional writer. There is but one thing wrong with it: like the myth that engendered it, the phrase has no basis in fact.

Actually, the general subject of missing persons contains very few demonstrable "facts," quite a few unchallenged assertions and what *Time* would call guesstimates, and four central myths that, after years of official repetition, have attained the weight of orthodoxy. These myths are worth brief examination.

Each year in the United States, one million people voluntarily absent themselves.

The figure is apocryphal. Even if every person considered "missing" were reported as such (and many investigators admit that probably as many as half are not reported), there is no central clearinghouse for such information, and hence no reliable source for such a statistic. If such a statistic did exist, it would still be misleading, since tabulation would be simultaneously inflated by premature alarms from anxious parents or spouses and deflated by untold numbers of people either too proud to report a disappearance or too poor— financially and/or spiritually—to care. One million is just a nice round number that attracts a lot of attention.

At the turn of the century, no police department in this country maintained a special bureau for missing persons. Nor were there other government agencies at any level that concerned themselves with much more than counting the population. The first specific discussion of missing persons as a social problem appeared in the November 21, 1925, issue of *Collier's*. The article consisted largely of an interview with Captain John H. Ayers, chief of the New York City Missing

Persons Bureau, which had been established seven years before. "Each year in this country," the article began, "about one hundred thousand free-born men and women, girls and boys—especially girls and boys—rise to a point of personal privilege and leave home, neglecting to inform parents, husbands, wives, sweethearts or the hired man where they are going."

Ayers described this phenomenon as "the strangest drama in American life." He told his interviewer that the 100,000 figure was a projection of New York City's experience. According to the captain, his special bureau had handled 103,-837 cases of this kind between 1918 and 1924; what's more, he and his men had "solved" 101,391. Giddy with this statistical triumph, Ayers pressed his psychic powers to the limit and announced that, of the 100,000 who annually vanish, "40,000 of these people are accounted for within a few days, 30,000 within a few weeks, 25,000 within a few months, 3,000 within a few years.

"Thus but 2,000 remain mysteries along the road of oblivion."

As the nation's leading authority on missing persons (primarily because he also was the nation's only authority), Ayers was also willing to explain the motivations of his quarries:

"Why girls leave home: Love entanglement, 25 per cent; lure of stage or movies, 25 per cent; dissatisfaction over home conditions, 40 per cent; miscellaneous, 'nerves,' etc., 10 per cent.

"Why boys leave home: ill-adjusted home conditions, too much coddling or too strict discipline, 50 per cent; romance, adventure, search for jobs of their own, 50 per cent.

"Why men leave: financial troubles, 25 per cent; domestic difficulties, 25 per cent; boredom, depression, love affairs, 40 per cent; miscellaneous, 10 per cent."

Unfortunately Captain Ayers offered no methodology for his ability to determine motivation, although he may have provided an inadvertent insight into himself by lumping under reasons men leave, "boredom, depression, love affairs."

The ultimate test of any projection, even a fatuous one like Ayers', is its credibility. Is the figure large enough to merit consideration, yet small enough not to strain belief? One hundred thousand apparently suited Captain Ayers and *Collier's*; it is worth noting that during his "seven years of painstaking statistical compilation," the U.S. Bureau of the Census first counted more than one hundred million people in the United States.

The Depression obviously added a new dimension—a visible dimension, with sizable blocks of the population in motion, in search of work, opportunity, or just surcease from the grinding boredom of unemployment. It also added one more zero to Captain Ayers' fanciful figure. Henceforth, the number of missing persons each year would be "approximately one million."*

This more impressive but equally fallacious statistic gained currency during the thirties, in newspapers, magazine articles, and through the vehicle of an immensely popular radio show, "Mr. Keen, Tracer of Lost Persons," that premiered on NBC's Blue Network the evening of October 12, 1937. In 1938, the figure received the personal imprimatur of Daniel M. Eisenberg, the founder of a New York–based detective agency called Skip Tracers Company. That year he and John N. Beffel published a book called *I Find the Missing*, in which the following remarkable assertion appears:

> Early in 1938 we made a nation-wide survey of disappearances. Questionnaires were sent to police departments in the principal cities and to private agencies. Answers received, plus information from our agents throughout the country, indicated that approximately 1,107,815 men, women, and children were reported missing in the United States in 1937. This was presumably an increase. We lack comprehensive figures for

---

* This figure predictably will be increased to two million shortly after the 1970 government census officially proclaims the population of the United States to be in excess of 200,000,000.

previous periods, but all available data point to an average of
about a million disappearances a year since 1932. . . . Public
agencies were informed of 417,567 of the 1937 cases. Private
agencies were requested to find 690,248 vanished persons.

[Captain Ayers, meet Mr. Eisenberg; Mr. Eisenberg, say
hello to Captain Ayers.]

Once established as the unchallenged annual estimate of
missing persons, "one million" has become the conditioned
response of every police official asked for his opinion. Pressed
for his source, a candid policeman will tell you he read it
somewhere. And he has, over and over and over again. As
impossible as it is to disappear, *Life* announced on April 14,
1952: "Still, the number of Americans, excluding criminals,
who try it every year is around one million. About one half
are juvenile runaways, almost one third are adult men and
the remainder are women." In its May 1961 issue, *Reader's
Digest* breathlessly revealed that "Each year an estimated *one
million* Americans vanish." On February 11, 1965, the Charlotte (N.C.) *News* informed its credulous readers that "Last
year almost one million Americans disappeared—some intentionally, some for other reasons." This sweeping and rather
inconclusive statement was echoed on July 8, 1966, by the
Salt Lake City *Times,* which announced that "Almost one
million people disappear in the United States each year—for
one reason or another." The *Wall Street Journal* carefully
investigated the subject for six months, then soberly decided
on the front page of its October 10, 1966, issue that "more
than 1 million Americans" disappear annually. On occasion,
even the FBI has lent its voice to the anxious chorus. But no
amount of "authoritative" repetition can convert a fanciful
estimate into a demonstrable fact.

*The police solve from ninety-five to ninety-eight percent of
missing-persons cases.*

What is especially misleading about this myth is the implication that the police have jurisdiction to look for everyone

reported missing. They do not, as will be discussed in Chapter IX. Moreover, a vast majority of the cases they do handle are "solved" by the voluntary return of the absentee—a circumstance that the police seldom attempt to make apparent in their annual summations of "cases successfully concluded."

Such statistics are entirely suspect, and with good reason. The actuality of being "missing" is not of itself a crime against society. Moreover, the search for missing persons is a service, not a function, of law enforcement. Hence, the police have less to gain by claiming an extremely high rate of solution than they have to lose by admitting a lower one. Having traditionally pretended to be almost infallible in this area of investigation, the police have no choice but to continue pretending to extremely high rates of solution, regardless of what their actual statistical experience might be.

Although this conclusion is impossible to prove, it should not appear unreasonable to anyone familiar with the self-serving habits of police statisticians in general. Nor was it contradicted by any evidence gathered or observed during the course of my research at various metropolitan police bureaus. In one such instance it was actually admitted. I had spent the morning examining the files and questioning the officer in charge about his unit's procedures. When I asked to see some examples of unsolved cases, he produced a large metal card index labeled "OPEN—1966."

I stopped counting at fifty-seven.

"I'm a little confused, sergeant. Are all these cases unsolved?"

"As far as we're concerned."

I asked him to explain.

"Well, some of those people have probably come back, and the families have never bothered to tell us so we can cancel the report."

"Then how was the department able to claim 97.6 percent solution last year?"

The sergeant just looked at me and smiled.

Before I left, I asked him about the cubbyholes bearing the

names of the major cities in the United States. He explained that the teletype alarms for missing persons were filed by cities, and that it was the routine for other departments to check the names of nonresident suspects with the bureau. It seemed curious to me that the box labeled "NEW YORK CITY" contained only two slips.

"Listen," he confided, "if we tried to file every bulletin we get, we'd need another man in the bureau just for New York City alone. Unless the requesting department has a specific reason for thinking their pigeon is here, we throw them away. We have to."

It is practically impossible to disappear in today's society.

This myth is a direct outgrowth of the vaunted infallibility of police investigations and the inflated boasts of private detectives. It is to the distinct advantage of both to perpetuate it.

The foundation for this myth is the mass of documentation that accumulates even in the course of a brief, uneventful life. The investigators would have the public believe that this great store of information is readily available (which it is not) and that, to the trained eye, it contains all kinds of clues as to why the person has disappeared, where he or she has gone, and what the man or woman will be doing when located (which is so much conjecture).

Armed with this trove of recorded knowledge, the investigator then proceeds to the so-called "digging in" stage. This consists of interviewing everyone who knew the missing person, and, through painstaking questioning, uncovering "subconscious" evidence that might disclose the instinctive destination of the quarry. Such information, the investigators insist, helps them overcome society's legal protections to privacy. Hobbies, avocations, former skills, military and travel experiences, youthful memories, casually uttered wishes at unguarded moments—all are represented as grist for the detective's mill. To be sure, a considerable detailed biography could be compiled from all this information, though it seldom is. What is debatable is the utility of such a personal history in locating the missing. Fingerprints and photographs abound, and people who preferred chili con carne and Humphrey Bogart movies before their disappearances will continue to eat it and patronize them afterwards. But is this knowledge really that useful to the public or private investigator? The answer is no—just as the most direct rebuttal to the myth that people cannot disappear in the United States is that every day people do.

Only a "small and select company" disappears permanently.

Although this might seem at first glance a contradiction of the assertion that it is impossible to disappear, it is actually offered in support of it. For this is the primary myth, which sums up the others and seemingly justifies them; this is the statistical tolerance that permits belief.

Unlike the first three myths, this one is seldom broadcast by anyone who claims to be an expert in the area of missing persons. It is, instead, particularly a literary device that has been used repeatedly in a series of nonfiction mystery books that focused on a handful of well-publicized disappearance cases. The statement was made directly in a *Life* article in 1952, describing the baffling disappearance of West Point Cadet Richard Colvin Cox. A sophomore from Mansfield, Ohio, Cox had served in the Regular Army in Germany before entering the academy, where he compiled a solid academic record and a reputation as a well-adjusted yearling. But in January 1950 a visitor identified only as George showed up at the Point, claiming to be a friend of Cox's from Germany. His visit upset the cadet, who told his roommates that he hoped "he wouldn't have to see that fellow again." The following Saturday, January 14, "that fellow" returned. And at 6:18 P.M., Cox slipped into his heavy dress overcoat and left the barracks for dinner at the nearby Thayer Hotel.

He never reached the hotel, and no one—at least nobody who has ever come to the attention of a regiment of federal and Army investigators assigned to the case—has since seen Cox or his mysterious visitor.

"He vanished—tracelessly, inexplicably, permanently," *Life* reported. "Thus he joined the small and select list of the permanently vanished, a list which includes Joseph Force Crater, the Manhattan judge who one night stepped into a taxicab on West 45th Street after a gay dinner party and was never heard of since."

Judge Crater is America's most famous missing person. Innumerable books and articles have been written about him since his disappearance on August 6, 1930; his name has entered the national argot; comedians joke about him; and he is a frequent and favorite subject of graffiti artists ("Judge Crater, please call your office"). The decades have hardly dimmed the press interest in Crater. When a pedestrian spotted what appeared to be a badly decomposed body in a trunk on a Manhattan sidewalk, the late *World Journal Tribune* devoted a third of its front page on January 19, 1967, to the "MYSTERY CORPSE UNCOVERED AT JUDGE CRATER'S HANGOUT." The trunk, with its grisly contents, had been used for many years as a prop at mock wakes conducted in the Harvey-Gautier Bar at 22 Beekman Street. During Prohibition, the place had been a speakeasy and had numbered among its "regulars" Mayor James J. Walker, Crater, and a host of Tammany Hall sachems. But the saloon was also frequented by a number of doctors from the old Beekman Hospital across the street, one of whom probably supplied the female cadaver, as a subsequent laboratory examination proved it to be.

Crater's disappearance, of course, would have warranted a great deal of publicity just because of his nomination to the New York Supreme Court bench in April 1930 by Governor Franklin D. Roosevelt. What converted the missing jurist into a national legend was not his cab ride to oblivion four months later but the subsequent disclosures of personal and professional chicanery. Crater was well known as a bon vivant; as a colorful and influential political figure before he went on the bench, he was a familiar sight in the livelier night spots and included among his wide circle of acquaintances socialites, theatrical personalities, and gangsters.

The night he vanished, there was a ticket waiting for him at the box office of a new musical, *Dancing Partner*. It soon developed that a number of Crater's "partners" danced to rather unsavory tunes. A sensational array of headlines revealed that the missing judge had been something of a philanderer; that his political activities involved kickbacks of the type that would soon bring about the famous Seabury investigation that toppled Mayor Jimmy himself; that his personal law practice included some receiverships that strongly suggested unethical practices. The mystery deepened when Mrs. Crater returned from their summer home at Belgrade Lakes, Maine, to find a large amount of cash and a variety of personal documents in their New York apartment —all of which had somehow eluded the police sleuths who had previously ransacked the place. She also found a note: "Am very weary. Love, Joe."

There were any number of reasons why Crater might have fled or been murdered; an equal number of theories were set forth, and numerous "sightings" of the judge were reported across the land, aboard cruise ships, and in other countries. Indeed, a large part of the public fascination with the case was engendered by the inability of the police to produce even the identity of the taxi driver who picked up the judge that fateful evening. For Crater, with his large robust frame and abnormally elongated neck and deformed right index finger, suffered in a car-door accident, should not have been difficult to spot. And yet an extensive investigation by several law-enforcement agencies, abetted by intensive nationwide publicity, did not uncover a single substantive clue to his whereabouts.

As further evidence of the "small and select" company of the permanently vanished, *Life* offered two examples. The first was four-year-old Charles Brewster Ross, the son of a rich Germantown, Pa., grocer. Young Ross did not disappear. He was kidnapped on July 1, 1874, and held for ransom, the first famous case of this kind in United States history. The negotiations with the criminals who snatched him were bungled from beginning to end, and the boy was probably murdered by his nervous abductors. The other example was Dorothy Harriet Camille Arnold, a twenty-five-year-old New York heiress. On December 12, 1910, Miss Arnold entered Brentano's on Fifth Avenue and, after browsing about in the stacks of new fiction, purchased a volume of gushy love stories entitled *An Engaged Girl's Sketches*. Outside on the sidewalk, she met a friend, and they chatted for a moment about the impending coming-out party for Dorothy's sister. Then she turned and walked off into impenetrable mystery.

Viewed strictly from the perspective of Crater, Cox, and Miss Arnold, the designation of "small and select" would seem to apply. But in fact the company of the permanently vanished is neither. State Supreme Court justices, West Pointers, and society debutantes do not disappear with much frequency. When they do, however, they merely follow, as we shall see, in the faint footsteps of a legion of lawyers, doctors, high-school teachers and college professors, insurance men, bankers, salesmen, managers, executives, writers, editors, musicians, policemen, storekeepers, contractors, industrialists, and housewives.

Myths, even outrageous ones, are not without some factual substance. To say, for instance, that the oft-recited figure of one million is a statistical mirage does not mean that each year about that many people do not try to disappear. There is simply no way of demonstrating it, and even a demonstration conceivably would tell us little beyond the percentages of men, women, and children involved. Numbers contain no revelations of motivation, economic status, or, more important, intent. And these figures would not and could not distinguish between those who methodically prepared a drastic and abrupt change in their way of life, and those who impulsively decided on a brief hiatus from responsibility and would like to return but cannot bring themselves to.

The absence of definitive statistics, however, does not totally obscure the dimensions of this phenomenon. If we can never know precisely how many people try to disappear, much less their reasons, there is still plenty of circumstantial evidence to provide a sharp sensation of social fluidity in this country, in which a sizable slice of humanity has become irreconcilably separated from family and friends—and creditors.

One important clue is provided by the Social Security Administration, which annually receives about 200,000 requests for information concerning the whereabouts of its clients. Most of these requests come from state and federal officials and involve the Aid to Families with Dependent Children program, tax investigations, immigration problems, and national security. But, according to Robert M. Ball, commissioner of Social Security, at least 20,000 are instigated by police, lawyers, credit organizations, and relatives, a figure that might be considerably larger were it not for the fact—which more and more people are becoming aware of--that the administration is prohibited by law and regulation from releasing such information.

In addition, this agency is frequently asked to forward personal communications by the relatives of missing persons. This little-publicized service was begun during the early 1950's, and is rigorously restricted to messages of a "humanitarian" nature or situations where the person sought would receive "a substantial monetary benefit."* To make sure of

---

* This procedure is not recommended in circumstances involving a time element. In a 1966 test of the system, a woman asked Social Security to forward a letter to her "missing" brother to the effect that their mother was critically ill. Six weeks later, J. L. Fay, director of the agency's data-processing bureau, wrote explaining that he would forward such a letter, but it would have to be written by the mother! When the sister answered and stated that her mother was on her deathbed and pleaded with Fay to forward the enclosed letter quickly, the administration

this restriction, the administration requires that the message be delivered to it in an unsealed envelope, with only the person's name written on the front. If the letter fits the category, it is then forwarded to the missing person in care of the last employer who reported quarterly earnings for him. Included is an explanatory letter from the administration, emphasizing that "We have not revealed your address, and we have informed the writer that we will not disclose whether the letter is delivered. You are free, therefore, to reply to the enclosed letter or not as you choose." Commissioner Ball estimates that his agency now annually forwards about five thousand such letters, of which a thousand are returned by the employers "with the notation that the individual cannot be located."

Another indicator is the number of inquiries received by the FBI concerning missing persons. Director J. Edgar Hoover insists that his bureau does not maintain a cumulative record of such requests; however, he said that between December 20, 1966, and January 20, 1967, the bureau handled 195 requests, eighty-three percent of which came from private individuals, ten percent from the police, and seven percent from Congressional sources. Hoover did not say whether this month-long experience might be considered average; the period was hardly the prime time of year for disappearances. But if it does represent an average, then the bureau receives more than 2,300 missing-person queries a year, of which about 1,900 come from immediate relatives. On April 30, 1967, according to Hoover, the bureau's active search files contained the names and/or fingerprints of 6,183 missing persons.

The statistical experience of the FBI and the Social Se-

---

relented and dutifully mailed it—forty-four days later—to the brother. It was addressed to a place of employment he had left five months before, and another two weeks elapsed before he received it. This means that about three and a half months elapsed between the sister's initial request and the delivery of the letter to the brother. How long this process might take in nonemergency situations can only be imagined.

curity Administration is not conclusive within the context of an inquiry into the nature and extent of middle-class anomie, except perhaps by implication. The act of pursuit itself by the relatives—especially the audacity required to enlist the Federal Bureau of Investigation in a personal affair—would strongly suggest a certain means and sophistication that are simply not possessed by the less affluent members of this society. Attitudes are operative here which would indicate the presence of those twin foundations of middle-class identity: possession and position.

Both of these characteristics are even more clearly involved in what would be, were it available, perhaps the most meaningful statistic: the number of people who are annually declared dead by our courts. These presumptive declarations, which will be discussed in Chapter XI, are bench decisions in response to petitions; as such, they do not become part of the official court record and hence are not filed in any readily accessible manner. To make meaningful tabulation even more difficult, the actual "presumption of death" is frequently contained deep within the text of a different kind of declaration, such as guardianship, child custody, or estate assignment.

Nevertheless, it would seem that approximately 2,000 Americans are so declared annually—if New Jersey may be considered a demographic microcosm of the country. According to the cumulative responses of that state's twenty-one county clerks, in whose offices such declarations are recorded, presumed deaths have been occurring at a fairly consistent ratio of about one per 100,000 residents.

This projection is supported by the ten-year experience of the claims division at the Prudential Insurance Company of America, the second largest in the nation. From 1957 to 1966, the company received a total of 3,709 claims based on presumptions of death (the count by years: 462, 468, 345, 390, 409, 332, 379, 318, 273, and 342). The last year, 1966, although below the decade average, represented .006 percent of the some 525,000 death claims processed by the company.

Since the entire life-insurance industry handled 2,502,000 such claims that year, this could conceivably mean that as many as 1,500 death claims in 1966 were based on legal declarations of death.

Some of these claims, to be sure, involve "specific peril" situations (e.g., persons known to have been killed in airplane crashes at sea but whose bodies were never recovered), and hence do not involve missing persons in the usual sense. And a certain amount of duplication between more than one company insuring the same policyholder would further decrease the total number of presumptive death claims. But even a smaller figure than 1,500 would not necessarily contradict the New Jersey projection of 2,000 declarations nationwide, insurance death benefits being but one of several reasons for seeking such declarations.

Ultimately, of course, there can be but one certifiable indicator: there is within all of us the impulse to flight. Although it persists in varying degrees from man to man, woman to woman, child to child, it exists as a basic shared impulse. We exercise (and, to a limited degree, control) this impulse through a thousand escape mechanisms. Whether we go to a movie or the theater, turn on the television, read a book, drink, indulge a hobby, attend a daydream, sleep when we are not tired, eat without hunger, travel, overexercise, lie, worship, extend our credit, become too deeply involved in work, change vocations, join an organization, take narcotics, break the accepted pattern of sex, or renew our subscription to *Life*, we are still merely responding to this shared impulse. For most of us, these calisthenics of momentary escape suffice. But it seems equally obvious that all of us, at one time or another, have experienced the fleeting temptation to walk away from our present condition, to pursue an unarticulated longing into the empty, trackless night.

The impact of this impulse cannot be totally negated by the myth that such flight is impossible. Nor is there much sustaining solace to be found either in statistics or the absence of statistics. The computer can count us and divide us and subdivide us, but it can never begin to understand us. Ambrose Bierce, the misanthropic author and columnist, intuitively sensed this when he wrote in *The Devil's Dictionary*: "According to the most trustworthy statistics the number of adult Dullards in the United States is but little short of thirty millions, including the statisticians."

In 1913, Bierce went to Mexico in search of "the good, kind darkness," and disappeared.

IV

One Luminary Clock

Something incredible happened to Lawrence Bader the night of May 15–16, 1957, on storm-tossed Lake Erie. One minute, just at dusk, he was talking to the crew of a Coast Guard launch; no, he told them, he did not need their help. The rescue boat pulled away; darkness enveloped the lakefront; the wind picked up, and the whitecaps churned against the beach. He was alone, he was adrift, and suddenly he was gone.

The effect of Bader's disappearance was to create—at the time—a circumstance unsupported by fact. The storm, the damaged boat, his car parked at the boathouse, all pointed to a reasonable presumption that he had drowned. Later, after he had been identified as Fritz Johnson, a new line of speculation developed. Had he methodically planned his disappearance or had he been the victim of a freak accident? Did he deliberately stage his "death" on Lake Erie and somehow make his way unseen to Omaha, or was he a true amnesiac, washed up on the lake shore to wander off in search of an identity? How and why had it happened?

The questions are unanswerable. There are, to be sure, numerous theories, each supported in varying degrees by incomplete evidence and intuition. Only one thing is certain: at some appointed moment that May night, Lawrence Joseph

Bader, or at least the person known to his family, friends, and associates as Lawrence Joseph Bader, ceased to exist. Whatever the cause and whatever the motive, Bader had reached his departure point. . . .

No man or woman traverses this mysterious point in precisely the same manner, primarily because no two people ever approach this traumatic act the same way or from the same direction or with the same reason. Some, like Bader, go by boat. Others, following the example of Judge Crater, step into cabs. Many simply disappear into subway entrances or onto trains and buses or board airplanes. Quite a few go out for an evening newspaper or to view a movie. A lot drive away in the family car. One man had his wife along when their auto broke down on a California freeway. He told her to wait in the car while he walked off in search of help. The investigators were able to trace him only as far as the municipal airport.

Some leave notes, some hints. A sizable (though again unmeasurable) percentage embark on trips—business, professional, social, recreational, vocational—and just keep going. An angry handful pause to stuff a suitcase before storming out of the house at the sullen end of an argument. But mostly the farewell consists of a routine telephone call, a postcard, a casual kiss, or a final wave, almost as afterthought, at the curb. Crater was neither the first nor the last to dine pleasantly with friends prior to vanishing into the night. An inventive minority collect their vacation pay but not their wives or husbands, then flee in the opposite direction. One New York City patrolman aborted red tape simply by tossing his badge onto the subway tracks. The majority walk away without any explanation.

The departure point for Mrs. Gertrude Jones came at 10:45 A.M. on May 10, 1964. It was Sunday, and her husband, Bruce, was outside setting bricks for some new front steps on their California home at 301 Richardson Way in Tamalpais Valley. As the forty-two-year-old woman came out the door and passed him, she muttered something that sounded like "good-bye." The last person to see Mrs. Jones was a neighbor driving home from church along State Highway 1; he slowed down and asked her if she wanted a ride, but the woman walked on without replying. She had about thirty dollars in her handbag.

"I thought she was just going out to visit neighbors," Jones told reporters. "When she hadn't returned by sundown I became frantic. I called all of her close friends, but nobody had seen her. I was awake all night, and the next morning I called the Marin [County] sheriff's office."

The police soon uncovered two puzzling facts about Gertrude Jones, who was an honor graduate of Hunter College in New York, with certification as an elementary teacher. Almost three weeks before she disappeared, she had purchased a round-trip airplane ticket to Los Angeles, using the name Mrs. R. Cooper. But she had apparently become confused about which plane to take at the San Francisco International Airport and returned home, without a word to her husband, in time to attend an adult class that night at Tamalpais High School. Secondly, the only documents she took with her were the original of her husband's will and a photostatic copy of her birth certificate. "It was either a planned disappearance," said Jones, "or the wandering off of a confused person who may be suffering from some kind of amnesia."

Bruce Nelson Campbell departed in bright green monogrammed pajamas, without benefit of a mumbled farewell. His point of departure came shortly before 2:15 A.M. on April 14, 1959. It was at that time that his wife, Mabelite McLane Campbell, discovered him gone from their room in the Sandman Motel in Jacksonville, Ill. His clothes were still there, and on the dresser were his cigarette lighter, glasses, money, and car keys. The Campbells were visiting their son, Bruce N. Campbell, Jr., an assistant professor of chemistry at MacMurray College in Jacksonville.

According to the local newspaper reports, the fifty-seven-year-old Campbell, an investment counselor in Northampton, Mass., had been exhausted after the long automobile trip to Illinois. On April 13, he was treated twice for what his wife later described to police as "a lack of orientation." Several times that night, he woke up and asked his wife if their station wagon was locked; she assured him that it was, then fell asleep herself. When she realized that he was missing, she rushed to the car and canvassed a ten-block area surrounding the motel for about an hour before contacting the police.

At this point, a minor debate of sorts occurred. Mrs. Campbell insisted to the investigating authorities that her husband had wandered away "while in a state of confusion because of the drug" he had been given to quiet him. The attending physician, Dr. E. C. Bone of Jacksonville, disagreed. "This condition recurred during the day [April 13]," he reported. "I administered medication which would have relieved such confusion. It would not have added to it."

The initial phase of the investigation was conducted by the police alone. It should not, they reasoned, be difficult to spot a thin, six-foot-four man dressed in green nightclothes, who walked with a pronounced limp. Late that first afternoon, Chief Ike Flynn and Police Captain Charles Runkel scoured the area in a light airplane. The aerial search and a missing-person alert over the Illinois state police radio network failed to turn up any trace of Campbell.

The weather the next day, April 16, was clear and crisp. Shortly after 9:30 A.M., Chief Flynn marched off at the head of a three-hundred-strong search party, 235 of whom were students at MacMurray College, the remainder off-duty police and firemen and sheriff's deputies. This company was soon divided into ten-man squads, several of which were sent six miles along the Wabash Railroad right-of-way and down both sides of Mauvaisterre Creek. Other teams were dispatched to check wells, barns, and farm buildings in the outlying areas, plus the facilities of the Morgan County Fairgrounds. Late in the afternoon fifty high-school students joined the hunt, which was being coordinated by four radio-equipped cars, walkie-talkies, and a small observation plane.

By sundown, after all the teams had reported in, Flynn admitted that "We just about have run out of places to search," and reluctantly canceled the operation. "We want to find him," he told the reporters. "If anybody has any suggestions we'd be glad to hear from him." Only one person accepted the chief's invitation. "A fortune teller told us that Campbell was seven miles from Jacksonville, either northeast or northwest of the city," Flynn revealed three days later. "We've even looked there."

The Jacksonville authorities were stumped. Back in Massachusetts, Campbell's friends and associates were confounded. They remembered him as a quite, rather intense individual, who often sported a tam-o'-shanter for his evening walks about the neighborhood with his favorite dachshund. His father, the late Louis L. Campbell, had been Northampton's postmaster for almost a quarter century, before buying the J. A. Sullivan Company hardware store and becoming president of the Northampton Cooperative Bank. Bruce had worked in the store for a number of years after his graduation from Williams College in 1923. His brokerage work seemed to be thriving; he was, in fact, planning to conclude a profitable mutual-fund transaction with the Stanley Products Company when he returned from Illinois.

The lack of motive heightened the aura of mystery surrounding a pajama-clad man who vanished from his wife's side in a strange town in the middle of the night.* What had happened to him? Was an accomplice waiting outside that motel? Could he have stumbled into the rain-swollen creek,

---

* On March 10, 1967, Bruce N. Campbell, Sr., was declared dead by Judge Harry Jekanowski of the Hampshire County (Mass.) Probate Court. The private testimony relating to his disappearance was impounded by the judge, the seal to be broken with his permission only for "persons with sufficient reason."

with his body swept downstream toward the Illinois River
and eventually to the Mississippi? These questions were still
being asked three years after his disappearance, when a family friend in Northampton noticed a curious letter to the
editor in the June 14, 1962, issue of the New York *Herald
Tribune*. The writer was protesting the invention of a martini
machine, which, he jested, would seriously interfere with the
bartender's traditional role as an unpaid adviser in such areas
of expertise as investments. Campbell worked with investments and his favorite drink was a martini. But what obviously excited the friend was that the letter was signed
"Bruce Campbell, New York." She promptly wrote a letter to
that newspaper, explaining the situation and asking for more
information about the author of the martini-machine letter.
No answer was ever received from the *Herald Tribune,*
which, on April 24, 1966, itself disappeared.

The one-column headline was succinct and innocuous:
"SYMES RESIGNS BANK POST DUE TO POOR
HEALTH." It appeared in the September 10, 1963, issue of
the Lockport *Union-Sun and Journal,* and the story that fol-
lowed did not begin to tell the residents of that insular New
York State community what had really occurred:

> Resignation of John T. Symes, Jr., as vice president and a
> member of the Board of Trustees of the Farmers & Mechanics
> Savings Bank was accepted by the trustees at a meeting Mon-
> day.
> Although Mr. Symes, an attorney, gave no reason for his
> action in his letter of resignation, it was learned that it was for
> reasons of health.
> William B. May, his law partner, said that Mr. Symes is
> undergoing a series of tests at a New York City hospital.
> Mr. Symes was elected to the Board of Trustees on Jan. 14.
> On June 11 he was elected vice president by the Board of
> Trustees.

The rest of the article explained in considerable and pomp-
ous detail how the trustees were going to increase the fourth-

quarter dividend on all of the bank's accounts to four percent. What the trustees neglected to announce was that at the
end of that quarter, Symes was going to be elected president
of the bank. They also forgot to mention that, fifteen days
before his resignation was formally accepted, John Thomas
Symes, Jr., had disappeared.

Others besides the trustees and his family knew the truth,
but it did not become general information in Lockport until
October 4, when the full story appeared in the New York
Daily News. Symes had left home as usual the morning of
August 26, his wife told the *Daily News,* and gone to his law
office to collect some legal forms. Then he proceeded to the
bank, where, about 10:30 A.M., he made a $1,500 withdrawal
and left the building. Before leaving for Buffalo to board an
airplane for New York City, Symes handed a sealed envelope
to a driver for the Lockport Star Taxicab Company and
asked to have it delivered shortly before 6 P.M. to his home at
552 Locust Street. "I have to get away for a while," Symes
wrote. "I love you and the family. John."

The bank received his resignation, postmarked Lockport,
the next morning, and a special audit showed that no funds
were missing. During the next two weeks, Dorothy Symes
received a telegram and several letters from her husband, all
of which indicated that he was somewhere in New York City.
"I showed the letters to a psychiatrist, and he said that John
was sick, needed help, and that I should try to find him," she
explained to the *Daily News*. "That is why I am here."

The *Daily News* responded with a heart-wrenching article
that featured a photograph of John Symes staring across the
page at a demure Dorothy Symes. "SOMEWHERE HERE,"
the headline sobbed, "A LOST, TROUBLED MAN." As a
result, more than a dozen telephone calls were received at the
West 47th Street precinct house, the most promising of
which, the police decided, came from Mary De Palma, a
waitress at the Woolworth's store on Broadway at 44th Street.
The day before the *Daily News* article appeared, she insisted,
a customer resembling Symes had told her that she reminded

him of his daughter. Mrs. Symes rushed to Woolworth's for a look, and then told the police that Mrs. DePalma did indeed resemble her thirteen-year-old daughter, Marilyn. On the basis of this reciprocal identification, detectives carrying photographs of Symes staked out the entire Times Square area that night, but to no avail.

The man they sought was a native of Lockport, where his father, prior to his death in 1950, was president of the Niagara County National Bank & Trust Company. He majored in geology and political science at Hamilton College, and was named one of the five outstanding seniors in the Class of 1941. He attended the Yale University Law School for one semester before accepting a commission in the Navy. He served as a photointelligence officer for two years in the Pacific aboard the destroyers *Kimberly* and *Wickes*. Later, he was reassigned to the Navy's Patents Division in Washington, where he was released from active service in September 1946, with the rank of lieutenant commander. The previous year he had married Dorothy Jackson of Middleport, N.Y., and the couple stayed in Washington while he completed his law training at George Washington University.

He received his law degree in February 1948, passed the New York State Bar examination thirteen months later, and joined the Lockport law firm of Lewis, Lewis & Bell. When the local Junior Chamber of Commerce named him its Young Man of the Year in 1954, its specifically cited his "qualities of leadership, his business abilities and last but not least his personal integrity." Among the activities that brought him that group's Distinguished Service Award were his work with the PTA, the Red Cross, the Community Fund, the Youth Committee of the YMCA, and the Junior Service League's "'53 Follies." In addition, he was a deacon of the First Presbyterian Church, a director of the Lockport Rotary Club, and a member (for six years) of the Lockport Board of Education.

His private life was equally active. Symes was a low-80's golfer, and he and his son owned and operated the Trans-

Golf Driving Range on the outskirts of town. He was an avid reader, a gifted public speaker, an accomplished parlor magician, and a skilled cabinetmaker, and he was known on the ham radio network as WA2ZWS. At the time of his disappearance, he was preparing to solo for his private pilot's license at the Amherst, N.Y., airport.

Six years have now passed, and no one has heard from or seen John Symes. Nor can anyone—except perhaps Symes himself—explain why a forty-four-year old man on the threshold of financial security and community prestige, a man described by the *Daily News* as an "attorney, banker, devoted husband and loving father of three," would abruptly go off for a few days and not come back.

What Orja Glenwood Corns, Jr., needed was not solitude but companionship. His wife and daughter had gone to Virginia to visit her parents, and Corns faced the prospect of spending the Fourth of July weekend by himself in their Winnetka, Ill., home. On July 2, 1948, his departure point, he decided to go out on the town. It turned into a night on eternity.

The son of a successful investment banker, Corns was born in Chicago in 1914. His childhood was a comfortable succession of private schools and exclusive clubs. It was marred only by the financial setbacks his father suffered in the Depression, which, combined with his mediocre academic record at Georgetown University, terminated his college education in midpassage. He went to work for several brokerage houses, but these were not prosperous years for the stock market, and after his marriage in 1938 to Betty Johnson, he started casting about for a new job.

The change was made in April 1942, when he became a clerk at a toolmaking concern. Two years later he was upgraded to salesman, and in January 1946 he was promoted to district manager in Chicago, with a tristate area to supervise. It was about this time that he and his wife purchased a white frame dwelling at 421 Linden Avenue in the quiet, exclusive North Shore suburb of Winnetka, beside Lake Michigan. He was earning in excess of $12,000 a year, and if the income did not quite cover the expenditures, it was merely another of the constant pressures that rising young executives, then and now, must contend with. His home life was not unusual. He enjoyed an occasional practical joke, and was known as an outgoing, convivial host. At thirty-four, Orja Corns was a good sales manager with a promising future.

He spent the week before his disappearance in touring company installations in Wisconsin, returning late Friday afternoon to the Willow Inn, about a mile from his home. He rolled the dice for drinks with the bartender, Dick Gipp, and lost. After several Tom Collinses, Corns had Gipp cash a $100.72 check for him, and made a date to go with the bartender to the horse races at Arlington Park on Monday, July 5. He left about 6 P.M., and Gipp had the impression that Corns would return to the inn for dinner.

Corns went home. The house, closed for five days, was hot and stuffy. He opened the windows and doors, took a shower, and changed into fresh clothes. His suitcase remained unpacked. On his dresser was eighty dollars. When he left the house about 7:30, he did not close the doors or windows, and he did not turn off the lights. He drove away in his green 1947 Oldsmobile.

How Corns spent the next few hours is as much a mystery as his ultimate fate. He had left home with twenty dollars from the check he had cashed at the inn, plus another thirty or forty dollars. Yet at some time that evening, he stopped at his Chicago office and left a receipt for eighteen dollars in the petty-cash box. Then, about midnight, he walked into the Parody Club on North Clark Street, where he was well known. During the next three hours, he cashed two personal checks for twenty-five dollars each. He left as he had arrived—alone.

Corns did not show up for a golf date he had made for Sunday; nor did he ever contact bartender Gipp about going to the racetrack. Neither man was disturbed at being stood up. It was not until Tuesday, July 6, that he was first missed. When he did not get in touch with his secretary that day, she called his relatives. What they found was an open house with the lights burning. They called the police.

The investigation quickly centered on the Parody Club. Clark Street, with its strippers and B-girls and touts and pimps and loud music and watered drinks, had a reputation for often repaying its high-living, free-spending patrons and conventioneers with violence. Muggings were routine, and there were more variations of the badger game than neon signs. "Accidental" deaths occurred, from the police point of view, with annoying and inhospitable regularity. Corns had obviously had quite a bit to drink between 5 P.M. on July 2 and 3 A.M. the next day, and he was apparently carrying a lot of money. Had he become the Street's latest victim?

A neat theory, satisfying on all but two counts. The proprietor of the gas station where Corns had his car regularly serviced swore—and could not be shaken from his testimony—that Corns had appeared at his place on July 6, four days after his nocturnal visit to the Parody Club. Two employees at the station agreed with the proprietor's recollection. Secondly, Corns's automobile was never found.

Mrs. Gertrude Jones is gone. Bruce Campbell is gone. John Symes is gone. And Orja Corns is gone. All four departed without warning, without explanation, without apparent reason, without preparation. Mrs. Jones mumbled a farewell; Campbell did not bother to dress; Symes gave his wife a routine kiss; Corns left the lights on. The only thing really unusual about their last days or nights was that these particular days and nights were unexplainably their last.

Or were they? Conventional wisdom demands that this quartet of the missing—surrogates in this instance for thousands of vanished compatriots—could not have survived. Mrs. Jones, for instance, was depressed and confused by a recent investment reversal. She had taken very little money with her, and she had reacted in a very peculiar manner when accosted on the highway by a neighbor. Obviously she was in no condition to fend for herself. Ergo, she must be dead. Similarly, Bruce Campbell. He was disoriented, under sedation, in his nightclothes, without funds. Obviously he must have suffered some mysterious fatal accident. John Symes had money, but he was "sick" and had, according to his wife, "cracked under the pressure of too much work." Alone, wandering the unfriendly streets of New York with a large sum of money, he had obviously unfavorable odds against survival. Orja Corns must have been murdered, despite the contradictory testimony of the service-station owner who claimed to have seen him four days afterward. How else to explain the failure of the police to find his car, which only a professional criminal would have known how to conceal or sell or demolish?

Obviously. And yet, conventional logic does not always suffice. It requires too many assumptions, most of them based on the comfortable but unsupportable presumption that life patterns and instincts cannot be drastically altered, that middle-class adults especially are locked in the unyielding vice of established and predictable behavioral modes. We frequently sense that this is not so, but for most of us the doubt remains unchallenged. It is infinitely easier, in certain cases, to invalidate a disturbing possibility than to discard or even resist it.

One such case was the apparent drowning on Lake Erie of Lawrence Bader. Logically, he was dead. Everything pointed to that eventuality. The only missing evidence was the body itself. The same circumstances obtained on Friday, July 28, 1961, when Jersey City physician Larry L. Feder vanished while skin diving in the vicinity of the Statue of Liberty in New York Harbor. The same inferences were drawn after Ionel Grigoriu, a teacher, parked his car along Highway 1 in California, five miles south of Carmel Highlands, and walked into the Pacific Ocean on Saturday, October 6, 1956. And the same conclusion was reached after the outboard motorboat in which attorney Philip S. Bird of Waterville, Maine, was last seen was found wedged into the bank of the Kennebec River on Tuesday, April 5, 1966.

Larry Feder's disappearance touched off an intensive air-and-sea search of the harbor. Coast Guard cutters and police helicopters scoured the area, and six professional divers checked a number of the favorite underwater haunts of skin divers. But they found no trace of Feder, a native of Austria and a U.S. Air Force veteran, who had been introduced to scuba diving during a recent vacation at Montauk Point on Long Island. Since his return to Jersey City, he had continued this interest, renting small boats and working the clear waters off South Beach on Staten Island. Once he was warned about steering his boat too close to the thrashing propellers of the ships entering and leaving the busy harbor.

The day he vanished, Feder had visited his office and then made his customary rounds of his hospitalized patients. Around noon he drove to Leonia's Yacht Club, where he rented a gray-and-white outboard-equipped boat. When he did not return at 5 P.M., the alarm was sounded.

While the harbor search was proceeding, the investigation ashore was turning up several disconcerting clues. The day after Feder was reported missing, a ticket clerk at the Port of New York Authority bus terminal in midtown Manhattan told police he thought he saw a man resembling the doctor seated in the waiting room. Jersey City detectives also discovered that Feder had discharged his office nurse a few weeks before, and had given up his post-office box in that city about the same time.

These suspicions became much more than bizarre speculation on August 8, two weeks later, when a medical colleague of Feder's turned over to the police a letter he had received from the missing doctor. Feder was in Amarillo, Texas, working at a Veterans Administration hospital and living in an apartment he had rented by mail a month before his "accidental death" in the harbor. Feder asked his colleague to deliver a sealed enclosure to his wife, Marilyn, at their apartment at 47 Duncan Avenue. "I ran away," he explained to his wife, "to start a new decision in life to get out of the old dying rut."

The day before Ionel Grigoriu vanished, he put his house at 860 Fine Avenue in Pacific Grove, California, on the market. His resignation as an instructor of Rumanian for the Army Language School at nearby Fort Ord was on his superior's desk; the effective date was October 31, 1956, and the reason he gave for quitting the post he had held five years was that he planned to reenter college for further studies.

The job meant a great deal to Grigoriu. He had secured it shortly after emigrating from Rumania with his wife, Maria. Only a few months before his disappearance, he had proudly become a naturalized citizen. But a promotion he had been expecting had not come through, and he was despondent. He did not mention this to his wife at lunch that final Saturday. Nor was there any mention of his vocational problems in the note she found on his dresser when she returned that evening from her job at a local department store. Instead, he advised her to forgive him, although he did not specify for what, and not to grieve for him but to make a new life for herself.

The implication of suicide was strengthened the next day, October 6, when Grigoriu's abandoned two-year-old sedan was found near the ocean on Highway 1, between Monterey Bay and Big Sur. Two bloodhounds quickly picked up the scent, leading the police half a mile down the highway across a field and down to a rocky beach. The trail ended in the surf. Grigoriu's car keys and wallet could not be found.

The rugged coastline where Grigoriu's footsteps ended has been the scene of numerous suicides in the Monterey area. A strong ocean current rapidly sweeps the bodies out to sea; generally, though not always, the corpses are eventually recovered. But it was not the failure of the sea to yield Grigoriu's body that puzzled the investigators. Rather it was the discovery in his closet of the trousers he had worn to his last meal with his wife: they were soaked to the knees with salt water. Had he lost his nerve the first time, driven home and changed his clothes, then returned to the scene and destroyed himself? Or was he involved in an elaborate hoax to feign his own death? The Monterey Superior Court accepted the first premise twenty-two months later and, on July 31, 1958, declared Ionel Grigoriu legally dead.

Kennebec County Probate Judge Lewis I. Naiman was satisfied a mere three months after Philip S. Bird vanished that the Maine attorney was deceased. In admitting Bird's will to probate, Naiman concluded: "A reasonable inference of death arises from his disappearance under such circumstances as would warrant the presumption that he died at the time of his disappearance. Death is established by the showing of facts inconsistent with the continuance of life and such as would lean to the conclusion that death had taken place."

The "circumstances" referred to by the judge appeared rather conclusive. On April 5, 1966, Bird drove to Gardiner, about thirty miles from his home, and asked to test-drive a fourteen-foot outboard motorboat. Although the water was quite choppy, he could not be dissuaded. When he did not return, the sales firm instituted a search, and the empty boat, its motor still idling, was found about six miles down the Kennebec River. A river watch of several weeks failed to recover the body of the thirty-six-year-old lawyer.

The missing ex-Marine, it soon turned out, carried life-insurance policies totaling some $350,000 in benefits, not unusually high for a successful attorney with three children. A member of a prominent Waterville family and an unsuccessful candidate for mayor, Bird practiced law with his father, Stanley Bird. There was absolutely no reason, the family assured the probate judge, why Bird would want to disappear. He had left no notes of any kind, had not attempted to contact the family, and had not withdrawn any money from his bank accounts. In addition, the dragging operations conducted by the local sheriff's office had snagged a piece of cloth that was identified as part of Bird's jacket.

In fact, however, Bird was not dead. Having abandoned the boat he was testing, he had driven a recently purchased used car to the West Coast, arriving about ten days later. Identifying himself as Earl Brecher,* he secured lodgings at 206 School Street in Daly City, California. Within a few days, he was hired as a salesman by a local Pontiac agency. After his true identity became known, he was described by his fellow employees as "normal and hardworking" and able to fulfill his sales quotas during the two and a half months of his employment.

On July 9, a few days after the judge had probated his last will and testament, Bird telephoned home. Within hours, his father, a former special agent of the FBI, was on an airplane to California. The next day Bird's wife, Marilyn Jean, was reunited with her husband at San Francisco International Airport. He was then committed to San Mateo County General Hospital for observation, pending a sanity hearing later in the week. The six-minute hearing was closed, but afterwards Superior Court Judge Frank B. Blum announced that Bird could return to Maine as soon as arrangements for psychiatric treatment were made there. The only public explanation for Bird's action came from Dr. Richard Levy, chief psychiatrist at the San Mateo hospital. "He apparently became discouraged," Levy told the press, "because he felt he was not matching up to his own standards."

Four men—a salesman, a doctor, a teacher, a lawyer. Three of them were "lost" in boating accidents, of whom two returned voluntarily; the other, Lawrence Bader, was recognized by chance years later. The fourth scribbled a cryptic note and walked from his car to the ocean—twice; he alone is still missing. The conventional presumption is death; the common denominator is water.

For the tiny minority of the voluntary absent who attempt

---

* The name of a Maine client, who had died before Bird's disappearance.

to simulate death, the point of departure almost invariably involves water. Oceans, lakes, rivers, reservoirs, quarries—any type of water, provided it is deep or swift-flowing or both. The main reason should be apparent: the absence of a body. Few other "circumstances" offer such a ready-made, inexpensive vehicle for certifiable doubt. The water death, moreover, has another advantage. It often resolves the moral dilemma that self-destruction poses for some people. If the event is staged properly, the investigators and the "survivors" are usually left to make the distinction between accident and suicide. At times, it becomes a fine distinction indeed, since mystery merely magnifies doubt and multiplies uncertainty.

Obviously, not many people fall "accidentally" off the Golden Gate Bridge. Quite a few jump intentionally, however, and a glance at the fatal record of that famous span might provide one specific insight into the probabilities involved. According to Lieutenant W. H. Porter of the California Highway Patrol, a total of 428 suicides from the Golden Gate were reported between 1938, when it was opened, and June 18, 1967. Three hundred and seventeen of these are considered "definite," Porter said, though only 211 of their bodies were ever retrieved from the surging tidal waters below. The remaining 111 reports (about twenty-one percent) are described as "possible suicides" by the police.* As Porter explained it: "Under 'Definite Suicides' are placed the names of persons who were definitely seen going over the bridge by witnesses, or who had left suicide notes and their bodies were later recovered. Under 'Possible Suicides' are listed persons who left notes, or their cars were left on the

---

* Unfortunately, no study has ever been made of the Golden Gate suicides—who they were, what ages, occupations, motivations, etc. The only discernible annual pattern is a sizable increase during Presidential election years, with the exception of wartime 1944. An especially difficult year was 1964, with twenty-eight, although it is impossible to tell whether they were liberal Republicans before the election or conservative Republicans afterward.

bridge, or otherwise indicated they would jump, and disappeared, but no witnesses saw them jump."

Nor, he did not need to mention, were the bodies of any of the "possibles" ever recovered from the tidal currents. Porter said that his department does not keep any statistics under the heading of "Faked Suicides." Any that may have occurred would presumably be included in the "Possible" category. As it happens, he added, his investigators have serious reasons to question the validity of forty-one of the 111 "possibles" thus far recorded.

Of the six "possibles" registered in 1966, only one was considered of extremely dubious validity. It occurred early on June 27, and it rapidly developed into one of the strangest manhunts in California history. The Volkswagen on the bridge belonged to an Edith Fisher, but the motorist who reported the parked car to the police claimed to have seen a short, stocky man walking away from it toward the bridge railing.

The standard procedure in such cases immediately went into effect, and within minutes a police cruiser had reached the abandoned auto and a Coast Guard vessel was maneuvering below on the incoming tide. There was no sign of the man, on the bridge or in the water. A search of the car, however, produced a loaded shotgun rigged by wire into a suicide weapon, several kerosene cans, and a handwritten note from Edith's husband, Max Fisher: "I intended to burn this too. But then, what the hell, it was a lemon anyway."

Later that day, the police discovered the added meaning of the arson reference. Four hours before the bridge incident, Fisher had put a torch to the cottage he had laboriously built in the foothills of the Diablo Mountains, five miles north of nearby Gilroy. Outside the gutted cabin, the detectives found a bloodstained pillowcase in a garbage can. The incriminating evidence accumulated quickly. A San Jose taxi driver remembered driving Fisher out to the cabin Sunday night, June 26. A neighbor saw Max drive away early Monday, just before the dwelling exploded in flames. A couple at the

Sausalito end of the Golden Gate told how a man resembling
Fisher had banged on their door about the time the car was
found on the bridge above and asked them to call a cab for
him. The police also learned that Fisher had stayed at a San
Francisco motel for the three days prior to his disappearance.
He had been alone. Mrs. Fisher had not been seen for five
days.

What it all added up to seemed painfully clear. Fisher had
murdered his wife, burned the cabin to destroy the evidence,
and then staged his "death" on the bridge. The detectives
rushed back to the couple's San Francisco apartment at 378
Golden Gate Avenue. Someone had been there since the
police had inspected it shortly after the suicide report: a pair
of black trousers and a dirty white shirt now hung over a
chair; nearby was a copy of a San Francisco newspaper with
the story of the bridge suicide carefully clipped out.

About the same time, the police located Max's Chevrolet
parked in San Jose. It contained a .22-caliber rifle, and in the
trunk the police discovered a sealed sack of quicklime. A two-
day stakeout of the car did not produce Fisher, but his non-
appearance did not especially bother the police, who had
issued a fugitive warrant charging him with arson. The only
loose end, they reasoned, was the body of Mrs. Fisher, and
they knew exactly where to look.

At least it all sounded perfectly logical at the time. She
must be buried in or around the burned mountain retreat,
which Max had sentimentally christened "Suits Us." The
cabin ashes yielded nothing, however, and suddenly the investigators experienced an intimation of doubt. If not to
dispose of a body, why had Fisher destroyed his cabin? And if
he was trying to obliterate the bloody evidence of a slaying,
why had he so carelessly left the pillowcase in the outdoor
garbage can?

The search continued. Bloodhounds were imported and
programmed with the scent of the missing fifty-four-year-old
woman. Each time, the dogs unhesitatingly plunged off toward a ranch pond a mile away, but divers and grappling

hooks found nothing. Numerous caves and abandoned mines in the area were carefully searched, also fruitlessly. Then a bulldozer lumbered up to clear away the charred debris, and squads of prisoners from the county jail systematically gouged trenches around the cabin site and bored holes at ten-foot intervals, still to no avail. Reluctantly the police came to the conclusion that there was no grave in the vicinity.

What really upset the investigation were the revelations that followed a routine police check into the backgrounds of Max and Edith Fisher. In a very real sense, the case began to disintegrate with a canary in a gilded cage. The building manager had seen Fisher carrying it from his apartment three days before he disappeared. And yet no trace of the bird or the cage was ever found. In the context of a possible murder and faked suicide, the removal of the pet canary began to assume a baffling complexity. Just what sort of person was Max Fisher?

The attempt to answer that query soon posed an even more pertinent question for the investigators: *who* was Max Fisher? He was, first of all, a superb waiter, whose Germanic accent and suave manner gave him a continental air much in demand at the Bay area's best restaurants. He had but recently quit his job at San Francisco's World Trade Club. But this was not that unusual. Fisher's valuable talents enabled him to work when and where he pleased. He received big tips, and he was himself a big tipper. His income was large enough for him and his wife to live very comfortably, with more than enough left over for him to indulge his taste in expensive cigars and vintage champagne. He was a physical-culture enthusiast.

Beyond that, it soon became apparent that a lot of people knew a little about Max Fisher, but no one knew much. Fisher would tell personal anecdotes, but he was notably reluctant to fill in the connecting links. On employment questionnaires, he had a habit of changing his birthplace each time. The two items in his biography that seemed consistent were his age, fifty-five, and his reference to his Army service in the Panama Canal Zone during the 1930's. When a search of the appropriate military records failed to disclose anyone by that name, the police began to wonder just what Max Fisher's real name was.

The investigators had been told that Mrs. Fisher was Mrs. Fisher without benefit of clergy. She had been positively identified by a San Francisco jeweler as the woman who had recently come into his store to look at wedding rings. At this point all the police knew was that the couple had come to the West Coast together from Miami about fourteen years before. In that Florida city, she had been known as Mrs. Edith Kelly. Routinely, the police began checking out the references Edith had listed for a job in Miami. What they learned confounded all the murder-suicide theories that had been developed.

Edith was not Mrs. Edith Fisher. She was not Mrs. Edith Kelly. She was actually Mrs. Edith Dunleavy Sadlier, and one June afternoon in 1945, after chatting pleasantly with her sister, Mrs. Louise Kelly, on a street in Providence, R.I., she had disappeared. "She just up and left," Mrs. Kelly told the incredulous investigators. No one in Providence ever received a word from her, including her husband, Clement Sadlier, who divorced her a decade later in absentia and remarried.

The startling news that Edith had vanished once before, coupled with the inability of the police to discover who Max Fisher really was, ended an active investigation that had already exhausted every available clue. Had Edith staged a second disappearance? But if so, why had Max gone to so much trouble to make it look like murder? If it was murder, what was the purpose of removing the canary three days before the fake suicide attempt?

While the San Francisco authorities pondered these sensational new possibilities, an unconnected and unspectacular but equally mysterious incident occurred in Tucson, Arizona. Charles Keith Beth, a forty-one-year-old salesman, registered unobtrusively at the Ramada Inn there. The part owner of a vending-machine company called Frosty Shakes, Inc., Beth had left his home in Denver a few days previously for a sales swing through Phoenix. When he did not return as scheduled on Tuesday, August 9, 1966, his wife became alarmed and contacted the Denver police.

Tucson detectives quickly traced him as far as the motel— but no further. He had arrived Friday, August 5, telephoned home to inquire about his wife and two children, and then made a few business contacts the next day and Monday. He was last seen at the Ramada Inn Monday night. Sometime that evening or early the next morning, Beth left his room and drove away in his 1965 Buick Electra. When the police arrived Wednesday, they found his clothes, personal papers, and shaving gear in the room. There was no evidence of foul play.

Three days later, Beth's locked car was found parked near the U.S. Immigration complex at Nogales on the Mexican border, some sixty-five miles south of Tucson. An extensive search of the area on both sides of the border ensued, but no information on the whereabouts of the Denver man, described by his family and friends as "very reliable" and "absolutely not" the type to disappear voluntarily, was uncovered.

The few notices that appeared in the local newspapers were short and perfunctory. There was very little to write about. No buildings were burned, no suicide staged, no investigation with bloodhounds and bulldozers and convicts. Beth left no notes, gave no indications, offered no explanations. One minute he was a dutiful husband, a loving father, an enterprising businessman who pursued without complaint his daily ritual of obligation. One day he reached his departure point.

And suddenly he was gone.

V

Journey to Redoubt

Everyone who has traveled knows the pervading sense of aloneness that infects the wayfarer as he stares at the unfamiliar door of a hotel room. This transient sensation is, however, of temporary moment to the normal traveler, who pivots like the free leg of John Donne's memorable compass, measuring instinctively his separation from a fixed point. His itinerary is circumscribed and of planned duration; round-trip tickets are purchased; someone is always there to accept his collect phone calls.

The voluntary absentee, moving through an open-ended and impulsive journey, lacks such basic assurances. He or she approaches a future unconnected to any past. To the uncertainties of geographical distance must be added the inevitable alterations of social status; the strangeness of the terrain is exacerbated by the emotional upheaval of unexplained departure.

There seems no way to generalize the awesome impact this transition might exercise on, for instance, a middle-income executive with a wife and children in comfortable suburban surroundings, who overnight becomes a $1.75-an-hour laborer in another city hundreds of miles away. The incongruity inherent suggests near-impossible obstacles in temperament, attitude, intent, purpose, outlook, and skill. The very magnitude of required change implies, at the least, an extended period of introspective anxiety and a painfully gradual accommodation to a vastly different set of circumstances.

Or does it?

Voluntary absentees seldom, if ever, have the time or the training to record their thoughts and reactions and experiences during this traumatic interlude. Those who have returned, for whatever reason, are either legally unable or personally unwilling to discuss it. We can, however, at least glimpse the essence of this experience in the private journal kept by a former newspaper editor, whose purpose was not so much to disappear as it was to escape from what had become for him an intolerable existence. Before he departed, he quit his $12,000-a-year job, obtained a divorce (there were no children, and the decree did not specify any alimony), and paid his outstanding debts. A small suitcase and a portable typewriter were all that he carried.

He had no specific destination in mind and little idea what he would do when he got there. He was, for the most part, acting on almost irresistible impulse, and, although he made no secret of his departure, he carefully avoided telling anyone in which direction he was headed. In all probability, the only person pursuing him when he left New York on an overcast January afternoon was himself. The diarist, like Larry Bader, had recently observed his thirtieth birthday.

January 24

I am squatting here on the Delaware-Maryland border with my belly full and my bowels empty. So ends the first day in the quest for my redoubt. Driving, even through six inches of Jersey soot slush, gave me hours to use in thought and use them I did. I thought of how easy it was to turn my back on that which never was—my life. Who is to say that it was not the bravado born of cognac a month ago which brought me to this place. Not I. But unlike the countless times before, when the brandied euphoria gave way to the more subtle narcotic blend of petty success, petty prestige, petty power, and sickening fear, this time I left. Yet I believe that I left nothing, for I had nothing, and indeed, perhaps until the moment I was on the way to the road, I was nothing.

But I am truly afraid now. There can be no more bottom-glass wailing against those who constrain me. There is nothing constraining me now. There is no one to blame now. . . . I am frightened, because I realize how ill-prepared I am to seek, let alone find, the answers to the questions welling up within me. In a few short hours [after my departure], the burden of freedom pressed down on me relentlessly. I may become more accustomed to it as days, weeks, and months pass, but I will always feel it there—its packstraps cutting into me. I have never been a free man before. It hurts and the pain frightens me. The elation I feel completes the paradox. . . . But hear this: I, the boy wonder, the purveyor of potential, the raiser of eyebrows, the master of the cynical sneer and the shivering child of my own timidity, I have submitted my resignation to the warder of compromise. I am free. Free to try, free to fail, and, perhaps, free to find my redoubt.

This initial entry, written at a motel in Laurel, Md., went on to cite the price of the room (six dollars) and the fact that his car, which he was delivering for a "transfer" agency in New York to its owners in Fort Lauderdale, was consuming gasoline with the "abandon of a wino at the marriage feast of Cana."

He was on the road early the next day, and by evening had reached Myrtle Beach, S.C. Perched on a bed at the Haywood Motel, he recorded his first impressions of the South, as seen from Route 1. A soaring hawk had captured his attention, and for a few paragraphs he tried to summon some sort of analogy with society. But the attempt depressed him.

27 January

I am an idiot. I have earned my first piece of money as a free man. "Piece" is the right word, since it was a half dollar. That was the sum of my wages for driving 1,500 miles through sleet, snow, slush, and dark of night. Worse than an insult, my half dollar was an afterthought. I put $2 of hi-test gas in the tank this morning. Then I took the car to be washed and even argued with the attendant because the ashtrays weren't quite clean. I simply wanted to do an honest job.

The owners of the car had not arrived yet, so he located the manager of their Fort Lauderdale hotel, one Mister Mc-Carthy, "a small flabby man with trembling hands and the hard eye of a teller who has finally made vice-president." After inspecting the car for dents but without commenting on its appearance, McCarthy handed him forty dollars, repayment of the $37.50 gas allowance.

I gave him two singles and was flapping around for the half dollar when he said, "That's all right, you keep it, *boy*." Mister McCarthy came within an instant of requiring surgery on his colon for the removal of a metal object the size of a fifty-cent piece. But I managed to spurt out, "Thank you, sir," and suddenly felt the bitter cotton of servitude clinging to my throat.

The McCarthy episode had a decidedly unsettling effect on him. Until then, he had been contemplating the implications but not the reality of his abruptly reduced status in society. Not since recruit training had anyone called him "boy" and remained standing. He spent one night in Fort Lauderdale, was appalled by the prices, and boarded a bus, instinctively continuing south.

My bus left on time. The ride to Key West was made in soft darkness, interrupted only by the hysterical screams of a little girl who tumbled from her seat and cut her forehead slightly on the seat in front of her. . . . We pulled into Key West at midnight, with a fresh ocean breeze rattling the shutters of the clapboard houses and playing zither music on the fronds of the palms. Key West, my first impression tells me, is for burnt-out cases like myself. I may be here for some time.

Writing two days after his arrival, he struck an optimistic note for the first time since his departure six days before. The trip had proved exhausting and somewhat humiliating. But now he was settled at last, and the prospects exhilarated him.

I am in my heart an islander. The sea is my barrier, which keeps at bay that which I flee. Key West is an island, despite the two-lane concrete causeway that links it, like a relief tube, to the mainland. A man can think on an island. The air is as clean as the fresh salt water that laps the beach before going out with the tide for its Gulf Stream journey north to a foggy union with the Labrador Current.

My mind is being scrubbed clean by the sun, air, and water. My eyes are opening as the sticky pus of three thousand nights of nothingness dries in the morning breeze. My senses tingle with an awareness of life. I respond to beauty again. My mind cartwheels from one thought to another. . . . The sand between my toes, with gentle abrasiveness, is rubbing away the tight-shoe calluses that linger as a brand of my previous condition of servitude. I do not, at this wondrous moment, own a pair of dress shoes. I may, should the need arise, buy a pair of loafers, but such an act will demand much reflection first.

This immediate euphoria, however, was dampened by his gradual awareness that for the first time in his adult life he was faced with a limited amount of funds and no prospect of income. The question of money had been raised the moment he reached Key West.

. . . I trudged to the Southard, my heart somewhat more burdensome than my bag. I envisioned a repetition of Fort Lauderdale and began to mentally chart my next destination. . . . The lobby of the Southard is divided into two parts. The foyer contains a proper hotel desk, mailboxes, a stair, and bell to summon the sleeping night man. The larger section is barred by a wooden accordion fence. Behind it was a television set and a passel of comfortable-looking chairs and couches. The room was clean. The night man was either absent or dead, too, or he might have been visiting his competitor in the hospital. I hadn't finished a chapter of the book I was working on before he sailed in, listing alternately from port to starboard as his cargo of booze shifted. I asked him what his rates were and was told, a little too evenly, $8.64 a night. "Friend, I don't want the bridal suite," I said, mentally multiplying the sum to $60.48 a week or $241.92 a month. I had been warned in

Lauderdale that Key West was expensive in the winter, but I wasn't prepared for this. Still, it was now close to 3 A.M. and I knew I couldn't get a bus before sunrise, so I started filling out a registration card. As I reached for my wallet, the manager, a somewhat beefy blond fellow named Jack, said, "Are you staying long?"

"Not at sixty dollars and forty-eight cents a week, I'm not."

He looked at me for a long time and said, "Look, I run this hotel, and you can stay here for $30 a week if you want, and I don't think you will be disappointed when you get upstairs either."

So it is to start in Room 309. It is a spacious room—I paced it off and found it to be roughly fifteen by twenty-five feet. The wall-to-wall green carpeting is neatly complemented by pastel walls, and three watercolor prints of fishing-boat scenes hang there. The air-conditioning unit is also a heater, and the room is furnished with a chest of drawers, two chairs, a good-sized table, a bench, twin beds, a night table and lamp, a mirror, and a closet. The bathroom has a large tile shower, and the whole place sparkles, since an invisible genie of a maid arrives sometime after I leave and cleans my droppings. I slept well last night. There is peace in Room 309. Peace that allows me to think and write. It may be that circumstances will force me to leave 309 before I wish to, but I doubt it. The peasant does not give up his land without a fight. Nor will I quit my island quietly.

The next two days were spent ogling the tourists, learning to eat conch chowder and pronounce it "konk," and investigating the local flesh-and-booze traps for the resident Navy population along Duval Street, which, he reported, "holds no mysteries for me, a diploma holder from Charleston's Market Street, Savannah's Indian Street, and who did graduate studies at that M.I.T. of such places, South Hotel Street in Honolulu." Still, a night of watered gin-and-tonics watching the hustlers work over the young swabbies in the Boat Bar cost him thirteen dollars and caused him to retreat to Room 309 with fresh evidence of Barnum's famous maxim. The money was not inexhaustible, and he resolved to begin conserving his resources.

January 31

. . . The chowder is made from the giant conch that lie in the shallow waters of the keys. Lone men working from stubby, low-riding pirogue-like boats put-put along the shallows gathering the harvest with hooks attached to about three fathoms of line. Some, I am told, dive for the conch, but that is harder work and is considered a waste of energy. The world's best conch chowder, without a doubt, is made by John at the beach where I swim, pitch horseshoes with the old men, and get my brains knocked out by these same old men at volleyball. For 35 cents you get what is described as a "cup" of it, which looks something like Manhattan clam chowder. Fifty cents buys a larger bowl of this delicacy, and it makes, I soon found out, a very satisfying meal, indeed. It is highly seasoned, and John is lavish with the conch meat and the fresh vegetables that float alongside it. I also learned soon enough about the 29-cent breakfast at McCrory's (two eggs, grits, toast, and coffee), so that in less than a week I have discovered how to eat well on less than a dollar a day without cooking for myself. In fact, within three days of my arrival, I was a "conch" myself, making nasty remarks about the tourists. This is curious, because when you leave one life for a new one, the old time relationships become distorted. A day seems like a week, a week a month. . . .

The next afternoon his time continuum was shattered, perhaps irrevocably, by a letter from a friend, the only person who knew the box number at the Grand Central post office in New York City, from which his mail was automatically forwarded, in this case to General Delivery, Key West. The journal entry for the day consisted of a copy of his reply.

February 1

Only once did fear grip me coldly by the throat. A single sentence you wrote on [his former wife] was enough to plunge me into deep gloom. Why can't she and they leave me alone? It cannot be love that prompts phone calls such as hers. Is there a pact sworn to in the darkness that none must be allowed to escape? Am I to be hounded? Am I suddenly, one day, to see the hated past before my eyes, smiling a thin grasping smile here in Key West?

Write no more of this, for God's sake. And please do not tell any of them where I am. Protect me, for I am helpless against them. My break consumed all the courage I have. I cannot survive another round.

He mailed his answer, then joined a group of men he had met on the beach. But what started out as a convivial evening of conversation and drink became, for him, a traumatic identity crisis.

February 2

Today I celebrated Groundhog Day as a guest of the city of Key West. I didn't all of a sudden wake up and find myself in the drunk tank of the city jail. It was a gradual awakening. . . . I was aware of where I was but not the particulars of just why I was there. My hotel key was in my pocket, as was my wallet with its papers and $16. I was cold, and I paced the empty tank to keep warm. . . . The Key West drunk tank is about eighteen feet wide and thirty-five feet long. The ceiling is about twenty feet from the cold concrete floor, with its center drain that serves its inmates as an informal urinal. There is a slatted bench fixed to the rear wall, but I did not avail myself of this bed since some earlier guest, finding no bucket or the like in that barren place, had defecated on it. . . .

I could recall nothing beyond a point when I was sitting, quite drunk, talking to newly made friends and listening to Sinatra records on the front porch of their rooming house about ten blocks from my hotel. . . .

Three of them—Doc, a paratrooper who got a medical discharge for either being wounded in Vietnam or claiming he was; Harry, who seems to be a tattooed Spanish-speaking attorney of about thirty-four; and Eddie, another man in his early thirties, who was not on the beach because he was in juvenile court explaining why he had not paid the Cuban woman who cares for his motherless child—had all gotten jobs that morning. They had, more on a lark than in earnest, gone out to the Boca Chica Naval Air Station and asked work of the contractor building some defense installations there. To their surprise, they were hired at $1.50 an hour, with the promise that their wages would be raised if they proved themselves willing workers.

There was to be a party celebrating this event, and to the quartet already named was added Jack, a fortyish ex-investment broker who does not work but who spends money freely since he fled California and the imminence of a nervous breakdown; Steve, a huge gross queer with curly blonde hair; Jason and Frank, a pair of twenty-year-old University of Bridgeport students down to the sun between semesters, and Diana, a beautiful blonde nineteen-year-old coed who had accompanied them and who, I think, warms Frank's bed these cool evenings. This was the cast that took up station on the wide roominghouse porch and watched the sunset, after several bottles of rum had been secured and a parakeet had been purchased to replace the landlady's canary, which had gone to glory that morning. . . .

The time between sunset and my personal dawn in the drunk tank spins like a centrifuge in my mind. As I paced and paced, the phrase "car radio antenna" popped up, but I did not know what to make of it. . . . I had reasoned that I was arrested for being drunk and disorderly at least, and the minimum of security and supervision shown me and my personal effects convinced me that any other charges against me could not be too serious.

They came at about five o'clock: two trusties to sweep and mop the outside floors. One of them, a grayheaded old man, with the skin and countenance of a turtle, bade me good morning and asked if I could use some coffee. I said yes and asked for a cigarette, too. . . .

He extracted some cigarette paper and a tin of Prince Albert tobacco from his denims and expertly rolled a cigarette for me.

The trusty brought him coffee and, for a dollar, produced a pack of tailor-mades. He also managed a look at the desk blotter to learn the exact charge: disorderly conduct and destroying private property. Only nine days before, the dia-

rist's name and position on his newspaper would have earned
him a ride home in a police cruiser and a promise to keep the
incident out of the official records.

At 6:30 A.M. a tall young policeman came, opened the cell (I
later learned he was the arresting officer) and said, "Buddy,
you are allowed one phone call." My first thought was to call
New York and have some money wired down, since I didn't
think I had enough left at the hotel to cover the bail. But the
cop reminded me that I would have to stay in jail until the
money arrived. "You'd probably be better off to get yourself a
bail bondsman," he said. My instincts as a journalist who has
spent more than his share of time in filthy little cubicles
tucked away behind a dozen detective bureaus had begun to
function again. "You're right," I answered. "Who do you
suggest?" He gave me a wary glance, "I can't take sides," he
said, and then listed three resident bondsmen. I raised my
hands in a gesture of helplessness, and he added: "Do you
want Jim Dolan?"* Of course I did, and I said so.

He went to call Dolan, and I went back into the tank. For
the first time waves of nausea swept over me like the incoming
tide of reality. This was not funny any more. There I was:
thirty years old, 1,500 miles from everything I knew and
understood, and powerless to control my situation. I was
actually shivering. I had lost my hard-found freedom less than
ten days after I had won it.

Dolan arrived with briefcase in hand at 7 o'clock. We talked
a bit while various papers were signed and my bond was
posted, the bondsman having satisfied himself that I was a risk
worth taking. The process was almost completed when I began
to pass out. I asked if I could go to the toilet, and the cell was
quickly opened and I hurried—unescorted—down that long
corridor and to the right where the men's room was. I sat on
the commode, my head between my knees, my mouth filling
with the rhythmic discharge of saliva as my body prepared to
rid itself of the contents of my upper stomach. I stood, my face
hot, my vision blurred, and tried to throw up in the bowl. I
failed, and seconds later the nausea vanished, I stepped back

* Fictitious name.

into the corridor and found Dolan, who had come to see what was keeping me. . . .

I returned to the Southard with Dolan, and got $125 for him, leaving myself with $15 (I had paid a week's rent in advance the day before). . . . Dolan said my letters of reference, letters designed—if necessary—to open doors that might be closed to some of Key West's most prominent citizens, were all right. He said that if I make restitution, it is likely that I will get off with a $25 or $50 fine on a plea of guilty. He explained that I was charged with a misdemeanor and that the city court where I was to appear was not a court of record. The only record of my transgression against the public weal would be in the voluminous drunk files of the Key West police.

Dolan promised to talk to the arresting officer to learn whose antenna I had destroyed (it was never made clear whether I had ripped it off the car or was merely trying to lean against it) and whether a complaint had been filed by that person. I promised to return tomorrow. I left his office, and in doing so, I left part of myself behind. I don't know exactly what it is, but I suspect that it was part of my middle-class background, which does not allow things like this to happen to people like me. I do know that something dramatic—if nebulous—happened to me. For when I was sick, frightened and ashamed and cowering in a barren jail cell, I was not, even at that moment, prepared to change places with another, who a few short weeks ago had been city editor of an influential city newspaper and hence exempt from the petty laws that rule the lives of unimportant, rootless people like me.

This particular entry ended with an introspective examination of his previous drinking record and the conclusion that, although he was at worst a problem drinker and not an alcoholic, he must abstain from all intoxicating beverages in the future.

February 3

After thirty years and a hundred days, I finally did it! I did an honest day's work. Again, in less than twenty-four hours I jumped one giant step from bum (Drunk, Model 1934-Y) to working man. I made the "shape"—as we say in my new

circle—at 6:30 A.M. at the Casa Blanca Guest House to ride to
Boca Chica with Doc, Harry, and Eddie. I did not bring lunch
or my new work gloves, as I suspected that even if I were hired
I would not be put to work until tomorrow. We stopped for a
sleepy cup of coffee and an order of toast, while Doc dominated the conversation with speculation on how much he
would get at the pawnshop for his portable TV set. It wasn't
that he needed the money that much; it's just that the set is
useless, since one must pay $8.50 a month to a corporation in
order to hook in a cable which brings in the Miami stations.
. . . So Doc's move was one of prudence. Rumor has it that
the controlling interest in this cable company is held by a
snaggle of Florida state senators. I believe it, whether it is true
or not.

When we reached the main gate at Boca Chica, I jumped
out of the car, before the Marine sentry had a chance to
assemble a court-martial. I sauntered into the security shack
and felt for the first time the jobless man's fear when he is
seeking work and he finds many of his kind there before him,
all busy filling out forms, having photos taken, and picking up
I.D. cards. . . . I was equipped with the name of a hiring boss
with the Allan H. Campbell & Company of Texas, and I left
the security shack for the pay phone after asking a seaman
apprentice to look up Campbell's number for me.

I thought I could feel the toast making its way back up my
throat when the voice at the other end of the phone brushed
me off. But then he quickly gave me the number of another
foreman who might be looking for workers and hung up. The
second voice materialized at the shack in a few minutes, looked
me over, and, after I assured him that I could be relied upon
to handle a shovel, told the sailor behind the desk to issue me a
temporary pass and dashed out. It took all of two minutes; all
they wanted was my name, an address (I used a phoney one in
New York, since I had lied on the question of whether I had
ever been arrested for a crime other than a traffic violation),
and what was presumably my Social Security number. Nobody
asked to see anything remotely resembling identification, and
in minutes I was in a pickup truck, with a hard hat on my
head, on my way to a Hawk missile site within one of those
jerry-rigged Army compounds. Fifteen minutes later I was

scraping away with a shovel at what they call "marl," trying to smooth a path for a long board which is used as a form for concrete.

I was assigned to help two carpenters. White is a young man, somewhat my junior, whose accent places him far below Nashville; Joe is an old man of indeterminate years, who knows his craft much better. I scraped away and then flailed about with my pick for brief spurts to deepen the spots where the board rose above the taut piece of string they used as a level. Sweat trickled under my armpits, and my breathing was just a tiny bit labored, but I had no doubts, then, that I could make it through to lunch.

There is more to those wooden forms than just plopping them in a six-inch trench. They must be anchored—clasped fast to Mother Earth, locked in the embrace of thirty-inch metal stakes, which, of course, must be pounded down through marl, coral, and other rock strata until they reach the molten mass in the center of the earth. I got to do the pounding with a sixteen-pound sledgehammer. The first few stakes were all but agonizing. My muscles ached, my bleeding hands hurt, my vision blurred and my mind reeled . . . my strength drained as I slipped from pounding the stakes down sharply and without pause to pounding them slowly and, finally, to pounding them between weary pauses. My journeymen overseers were the essence of charity. They had shown me how to hold a sledge the right way, and no taunts or insults passed their lips. . . .

It takes an average of sixty-five eighteen-inch strokes to pound one stake to its proper level. I do not know how many I so pounded, probably eight or ten, but whatever the number, it was more than sufficient for me. That done, I grabbed the pick which had lost much weight during my absence and dug quietly while I regained my breath. . . . About a week later, it seemed, the four o'clock quitting whistle blew, and a couple of silent Southerners gave me a ride back to town and dumped me within a few blocks of Room 309.

. . . I caught a glimpse of my reflection in a shop window as I passed. I was filthy, my hair matted, and my work clothes white with powdered concrete. I looked again. I looked lean and agile and damned if I didn't look young. This was no

teenage actor passing a gin mill near the shipyard on his way
from measured labor with Daddy. I was real, that filth was
real, my cuts bled real blood, and there was no mistaking the
reality of my aching arms, shoulders, and back. I had done an
honest day's work for less money than I have ever earned for a
similar period in my life, and I felt good.

Eight hours of brutal, punishing menial labor had almost
wiped out eight years of detailed white-collar experience.
Almost, but not quite; rather than appear in court to answer
the charge of disorderly conduct, he paid out an additional
$75 in conscience money "to avoid something that my most
primal instincts told me was a disgrace." He was also learning
about the gray zones of society—quite removed by form and
content from the middle-class experience—where movement
is lateral and impulsive, questions far outnumber answers,
and first names predominate.

Some impressions amid the flotsam of Key West . . . the
people about the beaches here seem a trifle unwilling to
casually drop their surnames until they assure themselves that
you, a stranger, are not an agent from the world they fled,
come to drag them back, bound with paper subpoenas. . . . I
was frightened (i.e., after my brief jail experience) that they
might reject me as an unfit companion, but tolerance is a
hallmark of those in exile, and absolution was freely given,
with no penance exacted. In fact, there was only the most
perfunctory interest expressed about the whole incident. These
people, unlike my former associates, seem disinclined to gloat
over the personal troubles of others. They exhibit the same
apathy, to a lesser degree, toward current events. . . .
Perhaps Doc [the former paratrooper] is an extreme case of
imagination run wild, but the malady abounds here in Key
West, where virtually everyone you meet at the beach is in
flight from someone or something. Horrified at what they leave
behind, they succumb to the temptation to create a different,
more exciting, more glamorous past for themselves. Most do it
with a certain charm. Some are clumsy. Others are inexpert at
lying, and still others laughable in their pretenses. . . . I
should think that we have the civilian equivalent of the

Foreign Legion, where each person's past is his own business and his comrades know only what he chooses to tell or invent. The practice, however, provides Key West with some of its fascination and much of its gossip. . . .

His initial fear of rejection in the informal, fluid beach society had evaporated with the realization that such conceits of friendship belong to a different, more stratified ethic. Long, grueling hours in the sun with a pick and shovel had made him distinguish between mobility and freedom, had taught him to look within himself for the redoubt he sought. And he now knew that what separated his previous manner of living from his new way of life was not simply dress, housing, travel, and the quality and quantity of his food, but such intangibles as attitude and perspective and outlook. In the privacy of his journal, he confessed that it was only with difficulty that he could remember how he used to live. He had been in transit only *thirteen* days.

February 5

I am sitting here looking at the stub for my first week's pay, a little green slip of paper that represents fifteen hours of my life, hundreds of droplets of my blood, pints of sweat, countless aches, and a renewed sense of outrage coupled with the purely sensual mystique of renewed manliness. For fifteen hours, the Campbell company reckoned my worth to be $22.50. The federal government decided that I should contribute $1.40 in taxes to shore up my society and another eighty-two cents to make sure I do not become an embarrassment to the Great Society at age sixty-five by starving to death noisily in some still-dirty street. It is not much—$20.28 net, but it is important because it represents the first honest money I have ever earned. I make the distinction between money earned by toil and money made by guile. I have been expert at the latter in the past. My skills as an honest man improve with each passing day's trauma. I am now to the wrecking bar what Casals is to the cello. I am also entrusted, now and then, with the task of driving nails into wood at impossible angles that would cause my carpenter friends more discomfort than they are willing to suffer, while some young idiot (me) stands by looking eager.

In a few weeks, I will be capable of building a house—provided said house has no real need for indoor plumbing, electricity, or finished walls. But if what is needed is a cinder-block house, complete with concrete pillars, steel I-beams, cement floors, glassless windows, and a fifteen-foot crushed marl parapet surrounding it, then, sir, I am your man. All I ask in return is $1.50 per hour and thirty minutes for lunch.

For the tourists, fleeing the cold slush of the north, sunshine is a perquisite of wealth; on the job, the same clouds the tourists curse from their rattan chairs on the motel veranda are looked upon by day laborers as evidence of His concern for their well-being. On February 15, it began to rain shortly after the starting whistle had sounded:

Today I earned seventy-five cents, which will buy a pack of cigarettes, a yard-long seventeen-cent loaf of Cuban bread, a five-cent pack of Kool-Aid, five grapefruits at three cents apiece, and two pounds of potatoes, leaving me with two pennies left to pay the tribute exacted by the state of Florida. . . . And tonight I feel the need of a woman. I would go out and find a whore, if I thought I could find one who would work as cheaply as me.

VI

Biography of a Stranger

Author Ted Robinson, Jr., did not keep a journal when he disappeared, but later he did chronicle his experience for *Harper's*. In this self-exposé, he detailed his anguish and frustration during two depressing months of looking over his shoulder for imaginary pursuers, trying to alter his appearance, and writing bad verse. The magazine published the results of this misadventure in its March 1952 issue, under the heading "How to Disappear." It is almost a classic example of just the reverse.

"Life had lost much of its charm for me and I had tentatively decided to have nothing more to do with it," Robinson explained, "but I thought I ought to enter into a sort of trial separation first, on the chance that a thoughtful period of isolation might restore my curiosity, about the world around me and possibly even about myself."

Robinson did not elaborate on the nature or duration of this depression, nor did he give any indication of just how long he considered dropping out of sight before he actually tried it. He was born in 1910, the only child of Edwin Meade and Martha Robinson. His father, who was also known as Ted, was a lecturer in etymology and phonetics at Cleveland College of Western Reserve University; for thirty-six years, until his death in 1946, he conducted the popular "Philosopher of Folly" column in the Cleveland *Plain Dealer*. It was on that newspaper that his son started his journalistic career in 1931. Ted, Jr., soon moved on to a variety of other papers and magazines, landing finally on *Time's* editorial staff. At the time of his disappearance, he and his wife had five children.

There is no mention of his family in his *Harper's* confession. He speaks of his depression and his instinct for absolute privacy, ". . . attainable, I thought, only if I became, in effect, invisible to the rest of the world. The only way I could do that, short of living in the woods, was to become somebody else." This decision made, Robinson next considered the question of where. Foreign travel was rejected, both because of possible passport complications and because he felt that language difficulties would make him more conspicuous. Since he had traveled widely in the United States as a correspondent and was well known in the press establishment, he automatically eliminated any place he had previously visited or where he knew that a press associate was stationed. His ultimate choice of the west coast of Florida was dictated by his conviction that no one went there in July and by his desire "to reduce the routine miseries of living to a minimum."

Having selected a place called Naples as his destination, Robinson convinced himself that the best way to avoid detection would be to get there in the quickest way possible. He telephoned a travel agency for airline reservations and, after dark and a few "fortifying drinks," picked them up. That afternoon he had purchased what he considered an escape kit—some loud shirts and ties, a small traveling bag, sunglasses, a razor, and pair of scissors. Some of this he stowed in his desk, the rest in a locker at Grand Central Terminal. Instead of depositing his salary check, he cashed it.

He went to his midtown Manhattan office early the next day, pausing only to have a barber drastically cut and thin his normally long and thick hair. Arriving before any of his colleagues, he hurriedly shaved off his mustache and trimmed his eyebrows and changed into his new shirt and tie. Then he donned the sunglasses and headed for the elevator. He was "pleased to find that the operator was unfamiliar to me."

The next few hours were spent trying to look inconspicuous in airline waiting rooms in New York and Washington, lurking behind unread newspapers, avoiding uncrowded cocktail lounges, and speaking to as few people as possible. His plane landed (about 4 P.M.) at Fort Myers, where he elected to spend the first night. But by morning, he had convinced himself that the local police had been or would soon be notified to look for him. He nervously boarded the first bus to Naples, which he had imagined as a lazy fishing village but which turned out to be a somewhat stylish small resort. Terrified, he hitched a ride in a pick-up truck the forty-odd miles back to Fort Myers. The driver told him about quiet Sanibel Island, a sparsely settled sandbar a few miles offshore, noted for its seashells and served twice daily by ferry. The next morning, Robinson taxied from Fort Myers to the ferry landing at Punta Rassa.

On Sanibel, he rented an isolated beach-front cottage, explaining to his landlords that he was a vacationing teacher who wanted to be alone to do some writing. "By moving to an island I had got myself out of sight, but I had also cornered myself. There was only one entrance and exit: the ferry. If I ever wanted to get off the island ahead of unwelcome visitors it would likely be impossible." In the end, what made Sanibel "impossible" was not its limited access and egress but Robinson's temperament. For a man who wanted "a thoughtful period of isolation," he spent far too many hours socializing with his landlords at the island's main inn, changing first the subject of conversation, then his cover story (from "teacher" to "dissatisfied artist"). On one occasion, he worked far into the night with his scissors, trying to alter his appearance further. The results were so atrocious that he felt obliged to explain his action as a drunken impulse.

"I don't believe that any of them actually did think anything of it. They regarded me, I found, as a harmless eccentric, not *too* eccentric but just the slightly unaccountable sort of oddity they imagined the woods of art were thick with. Such a role was thrust on me at the outset, and I soon embraced it with gratitude. It relieved me of a great many responsibilities, chiefly the responsibility of being consistent, and I know that there was many a little mystery about me which might have worried them in another person but which worried them not at all in my case because I was just that way, that was me, *you* know artists."

But the more he told, the less he could say, and this gnawed at Robinson's very being. "I am a man of deep feeling and wide acquaintance, and it was a hard thing to have to hold my tongue every time an invitation presented itself to set somebody straight in a tone of authority." The basic problem, however, was that the one person he could not seem to set straight was himself. Long hours spent tramping the empty beaches, staring at the Gulf of Mexico, examining his navel or soul or both, brought him little solace and understanding. ". . . I was alone, and talked to myself, which was neither more nor less rewarding than talking with the others. I sat in the cottage and talked things over, either silently or aloud, and walked on the beach and talked, usually to myself but occasionally, when I was hard up, to the old herons that hung around there. I never got anywhere."

He mailed off some "bad verse" to a few magazines; it was promptly rejected. One night, when the fear of discovery again overwhelmed him, he painstakingly cut into tiny fragments all the clothes he associated with his former identity. The problem of disposal panicked him: if he buried them, someone might stumble onto them; if he burned them, someone might notice. His solution was to creep down to the water late at night and sprinkle the scraps into the gentle surf. He spent an hour the next day collecting them along the beach where the incoming tide had distributed them. The incident sums up his seven weeks on Sanibel Island.

Abruptly he left. This time Robinson stopped worrying about detection as he wandered on impulse around the South, staying here a few days and then going there. ". . . I made no effort at all now to be inconspicuous. I managed to dismiss from my mind completely the possibility of being recognized; I moved freely, went wherever I wished and did as I pleased, and it didn't seem to make any difference.

"In the end I came to the decision that I really ought to kick it around with an analyst, like everybody else, and returned to New York."*

Back home he could barely conceal his disappointment. "It developed," he admitted ruefully, "that the hunting that had been going on you could have fitted comfortably into a coffee spoon." The only public notice had consisted of a small item buried in the pages of a suburban daily. "At least a few of my friends hadn't heard I was missing," he complained, which may offer a substantial clue to the author's unconscious motivation for the entire escapade.

Robinson himself denied the title and point of his *Harper's* article when he described his trip as "two months of hiding out." The theme of his experience is flight, but the dominant motif is fright. This constant fear of apprehension became so insistent, even obsessive, as to suggest finally that Robinson's real anxiety was that he would *not* be located.

This inherent contradiction characterizes a distinct subcategory of the voluntary missing, who are more properly described as runaways—persons who disappear temporarily in a desperate attempt to force a confrontation with their environment. These people invariably leave a well-blazed trail for the investigators; and if this does not result in their being located, they make additional efforts, consciously or not, such as collect phone calls to relatives, letters and remembrance cards with no return address but a clear postmark, or the use

---

* In 1952, Robinson joined the staff of *Newsweek*, becoming its movie editor in 1956 and a general editor two years later, a position he held until he left the magazine in January 1965. On July 19, 1966, he plunged to his death from his room on the nineteenth floor of Manhattan Towers, at Broadway and Seventy-sixth Street. He was fifty-six.

of credit cards; when all else fails, they follow Robinson's lead and return of their own accord.

What—from the point of view of a person who really wants to vanish—were Robinson's "mistakes"? To begin with, his decision to fly directly from New York to his selected destination and his careless gesture of going in person to pick up his reservation. Had there been any publicity about his disappearance, the investigators would have been on the next flight, and their task would have been simplified considerably by his ludicrous attempts at disguise, which served only to make him more noticeable. Moreover, he exhibited a strong failure wish by going to his own office to effect his costume change, a routine and rather unnecessary operation that could have been done anywhere. And his "relief" at bumping into an "unfamiliar" elevator operator is less than convincing.

His choice of the west coast of Florida in the summer was, in a sense, defeated by its very logic. Certainly no one goes there then. Which is precisely why he should have avoided the area, since his presence merely increased his need to explain himself to his hosts. And the more he talked, the more he contradicted himself, which in turn added to his sense of anxiety. But the most conspicuous thing about Robinson— which from this perspective means, in effect, his most serious blunder—was his idleness. Indolence, especially without visible sign of support, breeds speculation; curiosity is soon converted into inquiry; and inadequate or contradictory answers lead to suspicion. Obviously, the voluntary absentee cannot afford this type of suspicion. Yet the thought of employment does not seem to have occurred to Robinson, or at least he never mentioned it. He was apparently content to subsist on the residue of his salary check; the instinct befits a man who was trying, unsuccessfully, to hide, not disappear. That he failed to make this distinction was, in a sense, the final indignity of his predicament.

There are many reasons why the condition of employment is endemic to the state of voluntary absenteeism. The jobless stand out, of course, but mainly in middle-class situations—which was but one more of Robinson's intuitive miscalculations. A person seriously attempting to disappear and begin a new and therefore different kind of life drifts naturally and instinctively into the ranks of the skilled or semiskilled. In the United States today, this means primarily an urban area.

Money, it would appear, is initially of only secondary consideration. The absentee begins with a substantial bankroll in his wallet or her pocketbook; this amount is often determined by circumstance. Since the majority seem to have abruptly succumbed to impulse, the size of this flight fund depends on how much they think they will need and how much they can raise quickly without creating undue suspicion. Robinson apparently settled for his last salary check; Larry Bader and John Symes, respectively, presented their personal checks for $400 and $1,500. The diarist in Chapter V used a Christmas bonus from his publisher as a nest egg. One private developer in the Southwest was carrying the down payments on three houses he had built; an accountant in Connecticut was paid cash for his automobile and then talked the buyer into driving him to the railroad station in Hartford; one enterprising Cincinnati salesman managed to charge two new car batteries every day and six snow tires on his company's gasoline credit card before he abandoned the vehicle—and his family and job—on a side street in Cleveland a fortnight later; a disability pensioner in upstate New York reaped a sudden and sizable windfall from the policy numbers, stuffed some clothes into a cardboard box, and left a farewell note in the coffee canister for his tea-drinking wife. But the award for the most ingenuity, above and beyond the limits of duty, must go to the spouse of a Los Angeles haberdasher, who, en route to the airport, managed to collect four of her husband's delinquent accounts.

Regardless of the size of the absentee's stake, the money evaporates at an alarming rate when there is no income. The central motivation to seek work, however, is neither an effort to dissolve into the faceless work force nor a fear of the background-probing questionnaires of the welfare or unemployment bureaucracies. It is, instead, simply habit. This habit is more than just the preconditioning of years of reporting each weekday to office or factory or store. For the average American, the habit of work transcends instinct. Unprepared by education or inclination for leisure, he endows the routine of occupation with the weight of ethical fact. If idleness has gradually lost the aura of sin, it retains strong implications of sloth. And it is intensely boring.

A new occupation in a strange city under a different name sounds unlikely. Viewed from the distance of inexperience, it seems all but impossible. The middle-class reference to employment involves educational background, an extensive and well-documented work record, credit checks, vocational achievements, certified accomplishments. That a man or woman could secure a job simply by asking for it contradicts experience. Yet it happens every day—in an Omaha bar, at an automobile agency in Daly City, Cal., on a construction site in Key West. The applicants all met the employer's minimal requirements. A bartender must be alert, presentable, and personable; the best conversationalists are good listeners. Car salesmen? Well, if there were any requirements, besides an ability to keep a straight face, our highways would not be so crowded. The daily test of a laborer on a non-union construction job is his ability to get out to the site on time.

What rankled the diarist—and eventually cost him his "position" in Key West with Allan H. Campbell & Company—was the example of a Texas-based company under federal contract paying its non-union workers at a rate below the "poverty" income level defined by a Texan President. The anomaly disturbed him enough to spend his lunch hours sounding out his fellow employees about trade unionism. Convinced that the men were interested, he went to Miami to talk with the proper AFL–CIO officials. Their reception to his ideas for establishing a building-trades union in the Florida Keys was, he felt, "lukewarm." Nevertheless, he persisted. Evenings and weekends, he proselytized the other laborers in their homes and at local taverns. For two months he patiently sought out a nucleus for a union.

Finally the company learned of his efforts. At 8:17 A.M., Tuesday, April 6, his foreman appeared on the edge of the trench he was digging in. "Go get your pay," he said, and walked away.

April 16

. . . I have found a job, the only one available in the entire Florida Keys, if I am to believe the newspaper ads and the Florida State Employment Service. I now dispense gas and oil at a Star Service Station on the 3 to 11 P.M. shift. For a mere six days' work, I receive $68.60.

That is, of course, just my base pay. All attendants, with the tacit approval of the manager, jack up the price of oil by ten cents a can and pocket the dime. I'm told by my co-conspirators that one can make almost $2 extra that way during a good week. And then, too, there are the tips. Last night a generous evangelist passing through town gave me three (3) Bible tracts. "The days of our years are threescore years and ten; and if by reason of strength they be fourscore years, yet is their strength labour and sorrow; for it is soon cut off, and we fly away." (Psalms 90:10) . . . I got so intrigued I forgot to overcharge the bastard for his oil.

His career in the "petroleum game," as he called it, ended abruptly with the arrival of the station manager's unemployed brother.

April 27

This Cuban gentleman, whose knowledge of English seemed to be limited to bobbing his head and smiling hopefully, was in need of a job. Needless to say, I provided him with one.

It was all quite funny at first, but then I realized that I needed that pitiful job, and I got highly annoyed about twelve hours later. . . . I have calmed down now. It is easy to spot some of the economic causes of prejudice when you are on the receiving end of its boot. Presume that I was a native-born American of limited education and no skills, who considered himself fortunate to land a dandy job paying $68.60 a week. What would my reaction be to being kicked out of that job, without notice or severance pay, just because my foreign manager's foreign-speaking brother decided to leave Miami? I suspect that I would be in the market for a white sheet complete with hood.

As it was I made no real protest, for the simple reason that I intended to keep that job only as long as it was necessary to find a better one. I am $91.20 ahead of the game and that will pay the rent. I could have been considerably more ahead had I had a day's notice or so to exercise the attendant's time-honored privilege of ramming his head into the Coke machine after hiding the night's receipts in an empty oil can and then screaming "robbery!" Oh well, there's always the 10 per cent that doesn't get the word.

This time a new job was harder to find. The local newspaper, the Key West *Citizen,* ignored his employment query; he had already been warned not to bother applying at any of the other construction companies operating in the area. A stint as a mate aboard a charter fishing boat proved interesting, but the work was too irregular, and he was repelled by the customers' attitudes (". . . they have no intention of eating their victim, nor have they any respect for their adversary"). Unwilling to quit his island haven, he accepted the interim offer of a local builder to work—"unsupervised and unmolested"—on the foundations of some row housing outside town.

August 11

. . . I am now gainfully employed again. I drive a truck for Lindsley Lumber here, and when I am not driving, loading or unloading the truck, I stack wood or bags of cement, etc., in the yard. In return for this ball-busting labor, I am paid $1.40 an hour, which just happens to be the Federal minimum wage for interstate commerce. Key West is one of those unhappy places where the whole town goes on a spree every time Congress raises the minimum wage.

I work 9.5 hours a day, five and a half days a week, for a grand, excruciating total of 52.5 hours. I receive $82.25 a week, since I must be paid time and a half for everything over forty hours. . . . Tonight I counted enough splinters in just one hand to build another Levittown. . . . To get this low-paying bonanza, I had to invent some more experience, and thus came into being the JRB Construction Company of Point Pleasant, N.J. Just in case Lindsley bothers to check, I sent John a note explaining that he was to tell them I had driven heavy equipment for his firm for about eighteen months, when in reality my experience on large vehicles is confined to riding briefly on the tailgate of a semi.

My stint as an ersatz teamster had the double advantage of pushing my newspaper career farther away. Another precaution against unnecessary questioning consisted of demoting myself from a former editor to a former reporter and cutting my pay in half, as I have found out that firms shy away if you list well-paying jobs you have held in the past. Since the job at Lindsley was offered only on a temporary basis, I suspect that there will be more applications to fill out, and on these I intend to further demote myself to the circulation department and mention only one year of my college background. . . . The man who interviewed me for this job seemed to accept my version of having been ill fitted for newspaper work and preferring to work with my hands. It is thus worth noting that several weeks ago I applied at another lumber company here in Key West, and I filled out the application form honestly. I have never heard from them.

For references, he provided the names of three friends in the New York area. Although each of them was identified by a spurious title (construction-company president, managing editor, and plumbing contractor), only their home addresses were provided. Which is where the reference forms were dutifully mailed by J. G. Baumann, assistant manager of employee and public relations at Lindsley's main office in Miami. "You may feel assured," Baumann wrote, "that your answers will be held in the strictest confidence." As Baumann did not ask for reciprocal assurances, the returns were uniformly satisfactory, and the diarist, who had himself written two and dictated the third, was soon made a permanent employee. But the work, he discovered, seemed out of proportion to the wages ("At the end of each day," he observed, "I feel like an old man on the brink of a cardiac arrest") , and he was soon casting about for a less taxing proposition.

He settled on an advertisement in the local newspaper for a "confidential inspector"—a job that promised a base of four hundred dollars a month, plus incentive bonuses for productive workers. The employer turned out to be the Retail Credit Company, the nation's largest commercial credit investigator. He was ordered to Miami for a battery of intelligence and "sensitivity" tests, the latter designed to measure his ability to draw inferences from stray bits of conversation.

Five days later he was rejected for the position, allegedly because he had scored too high on the tests. "I was told that personnel studies and surveys 'proved' that the company thrived when it hired men of above average but not superior intelligence. The company is apparently convinced that the perfect candidate had been a C-plus student in college. I insisted that there were damned few occasions when I rose higher than a C-plus, but my confession did not help my cause."

Irked by his failure to get the job, the diarist resolved to quit the lumber company and his island haven in order to resume his symbolic journey. His parting gift from Retail Credit consisted of a practical insight into perhaps the most serious difficulty the voluntary absentee faces in adjusting to a more menial condition: the intelligence gap.

No intelligence or "sensitivity" tests are required, for instance, by the Rockford (Ill.) Paint Manufacturing Company when it hires a pigment grinder. In 1962, the job paid $1.90 an hour, and one of the men thus employed on February 14 of that year was Verne Hansen. He had arrived in Rockford in early 1955, and, through an employment agency, secured a job as a common laborer and shipping clerk with the Grand Woodworking Company there; on his application, Hansen stated only that he had a high-school education.

Then, in 1959, he married a paint sprayer, Mrs. Mabel Ostling, a divorcée with two daughters, and the following year Hansen shifted over to the paint company.

The management had no complaints about his work, although, as the company's personnel manager later explained, "It was obvious when he first came to work that he was unaccustomed to physical labor." What set Hansen apart from his co-workers was his superior intelligence. "It was somewhat of a company joke," the personnel spokesman told reporters, "that a man of his mental stature, obviously out of character in a paint plant, was working with a group of semi-illiterates."

Hansen also drank, not enough to seriously affect his work but beyond what his wife could tolerate. When they separated in 1961, Hansen moved to a local hotel, where he decorated his room with rented prints of famous paintings and spent hours listening to classical music on his phonograph. The bellboy considered him a "nonentity" who paid his bills on time. On February 4, he was arrested for drunken driving and tailgating; the Rockford police routinely sent a copy of his fingerprints to the FBI. Ten days later the police in Syracuse, N.Y., announced that they had finally solved the seven-year mystery of the disappearance of Professor Carl Vernon Holmberg, an internationally known cellulose chemist.

A reporter from the Rockford *Register-Republic* brought the news to Hansen, who expressed disbelief. "It seems rather incredible to me," he replied. "I can't quite see myself as a forester. I suppose I will have to go check up to see if the story is true, but I don't see how a man could break off one life and start another."

The story was quite true. What began as a fingerprint comparison soon led to a matching of photographs ("That's Holmberg, all right," a former Syracuse University colleague declared), and finally to the discovery that the missing professor's place and date of birth matched those provided by the paint grinder on his Illinois marriage application.

When Holmberg-Hansen next met the press, he began by explaining that he had no memory of anything preceding an afternoon in 1955 when, as a hitchhiker, he had been given a ride from Elgin, Ill., to Rockford. "My mind was a complete blank when I came to Rockford," he said. "My suit had a New York label and I seem to recall the hills of New York. I recalled some other places too, mostly landscapes. When I got to Rockford I tossed lumber in the yard and picked up a few other odd jobs. I don't know what I'm going to do now."

Asked how he got his present name, Holmberg-Hansen explained that, although he did not have a billfold with him when he came to Rockford, he was carrying a briefcase with the initials "V.H." on it, and so he took the name Verne Hansen. He declined to comment on the fact that Holmberg and Hansen were both born on the same day forty-five years before in Sandpoint, Idaho.

Resolutely he insisted that he had no recollection of Professor Holmberg, or Mrs. Holmberg, or their three sons, or his job with Syracuse University's College of Forestry.* Naturally, he claimed to have no memory of the events of May 11, 1955, when the popular and—within his profession—renowned chemist, after exchanging routine pleasantries with his secretary, walked out of his college office and drove his 1939 Hudson sedan to a nearby intersection.

Three years later, in an article reviewing the mystery that still surrounded the case, the Syracuse *Post-Standard* wondered in print how the thirty-nine-year-old professor could have just walked away unseen from that car, as one leg was encased in a cast to the knee to protect the bones he had broken in his heel in a recent fall at home. Moreover, the writer went on:

---

* This was contradicted somewhat in a statement by his second wife, Mrs. Mabel Hansen, who recalled: "He was very happy in his work here. He read a lot and listened to classical recordings, and he did mention once that he was from Syracuse. That's an awful thing to have on your mind—not knowing who you are."

There were lots of strange circumstances surrounding his disappearance. But the professor's behavior for about a year had
been "strange" anyway. The pressure of his work and of the
many faculty activities he participated in were wearing him
down, according to police. He had been asked to see a physician, an appointment was set, but he failed to keep it. Then
another appointment was set—for the very day he disappeared.
He never kept the appointment. Because of the disappearance
without a trace, some of his associates think he may have
planned to go away.

His family thinks not. Just before he left, he withdrew $30
only from a checking account. He went to the safety deposit
box and took the birth certificate belonging to one of his sons.
He didn't take his own, and he would need one for a passport
to a country other than Canada, Mexico and some small Carib-
bean nations.

The article proceeded to review Holmberg's academic career at the Universities of Michigan and Syracuse, before
concluding with a thumbnail portrait of the vanished professor:

Dr. Holmberg was an active man, but quiet, interested in
camping and outdoor life. He was an excellent piano player—
a skill developed playing in his uncle's theater during the days
of the silent movies. In addition to being active in faculty
affairs, he took a deep interest in his students and their problems. Their worries became his worries. Despite the love of his
work, his family, his friends—he left. He parked his car in the
university section and hobbled away.

A more caustic appraisal was offered four years later, after
the professor's whereabouts had been disclosed by a routine
fingerprint check. "His home life wasn't too satisfactory," recalled a friend and former college roommate, "and we all
believe that was the main cause of his disappearance." A university colleague, however, attributed Holmberg's disappearance to vocational depression. Dr. Edwin Jahn, associate dean
of the department of physical science and research, stated that
Holmberg had seemed eager to change his way of life. "He

appeared to be considerably disturbed for some weeks before leaving," Jahn remembered. The dean also told the press that Holmberg had frequently expressed distaste for the built-in pressures of academe, especially the necessities of periodic publication and research achievements for career advancement.

Jahn was less specific when asked whether Holmberg would be welcome to return to his old position in the College of Forestry. Such a decision, he explained, would rest with the heads of the various departments and the board of trustees. His former position, of course, had been filled, etc., etc., etc. The dean's thinly disguised anguish was wasted on Holmberg-Hansen, who continued to insist that he was not conscious of any specialized intellect. The missing professor even ridiculed the suggestion carried to him by reporters that a $20,000 job had been offered him by a friend. "It sounds rather ridiculous," was his response. "Anyway, what could I do to earn that kind of money?"

In Menlo Park, Cal., the professor's first wife, who had divorced him in 1960 and later married a consulting electronics engineer, issued a statement: "I have no further interest in Dr. Holmberg, other than possibly satisfying my curiosity. We have no connection with him, either legally or emotionally anymore." While she remained in seclusion, her husband, Gordon Babcock, conceded that she was not particularly surprised by Holmberg-Hansen's reappearance. "She always sensed something was wrong," he explained. "Little ambiguities, evasions. We were rather prepared for his eventual reappearance." He did not elaborate.

Neither did the former professor, who appeared as uninterested in his past as he was vague about it. He continued to insist that "reading and hearing the story about Dr. Holmberg is to me just as though I were reading the biography of a strange man, a man I do not know." Locked incommunicado in his Rockford hotel room, he sent word to his employer that he would like to keep his present job. "He said he feels he is working at his capability level and wants to continue," a company spokesman revealed. "He said he doesn't know a thing about research chemistry." But the press remained skeptical about the nation's most brilliant pigment grinder, especially after an enterprising newsman discovered that Holmberg-Hansen had, the very day his real identity became known, returned a copy of *The Origin of Mathematics* to the Rockford Public Library.

In Syracuse, the police missing-persons bureau routinely issued a teletype canceling its seven-year-old bulletin on Professor Carl Vernon Holmberg.

The fact that Verne Hansen had more education than his co-workers did not prevent him from obtaining and performing the job; neither was the obvious intelligence gap instrumental in exposing his former identity. But it did serve to emphasize his apartness—a facet of eccentricity that the voluntary absentee cannot readily afford. The emotional price of such enforced estrangement from intellectual companionship can only be inferred from Holmberg-Hansen's situation.

A broad hint, however, was provided by Ted Robinson, the writer hiding out amidst the mosquitoes on Florida's Sanibel Island. "The ladies at the inn had very little to do at this time of year, and it was impossible to avoid a half an hour of porch-rocker conversation with one or another of them now and then," he complained in his *Harper's* article. "I could not speak knowingly of the things with which I was familiar, because the ladies were quite acute and in time would certainly have managed to reconstruct my background all by themselves. I had to profess ignorance of most general subjects on which I was actually fairly well informed, had to disavow any real familiarity with the places I knew best, and could never, of course, admit to a real acquaintanceship with anybody at all. This meant that I could never speak intelligently on any subject the other party to the conversation knew anything about, and could say very little, ever, about anything *I* knew anything about, and almost nothing at all—

to be on the safe side—about anything I really *didn't* know anything about."

One of the things that Robinson really didn't know anything about was, it seems apparent, "How to Disappear." And yet, despite the numerous "mistakes" he made, he would have proved extremely difficult to locate had someone actually bothered to pursue him. Why? First, because he unconsciously adopted Thoreau's dictum that ". . . the man who goes alone can start to-day; but he who travels with another must wait till that other is ready, and it may be a long time before they get off." In a somewhat different context, the man or woman who goes alone and tells or contacts no one has vastly diminished the possibilities of exposure.

And most importantly, Robinson changed his name.

VII

The Game of the Name

Names are habit-forming. Our own name is among the earliest speech accomplishments, often the first writing experience, ultimately a syllabic foundation of personality. Through time and iteration, our name assumes the force of identity and the substance of property. In many ways, it is our only irrevocable possession. After death, it is the only part of our estate left unappropriated by relatives, creditors, and the tax collector. While we are alive, these same people rely on that name to keep in contact with us, or, should we try to evade their scrutiny, to locate us.

When we write that name on a piece of paper late at night and then erase it, we experience a curious sense of disembodiment. When we discard it, we vanish. It is—as will become apparent in Chapter IX—almost that simple.

How simple is that? Well, it depends upon whom you ask. The private detectives insist that effective name switching is improbable if not impossible, and they have a vested interest in believing themselves. The police are generally more noncommittal; they admit that it is done with some regularity. Those who have accomplished it offer witness of a more convincing, less conjectural nature. They have, like Ted Robinson, Jr., taken the trouble to take another name. Unlike Robinson, who frequently changed his *nom emprunté* and accordingly experienced difficulty remembering who he was supposed to be at any particular moment, these people, after a brief period of adjustment, have adopted their pseudonyms to the point of instinct. In this they are not alone. Half of the married people in the world do just this every day.

Selecting a new name, despite a free abundance, is difficult. To a certain extent, it is comparable to assembling a jigsaw puzzle with blank pieces. The original name is suffused with memory and association and, perhaps to a lesser extent, purpose; a lineage exists, and an ethnic character. To presume another identity is to confront for the first time the potential relation between a name and a person and a function. The theatrical world has considered this problem for centuries, with the result that we are seldom called upon to reconcile a beautiful heroine named Myrtle Slockmüller or a dashing, virile leading man *né* Herman Nipples. To a smaller degree, the equally contrived world of literature has contributed its share of sacrifices to this impulse to make sound follow form.

One writer who succumbed for professional reasons, the immortal Lewis Carroll, whose mail came addressed to Charles Lutwidge Dodgson, explored the being of this impulse in *Through the Looking Glass:*

"Don't stand chattering to yourself like that," Humpty Dumpty said, looking at her for the first time, "but tell me your name and business."

"My *name* is Alice, but—"

"It's a stupid name enough!" Humpty Dumpty interrupted impatiently. "What does it mean?"

"*Must* a name mean something?" Alice asked doubtfully.

"Of course it must," Humpty Dumpty said with a short laugh. "*My* name means the shape I am—and a good handsome shape it is, too. With a name like yours, you might be any shape almost."

The first and fundamental meaning that a new name *must* have for a voluntary absentee is security. This consists for the most part in selecting a surname not readily connectable with his or her previous situation. The retention of the given name or the choice of new names with the same initials or even the same number of syllables is not—the testimony of the investigators notwithstanding—of demonstrable aid in the pursuit. One example of this is Professor Vernon Holmberg in the previous chapter, who was unsuccessfully sought by the police and private detectives under a variety of family names, but who, for seven years, lived and worked undisturbed as Verne Hansen.

But to shift to a simple familial variable is to risk eventual recovery, as James A. Schultz learned in 1962. Technically, Schultz was not a voluntary absentee; technically, he was a kidnapper. What he "kidnapped" were his two sons, Craig, ten, and Brent, three, whom he was about to lose in a custody battle with his ex-wife, Laurie. The couple had divorced in 1951. The older son continued to live with his father, the younger joining them on alternate weekends. But it was only a lack of finances that prevented the mother from gaining complete custody of both boys, and that hurdle was eliminated in April, 1953, when she married used-car dealer Frank Van Buren. On June 19, Schultz—anticipating a court decision that would provide Laurie with the bitter victory she had so long sought—took his two children and disappeared.

Mrs. Van Buren had a premonition that this might happen, which was confirmed by her first glance at Schultz's deserted home in Richmond, Cal., when she and her husband drove up to reclaim the two boys. What ensued was a nine-year personal manhunt by an unyielding and resourceful woman, who in July 1963 described her long search for the sympathetic subscribers of *Good Housekeeping*. Even before the police concluded their initial investigation, she had begun questioning relatives, associates, and officials at the various high schools where her ex-husband had taught. Letters from Mrs. Van Buren were dispatched to the American ambassador in Mexico City, other state boards of education, the Federal Bureau of Investigation. She even wrote to the headquarters of the Boy Scouts of America, in the hopes that that organization's records might lead to the location of her two sons.

Nothing she did, however, produced any results. Hundreds of leads were developed, only to be traced into blind corners by a friendly Richmond police detective named Allen Madruga, who took a personal interest in the case. Then, in 1956 Mrs. Van Buren presented her plight on the nationally televised "Queen for a Day" show. The emotional impact of her dilemma brought her the first prize—eighteen months of futile effort by a well-known Los Angeles private detective agency—and hundreds of new leads, all of which, after faithful checking by Madruga, who was by then even devoting his free time to the case, proved to be false.

As the years went by, the calendar was added to the obstacles Mrs. Van Buren had to face, because a boy's opinion begins to carry legal weight in custody battles after he reaches fourteen. But just as her pursuit seemed to have exhausted every conceivable direction, she awoke one night with an intuition that Schultz might have assumed his mother's maiden name of Howell.

At first, this new tack produced no tangible results. Hours of poring over a collection of telephone directories from across the country were fruitless. So was a check of the nation's private schools. About the only exciting possibility was a crippled professor at the Oregon Technical Institute, whose amazing publicized resemblance to Schultz in a newspaper photograph subjected him to a 2 A.M. confrontation, in 1958, by Laurie and her eager assistants.

Mrs. Van Buren, however, never gave up hope. She queried the armed services, various state licensing bureaus, even the Social Security Administration on Craig's eighteenth birthday, still without results. In desperation, she began pestering the members of Schultz's family in California. On August 25, 1962, while talking to one of them, Laurie began playing the "Is he in . . ." telephone game. The meaningful answers, she had decided, would come in the form of pregnant pauses, a sort of inaudible polygraph examination. She received two such verbal hesitations—first when she asked, while running through the states alphabetically, whether her former husband was in Florida; second when she inquired if he was living under the name Howell.

It worked. Ten days later, the police located a teacher in Hollywood, Fla., named Charles V. Howell.* Nine years before, Schultz-Howell had driven off in the night with his sons to nearby Oroville, abandoned his car, flown to Detroit, and taken a bus to Miami. Through a friend in Nevada, he had secured teaching credentials and taken a position in Hollywood, where he had posed as a widower.

The recovery of Schultz-Howell was facilitated by his retention of his profession and the contact he maintained with his relatives in California. But in the end, it was his choice of his mother's maiden name that led to his exposure. Another name variant frequently cited but of questionable use to investigators is the anglicization of foreign names. In theory it would appear rudimentary to trace someone who had switched from Schwartzstein to Blackstone or from Wilkiewiez to Wilson, but in practice the very multiplicity of foreign derivations complicates, rather than simplifies, the pursuit.

One man, Charles Mitchell Waterman, even reversed the process. A teacher of English at Westinghouse High School in Pittsburgh, Waterman left his Greenfield, Pa., home the night of October 19, 1960, after telling his wife he was going to a movie in the city. About 1 A.M. he called his wife and told her where she could find their car. Then he drove to a wharf on the Monongahela River. The keys were found *in situ,* and, according to the police, there was a note in his handwriting on the front seat to the effect that "This is the

---

* The older Schultz child was by then married, but Brent was only twelve. On September 2, 1962, after an acrimonious ten-hour hearing, the Broward County (Fla.) Court ordered him returned to his mother in California and granted the father custody rights for the summer months. The charges pending against Schultz in California were withdrawn at the request of Mrs. Van Buren.

best way out." Noting that the wharf was but a few blocks from the bus terminal, the Pittsburgh police declined Mrs. Waterman's suggestion that they spend some time dragging the river bottom.

But despite the firm conviction of the investigators that Waterman had attempted to fake death by suicide, the search for the thirty-year-old teacher turned up very little in the way of useful information. His employment record was spotty. Before becoming a teacher, he had worked for an insurance company and later with United States Steel. His military service consisted of twelve years in the National Guard. About the only meaningful clue uncovered by the detectives was that Waterman had frequently expressed a disdain for teaching at the high-school level and had seemed anxious, according to a faculty colleague, to "find something significant to do with his life."

The first real break in the case, however, was provided eight months later by Waterman himself, when he wrote to one of the administrators at Westinghouse High School, asking that his college transcripts be sent to an address in Tel Aviv. Armed with this purchased information, the investigators soon located him in a kibbutz near Haifa, where he was known to the other laborers in the orange grove as Chaim Wassermann.*

Beyond the basic consideration of security from detection, is there any tendency to *shape,* in Lewis Carroll's analogy, a new name in proportion to the intent and altered personality of the absentee? Quite frankly, the evidence is minimal, primarily because it would appear that only a small fraction of

---

* Waterman returned to Pittsburgh in 1962, when his mother became critically ill. After her death on March 8, he remained to manage the real-estate holding company that she had owned. On July 8, 1963, he was killed in a four-car accident while returning from New York City, where he had visited his ex-wife and their four children. At the time of his death, he was enrolled as a graduate student in the library-science program at the University of Pittsburgh.

the people who took new names have ever been located. From just the examples of Lawrence J. Bader, Thomas C. Buntin, and Norman H. Briggs, however, a tentative and limited "yes" might seem indicated. For example, a gentleman named Briggs might prosper as a nine-to-five white-collar salesman in an Eastern city, but he would hardly be as well equipped phonetically to swing into the saddle of a quarter horse out West and begin herding cattle; that, it seems obvious, is more properly the domain of a man with the handle of Clay Hollister.

Around Nashville, Tenn., the name Buntin is synonymous with wealth and position. Naturally, if a scion of that illustrious clan wished to palm himself off as an undistinguishable member of the masses, he would probably be inclined to adopt a less exalted title, such as Thomas D. Palmer.

Bader's choice of John F. Johnson bespoke the regimentation and alliterative anonymity of his invented background—a Massachusetts orphanage and more than a decade of naval service. Bader-Johnson added several mnemonic frills that offer one solution to the apparent problem of being consistent about the details of a new identity. First and foremost was his nickname, Fritz,* which he persisted in being called until it became common usage in Omaha. On more formal occasions, he had only to extend his first name to produce his last, using his preferred sobriquet to provide a middle initial. The cover story about the orphanage eliminated most of the questions about parentage and place of birth. As for the date of his birth, Fritz explained that the institution always assigned each child a birthday on the last day of the quarter in which he came to the orphanage. Since he had arrived during the second quarter, his birthday was June 30, which is quite easy to remember. Fritz Johnson and Larry Bader were both born, conveniently enough, in 1926.

---

* Fritz Zepht was the president of the company that employed Bader at the time of his disappearance.

Bader's wedding anniversary was April 19; Johnson's was April 11.

Bader-Johnson's use of such memory-prodding devices is hardly unique. Numerous instances were observed in which absentees listed their birth dates on national holidays or, more often, retained the original months and days but advanced the years, thereby making themselves appear younger. One man, asked to provide the names and birthplaces of his parents on a questionnaire for industrial group insurance, perversely listed his real name, identified in parenthesis as "stepfather," and then proceeded to identify his former wife as his mother.

Such a confabulation of fact and fiction, however, is hardly as necessary as it might seem from the well-ordered distance of middle-class consistency. Because we have consistently submitted our life documents over and over again on request, or at least have been consciously prepared to do so, we presume perforce that a complete and detailed biography is a prerequisite in every situation. It is not. In most instances, society is quite willing to take our word for it. And most of us are called upon daily to make similar assumptions—and do. Which is why we eventually come to feel distinctly knowledgeable about a wide circle of friends and associates, when in fact we know little more than what they have told us. And even that, if we stop to consider, is frequently much less than we think.

In the less affluent and more mobile sectors of society, according to those who have been there, the past tends to become more of a painful presumption than a present necessity. One does not casually plumb another background and memories. In part, this is an instinctive response to the unwritten axiom that the fewer questions one asks, the less answering one must do. But mostly it is a personal tolerance that approaches apathy. If a man shows up and wants to be called by a nickname and insists he was once a vice-president of General Motors or a paratrooper or a newspaper editor or a YMCA secretary, what's the harm? And if this person prefers a job obviously below his intellectual capacity, what difference does it make, provided that he performs adequately and without complaint? And if he is disinclined to speak of other times and other people and other places, well, he must have some reason. What matters, here and now, is not the meaning of the name but, as Humpty Dumpty ultimately discovered, the shape itself.

Essentially, a person in search of a new name under which to begin a new life has two choices: he can appropriate some-one else's name or he can make one up. If he elects the first possibility, it is for one of two reasons. Either he intends to impersonate that person or he is determined to acquire a solid documentary base for a new identity. This process is known in the trade as "repapering," and few people have ever developed a better facility for it than Ferdinand Waldo Demara, Jr.

Demara pressed this advantage brilliantly and quite fraud-ulently through a series of incredible escapades, chronicled—up to 1959—by Robert Crichton in his *The Great Impostor.* The various names that Demara masqueraded under all had one thing in common—they belonged to someone else. The people who owned the names had skills Demara needed, and, with an impostor's instinct for the procedural weaknesses of institutional record keeping, Demara developed techniques for instant documentation of education and experience that he could not claim, inasmuch as he had not bothered to finish high school under his real name.

Demara's most fantastic caper, the one he is invariably remembered for, was his brief tour as a lieutenant in the Royal Canadian Navy as an irrepressible surgeon named Joseph Cyr. During his service aboard the destroyer *Cayuga,* off the Korean coast, the impostor, who insists that as Demara he could not accomplish any of the exploits his impersona-tions can, actually treated nineteen wounded Korean com-mandos; he performed delicate operations on three of them while the ship pitched through a storm.

The Navy adventure, however, was really an aberration. Usually Demara operates within his life frame of reference— either teaching (he has been a member of numerous Catholic teaching orders, under a variety of names, including his own) or institutional work. These impersonations have ranged all the way from the deanship of the school of philosophy at Gannon College in Erie, Pa., a position he held as Dr. Robert Linton French, B.S., M.S., Ph.D., to working as Captain Ben W. Jones, the acting assistant warden of the maximum-security section of the Texas Penitentiary in Huntsville. Teaching is by now almost second nature to Demara, and during a series of accomplished professorial performances, he has picked up more than the equivalent of a graduate degree through extension courses. The insights he brought to his penological assignment were gained during a stint as an inmate in a federal prison for desertion (having gone AWOL from both the Army and the Navy, the second time after leaving his clothes, wallet, and a suicide note on a Norfolk, Va., pier).

Demara stole his first set of documents from a friend; he tried to use them to enter the Trappist order at the famous Abbey of Our Lady of Gethsemani in Kentucky. Past associations caught up with the novice even before the inevitable letter of exposure arrived from the bishop of his friend's parish. The attempt was a failure, but Demara, like all impostors, succeeds by failing (unexposed impostors, it would seem, are left with nothing but the bitter taste of testimonial dinners).

In subsequent impersonations, Demara carefully researched his borrowed identity, until he could recite all of the pertinent information on an employment form; the institutions named therein dutifully sent along the necessary documents, transcripts, etc. Sometimes he skillfully forged or otherwise altered the required documents and credentials. He was seldom without a trunkful of real or fake letterheads on which, with the aid of the post office's forwarding system and mail drops such as gas stations (he would arrange to pay a complaisant attendant for the privilege), he would write his own letters of recommendation. At the start of his Canadian Navy gambit, an unsuspecting surgeon voluntarily gave him all his personal documents, after Demara, then masquerading as Brother John Payne of the Brothers of Christian Instruction, promised to help the Canadian procure a license to practice in the United States. On the strength of those credentials, a startling ration of nerve, and a ringing attack on socialized medicine before the medical-officer selection board, Demara-Cyr was commissioned into the Royal Canadian Navy.*

Obviously, diametrically opposed motivations prompt the actions of the impostor and the voluntary absentee. The impostor bends his or her energies toward *being* someone else; the absentee, in effect, is trying to *unbecome* somebody. The former has a definite need for obtaining the certificates of accomplishment of another more qualified person; the latter feels obliged merely to secure a modicum of proof of his new name, meaning a birth certificate. The distinction—though the eye of the law might view them narrowly as one and the same—is between theft and appropriation. But there is, in reality and in practice, no necessity for either. It is much simpler and, from the absentee's standpoint, safer to merely invent another name and then document it.

One of the perquisites of middle age is the diminution of society's compulsion to make us constantly prove when and where we were born. Once a person is visibly past adolescence, bartenders and election-bureau officials stop asking; and it would never occur to a personnel interviewer to re-

---

* Author Crichton's absorbing account of this strange man's amazing career makes several attempts to explain why Demara has pursued a life of impersonation, but he does not consider the ancillary possibility that all impostors are at least partially motivated by a desire to demonstrate the ludicrousness of pretending that talent and skill can be effectively certified in the first place. For the other end of the needle also pricks, in that the more documented a person becomes, the greater the risk he takes, in this special sense, of turning into an impostor.

quest the draft status of someone obviously over thirty. The only occasion when an adult is required to furnish proof of birth is for a U.S. passport.

To be sure, the policeman is naturally curious about whether we are licensed to operate the vehicle we might happen to be driving. A driver's license, however, can be obtained by an adult for the asking and the testing. No special identification or documentation is necessary if the clerk can tell at a glance that the applicant is years beyond the legal minimum-age limit and the applicant in turn explains that he has just learned to drive.

The rest of the documents are for sale. The first "store" I went to for the express purpose of purchasing a set was a luncheonette, where there are considerably more incoming than outgoing calls on the pay telephones. The men at the tables nearest the booths were bookmakers and policy-number operators; the Shylocks tended to sit closer to the door. As a former newspaper reporter in that area, I knew some of these men, if not as friends then at least as crafty and formidable chess opponents. They informed me that there is a limited but brisk sale in such documents. But not, as I had imagined, for the purpose of covering the illegal entry of immigrants; rather they are used for such pedestrian matters as driving on a revoked license or deluding the Internal Revenue inspectors who might be waiting at the pari-mutuel window to record the names of the winners of unusually large payoffs.

Within ten days, arrangements were made for me to see two different sets of documents. The first, tentatively priced at $150, appeared a complete and somewhat inept forgery, although I was assured that similar documents had been used successfully to obtain a passport. The second and more comprehensive set, which was offered to me for only $50—because, I was told, I came well recommended—was an interesting mixture of forgeries and stolen official forms. It included baptismal and marriage forms, embossed with the parish emblem. The driver's license, my informant insisted, was genuine, although the validating stamp had been faked (it was impossible to tell from a comparison with my own license). For an additional stipend—he mentioned $10, then quickly raised it to $15—he promised to have the birth certificate (real) impressed with the county seal (real) and signed by the county clerk (forged). This would be done, he claimed, by an accomplice in the courthouse.

Both sets of documents were blank. The purchaser supplies the name.

If this procedure seems unnecessarily troublesome, and it probably is, there is always the mail-order industry. The firm I used was the Standard Forms Company, 626 Bond Building, Washington, D.C. 20005. At fifty cents each, I purchased a birth certificate (Form #101), a motor vehicle operator's permit (Form #102), and a high-school diploma (Form #106). I passed up, at the same price, wallet-sized copies of these certificates, plus a hypnotist certificate, a "Last Will & Testament," and, most intriguing of all, a "Certified Instructor of ———."

For its more impatient customers, Standard Forms will provide, in the same envelope, a marriage certificate (Form #103) and a divorce certificate (Form #108), which, the company brochure explains, "has space for two names and settlement agreement." Speed is only one of this unusual company's hallmarks. Another is secrecy. "We guarantee," it assures each potential consumer, "to place your order in a SEALED, CONFIDENTIAL envelope and mail it the day it is received." It does.

The authenticity value of the forms it provides, however, is questionable. They are printed on ordinary white bond paper, with a predictable amount of Tudor Black or English Gothic lettering and the inevitable textured border. The Certificate of Birth bears some resemblance to a genuine article, particularly after it has been folded and refolded, notarized, and reduced through photocopying. Interestingly enough, Standard Forms of Washington offers to photostat "any paper, certificate, or letter" for one dollar.

The one item not for sale on the document market happens to be the most useful one—a Social Security card. If it were carried in inventory, there would be no reason for buying it. The United States government gives it away.

At 1:17 P.M. on September 6, 1968, a man dressed in a business suit and carrying a borrowed umbrella strolled out of the rain into the narrow, empty lobby of 1657 Broadway and took the elevator to the second-floor midtown Manhattan offices of the Social Security Administration. He told the receptionist that he wanted to apply for a Social Security card. She handed him Form SS-5 PR (12-64) and asked him to fill it out.

At a nearby counter, he studied the eleven questions on the form for a moment before he began to write. He gave his name as John Lawrence Henderson, Jr. After date and place of birth, he wrote October 12, 1936, and Bethlehem, Pa. He listed his parents as John L. Henderson and the former Beverly Ann Hilton. Under sex, he checked the box marked male; as for "color," he had a choice between white, Negro, and "other." He hesitated over only one question, No. 10, which inquired whether he had ever obtained a card from the administration; he finally checked the "Don't Know" box. Then he wrote in an address and signed and dated the application.

He took his place in line and waited about ten minutes, while the clerk behind a small desk patiently explained to three aliens that they would have to go home and get their passports. When it was his turn, he moved forward and seated himself on the chair before the desk. The clerk audibly reviewed his answers to the various questions.

"You don't remember having a Social Security card before?" she asked.

"No, I don't."

"You haven't been employed?"

"No."

A pause. "All right, Mr. Henderson. You should be receiving your card in about two weeks."

"Thank you."

He left the building at 1:41. It was still raining.

His name, of course, was not Henderson, and to the best of his knowledge, there is no such woman, mother, or hotel known as Beverly Ann Hilton. As far as he was concerned, Bethlehem might be a nice place to visit but certainly no one would want to be born there. Nor had he been born on Columbus Day, and he had been several years old when Franklin D. Roosevelt campaigned for a second term. Nevertheless, twelve days later, a franked manila envelope arrived at the address he had given the Department of Health, Education and Welfare. Inside was the card he had requested. The account number assigned to him was 122-44-5765. Underneath had been typed his name, and below the space allotted for his signature was the legend "FOR SOCIAL SECURITY AND TAX PURPOSES—NOT FOR IDENTIFICATION."

This official admonition cannot and does not prevent the constant use of such cards for that purpose. Sometimes, the investigators have little else to go on. When Miss Cille Sommers died of natural causes while vacationing in the Hawaiian Islands on November 24, 1958, the Honolulu police, anxious to locate her next of kin to determine the disposition of the body, began their search with her Social Security number, 567-54-8799.

The Washington agency, however, had little more to offer than the information that she was thirty-four and worked at Whitney's-at-the-Beach in San Francisco. The San Francisco police were not much more helpful. Her employment records, the police soon learned, consisted entirely of fictitious information. When the detectives visited her apartment at 855 Forty-sixth Avenue, where the slender blonde had lived alone during her four years in the Bay City, they could find no clues as to her real identity. The only substantial lead consisted of a co-worker's recollection that Cille had once mentioned having attended Dickinson High School in Jersey City. Accordingly, the San Francisco authorities forwarded her photograph to the police in New Jersey, who, on the basis of the woman's estimated age, concentrated their search on the Class of 1942.

Midway through the class yearbook, the Jersey City Police found the name they were looking for. And at about the same time, the FBI discovered, at the request of the Honolulu police, that the fingerprints taken from the corpse of Cille Sommers matched those on file under the name Lucille Cobb Mayer. Mrs. Mayer, the mother of two sons, had been a mental patient at Graystone State Hospital in New Jersey when, on a "pass visit" with her husband, she had escaped in June 1954. Her fingerprints had been on file in Washington because, shortly after her marriage in 1942, she had taken a war-production job with the Western Electric Company in Kearny, N.J. At that point, her Social Security number was 147-18-9266.

Upon her arrival in San Francisco, Mrs. Mayer had become Miss Sommers simply by walking into the nearest Social Security office and filling out an application. If she answered "No" to the question whether she had previously been issued a card, she would have been issued this curiously vital document on the spot. When the applicant indicates that he is not sure, as Henderson did, he is required to wait two weeks, while the administration checks the name and birthdate against its giant computerized files in Baltimore. If no previous account is found, a new card is promptly mailed. It is not supposed to be used for identification, but with it a person can get a job, open a bank account, pay his income tax.

This is precisely what Cille Sommers did in San Francisco in 1954; this is precisely what John F. Johnson did in Omaha in 1957; this is precisely what John L. Henderson, Jr., did in New York in 1968. A person came attached to each application, but they were people with other names, other motives. Legally, none of them existed—except as numbered participants in the government's Old-Age, Survivors, and Disability Insurance program.

Since this program was instituted in January 1937, more than 170 million people have registered. At least 3.5 million, according to the administration's Commissioner Robert M. Ball, have signed up more than once. "There are no statistics available to indicate the reason for the issuance of these multiple numbers," he has stated. "Some name changes would be included in the 3.5 million figure. It does not, however, include name changes for persons who specifically applied for a name change; these persons would be issued cards with their old numbers and their new names."

Ball added that "The number of name changes for reasons other than marriage is negligible," but he readily acknowledged that his agency would have no way of determining how many people have applied—as Miss Sommers and Johnson and Henderson did—for a new number under a new name. Nor does the administration, given the nature and purpose of its operations, have any special need to know. It is up to the applicant himself to inform the administration if he already has an account number under another name. Most do; some don't. No one has any way of measuring how many they total.

Commissioner Ball's office counts everything else, though. And for 1966 the administration produced a singularly intriguing statistic: that year, about 230,000 Social Security cards were issued to men over the age of thirty.

VIII

A Permanent Mutilation

A person without family, friends, or creditors cannot really disappear. He has no connections to sever, no commitments to break, no obligations to rescind. If he does not return to his job and an audit of his accounts shows that he is without debt to his employer, his personnel folder will simply be shifted to the "Inactive" drawer. Should such a person decide abruptly and without notice to change his location, his occupation, and his life goals, he has no need to conceal his whereabouts, disguise his identity, or alter his background. He did not really belong to society before; he is under no pressure to join now.

The essence of this distinction lies in the intransitive verb "to disappear," which depends for its meaning on the implied preposition "from"—from someone, from something, from somewhere. "No one is really missing," begins one of the investigator's traditional clichés. "It's just that his whereabouts are not known to others. He knows where he is. Someone else doesn't, that's all."

Being that "someone else" is hardly a pleasant experience.

Lawrence Bader, for instance, did not return home that May night in 1957. His wife finally went to bed about 1 A.M. This sort of thing happens from time to time in many marriages. Generally the husband arrives hours after midnight to find his spouse sound asleep, somnolent testimony to her confidence that he will be there beside her in the morning. When he is not, the wife's initial anguish is mixed with anger, which, if he does not call by mid-morning, gradually turns to fright. At this point, she reaches for the telephone—relatives, friends, associates, and finally the police.

Mrs. Bader's telephone search was cut short by the discovery of her husband's abandoned boat on the Lake Erie beach. But when his corpse was not found and, during the following days and weeks, when shreds of inconclusive but nevertheless incriminating evidence were uncovered that indicated he might have staged his death and voluntarily absented himself, the doubts must have multiplied. They certainly did in the minds of the local police chief, a couple of insurance-claims investigators, and Bader's own father. Bader's wife, however, denied that she had shared this skepticism. In a copyrighted interview with the Akron *Beacon Journal* after her husband had been located in Omaha, she retrospectively insisted:

> I felt if it had been disappearance, rather than drowning, that it would have to have been something that was out of his control, definitely. Never once have I thought that he was wandering around the country.
>
> Q—You accepted the fact that he was dead?
>
> A—Yes, I had to accept the fact that he was dead. I always have come to the conclusion that the man was positively dead; that was the only conclusion that I ever came to.
>
> Q—You never got any information at all which would suggest otherwise?
>
> A—No; nothing.

She assured her inquisitor that she and Larry had had a good life and "a happy marriage," that he did not seem under any unusual pressures at the time of his disappearance, and that he had neither said nor done anything that final day which might have suggested what was about to happen. Eight years later, she was still able to recall vividly their last conversation: her request that he forget about going fishing that afternoon, and his reply, "Maybe I will and maybe I won't." Was it merely a cautionary concern about the worsening weather conditions, or was it rather some indefinable premonition of personal catastrophe?

The fundamental reaction to disappearance is an abiding sense of rejection. This feeling is especially painful in situations where the missing person has demonstrably taken flight. To be abandoned, without even the consideration of an explanation, is humiliating. How humiliating is often indicated by the intensity of the protective mechanisms at work; the resulting distortions make it almost impossible for the investigator to get an accurate assessment of the marital relationship from a deserted spouse. "You get the impression in this business," one police detective asserted, "that the only truly perfect marriages are those involving missing persons."

As painful as this postdisappearance introspection must be for those who have been left behind, it does not begin to compare with the hurt that is sometimes callously, more often casually, inflicted by outsiders. In its most malicious form, this assault may consist of ugly rumors about the actual fate of the missing person. One extreme instance involved Elbert O. Bolin, the foreman of the Attalla (Ala.) Pipe and Foundry Company. On an August afternoon in 1954, his eighteen-year-old daughter, Jimmey Faye, carried the trash outside, stepped over a low picket fence, and disappeared. Almost immediately, the local sheriff began receiving reports that the girl had been murdered by her family; an anonymous woman caller went so far as to hint that the body was buried under the garage. Poison-pen letters also were sent to the Bolin home. One featured a crude drawing of a large eye, with the legend "You're being watched." The pressure on the family mounted to the point where the Bolins actually volunteered to undergo polygraph examinations.

Not until twelve years later, when Bolin had suffered a

disabling heart attack, was the mystery finally resolved and the rumors laid to rest. The news of Bolin's condition somehow reached across the country to Mrs. Louis Drumheller in North Highland, Cal. The wife of a contractor and the mother of four children, she promptly placed a long-distance call to her father. "I can't ask you to forgive me," she told him, "for that would be too much to ask, I know. But I do want you to know that I'm happy." She promised to visit her family in the near future, then hung up before any explanations could be sought as to why she left home or what had happened to her in the intervening years. "We just couldn't ask her those things," a relieved Bolin told the press. "I hope someday she'll just volunteer to tell us. We're just glad to know she's all right. Also it puts an end to those dirty rumors. You don't know how something like that can cut at you."

The unkindest cut of all, in another sense, is the brutal raising of false hopes. The more unexplainable the disappearance, the stronger the resistance to the possibility of finite loss, and hence the greater the anguish when strangers intrude with cruel suggestions of assistance. Obviously, publicity vastly increases the numbers and nerve of these emotional vultures, which is precisely what happened after *Life* published a detailed report in 1952 of the mystery surrounding Cadet Richard Cox, who had vanished inexplicably two years before from West Point. His mother, Mrs. Minnie C. Cox, of 175 Bennett St., Mansfield, Ohio, had sorely tested her belief in her son's continued existence during the government's exhaustive investigation; numerous times the federal search would turn a promising corner into a blind alley. But through this entire process, Mrs. Cox maintained—as she has to this present day—her faith that Richard would eventually be recovered.

After the *Life* article appeared, however, the cranks descended en masse on Mrs. Cox. Dozens of letters containing meaningless data and worthless advice were sent to her home, and one night a woman tried to reverse the charges on a telephone call from Texas to give Mrs. Cox information about her son. Warily, Mrs. Cox told the operator to have the caller contact the nearest FBI office. The woman never did, of course.

Occasionally Mrs. Cox received informative letters that merited serious investigation. One such tip came from a woman in southern Illinois, who had noticed a strong resemblance between one of her neighbors and the picture of Cox in *Life*. Mrs. Cox asked her older son, Rupert, a salesman living in Aurora, Ill., to check on the man. Rupert drove to the address given and pressed the doorbell. He was quite encouraged when the child who came to the door reminded him of his missing brother; so did the father, who arrived home minutes later. But the man was able to prove that he was not Cadet Cox, and one more hope was dashed.

As the years passed, the flow of crank mail diminished and then stopped. Mrs. Cox continued to receive sympathy letters and, less frequently, requests from newspaper and magazine writers for interviews. Then, in 1966, the Coxes were victimized by a cruel hoax, when another resident of Mansfield, who knew the Cox family and saga, tried to convince a local woman that he was "Dick Cox," the lost West Pointer. The woman was sufficiently impressed to contact the police, who quickly unmasked the impostor. But not before Mrs. Cox was made to suffer another disappointment.

In the intensity and scope of the search, the Cox case is undoubtedly unique in the annals of missing persons. A total of 1,500 or so "leads" were checked out on three continents, and, in one instance, Army investigators actually went into combat in Korea to check the fingerprints of another Sergeant Cox, whose photograph had appeared in a national magazine. Such extensive resources are simply not available to the relatives of any other missing person, and if they were, few could afford them. They must content themselves with the most perfunctory of searches, and the outside chance that some relative or acquaintance will establish a meaningful contact—and then be willing to share this knowledge. For the suddenly abandoned, grief is denied expiation, and even sorrow is muted by uncertainty; there is, instead, only anxiety, compounded by doubt and apprehension and hope.

Perhaps no one has ever publicly probed the nature of this personal anxiety more poignantly than critic and lexicographer Wilson Follett, who in May 1941 addressed an "open" anonymous letter in the *Atlantic*, "To a Daughter, One Year Lost." His daughter Barbara, a poet and the precocious author of two novels, had walked out of her Brookline, Mass., apartment and her husband's life on December 7, 1939. More than a year had passed without anyone hearing from the twenty-five-year-old woman, who had not been carrying much money when she disappeared.

Follett began by describing his bewildering reaction to the indifferent attitude displayed by the police when the family reported Barbara as missing. He specifically cited the bored policeman who had taken the information, but basically Follett was expressing the dismay most people experience when they first learn that the police do not and cannot share the intense singularity of their concern. What seemed to shock the author most, however, was his own incredulous discovery of the rather orderless world that lies just outside the self-inscribed, documented limits in which the majority of us subsist and have our being. In other words, it was not so much the fact that *his daughter* had vanished that astounded Follett as it was the revelation that *anybody* can vanish, and, what was worse, that the police were not especially inclined to dwell on this distinction.

The passage of time had forced the author to face this unpleasant realization, and it had, in the process, imposed a new and unforgettable dimension on his life view:

A year, in common adult experience, is no eternity, but it is quite long enough to have told me to the last chapter the story of how I miss you. Surely you will not recoil from knowing just this: that simply, humanly, sorely, I miss you.

Follett had a specific reason for phrasing his fatherly affection so carefully. He and Barbara had maintained a close, warm relationship for the first thirteen years of the girl's life. Then his marriage had broken up, the girl had remained with her mother, and the two apparently had seen each other only infrequently. Somewhat petulantly, Follett complained that his daughter had no sooner grown up than she was married to a man with whom the father found it impossible to establish a rapport. Not seeing his daughter, however, had not diminished her importance to him. And to his personal loss was now added the even sharper pain caused by the mystery of her disappearance, which he compared to the sudden removal of a familiar mountain from view:

> A scheme of things in which I do not know where you are, do not probably know *that* you are—it changes, I assure you, the shape of my sky.

In Follett's soaring metaphor, loss, however painful, was merely change; the skyline remained without the mountain. But unexplained and fathomless disappearance—"I do not know where you are, do not probably know *that* you are"— was distortion; it affected not just the skyline but the actual "shape of my sky." If he could be assured that his daughter was alive, the anxiety, if not the pain, of separation might be eased.

By compressing his entire relationship with Barbara into twelve months of anguished contemplation, the author attempted to find an explanation, not just of her disappearance, but of her continued being, planted somewhere within his memories. By concentrating on their past association, he tried to evoke her physically in his present. This effort, Follett wrote, was complicated by those who tried to convince him that she was dead. But just as he was beginning to doubt his own confidence in her continued existence, he had a revelation.

It occurred about dusk, as Follett was attending some last-minute chores on his isolated farm in Bradford, Vermont.

Suddenly, he was aware of a car trying to negotiate his steep, snow-covered driveway, and he was inexplicably filled with the joyous sensation that his daughter had finally returned. His visitor turned out to be someone returning a typewriter he had left at a repair shop, but the disappointment had little effect on Follett's rapture. The sensation he had experienced was confirmation enough that his daughter lived.

Having rationalized, albeit mystically, his belief in Barbara's existence, a life he had merely been temporarily separated from, Follett next attacked what he considered the root of the problem. Modern society, he announced, is too impatient fully to enjoy the present and yet afraid to invest too much hope in the future. He had noticed—at the conclusion of the 1930's—that the younger generation had become restless with traditional values and was inclined to discard that which did not provide immediate dividends. He wondered out loud whether life, in his daughter's view, was not considered "a promissory note that is perpetually renewed"? And he frankly questioned whether her disappearance was actually a "one-woman strike against a system of deferred payments and for the right to live richly, fully, fulfillingly in the continuous present."

A perpetually renewed promissory note . . . a system of deferred payments . . . the continuous present. Follett did not quite believe it. He strongly implied that such a definition of life springs not so much from realistic appraisal as from the unbounded energy of youth, untempered by sobering maturity. Nevertheless, his love was deep enough to pursue this extreme possibility. He did so by asking Barbara —along with the many thousands of *Atlantic* readers—if she had found identity conversion either easy or satisfying. "Can you re-imagine yourself *de novo* as a more important and vital person than you were before?" Despite his assurances that his constant queries were "without ironic intention," Follett managed to infuse his distant interrogation with doubt, and he was less than convincing when he concluded by assuring his daughter that, if she were comfortable in her new identity, she was "indeed struck by the lightning of creative genius, and all the moral probabilities, the natural laws of conduct, are suspended in your behalf."

Aware that he was now sermonizing, Follett swiftly turned his critical acumen on himself. He wrote of the possible effect on Barbara of his own broken marriage and subsequent re-marriage. He retrospectively castigated his own commitment to progressive child-raising techniques, speculated on his child's actual reaction to her parents' liberal policy of non-interference, and lamented the lost merits of the traditional, dictatorial approach. Would it have been better for Barbara, he asked, if her mother and father had been more overbearing in their love for their daughter?

Follett left his own question formally unanswered. One must do, he seemed to imply, what one feels is the right thing at the moment, and later trust and pray that the others will eventually understand. Nothing can be guaranteed, only asserted; intent alone must suffice. His intent in writing to Barbara through the pages of the *Atlantic* was clear. Nevertheless, Follett tried to minimize any possible misunderstandings. ". . . I initiate this message wholly in the spirit of a person-to-person call, and by no means that of a moral subpoena," he emphasized. He did not ask much. If you cannot tell us where and what you are, he pleaded, then at least give one of us a sign that you exist. "Is it truly indispensable that you condemn a whole group of lives to the awful and unending suspense, the permanent mutilation, of not even knowing how or whether they have helped kill the thing they loved?"

Follett, an *Atlantic* contributor, hoped to reach his daughter's heart and provoke a response through the pages of that magazine, which, presuming her continued existence and interest in literature, she might have been drawn to. Framing his affectionate concern for her in a series of questions and confessions, he had broadcast an anxious person-to-person call. "I *wish* it were possible for you to answer it," wrote a tormented father, with a depth of emotion shared, less articulately but with equal intensity, by everyone who has been mysteriously abandoned.

Barbara did not answer, and her father's moving though unsigned message was still unacknowledged when Wilson Follett died in January 1963. Three years later, Harold G. McCurdy, a psychologist, in collaboration with the girl's mother, Helen Thomas Follett, published *Barbara: The Unconscious Autobiography of a Child Genius*. At the end of the book, McCurdy tried to demonstrate that Barbara might have prefigured her own fate in her fiction. His tentative conclusion was that Barbara may have retreated, in dead winter, to some hidden recess in the beloved Maine woods of her cherished youth, and there, like Eepersip, the heroine of her first novel, *The House Without Windows*, "dizzy with the colour and the beauty, [fallen] asleep, her fingers clutching the rosy snow."

McCurdy found this prophetic analogy reasonable. "How consistent it would have been," he hypothesized, "if Barbara, on that December evening, had carried her loneliness northward to her friendly woods and mountains! A snowstorm may have embraced her, an avalanche rapt her away." Consistent it may or may not have been, but convenient—and, to a degree, comforting—it certainly is for the people she abandoned.

Dead or alive, lost or hidden, Barbara Newhall Follett has achieved the continuous present. By her passing, she has left all whose lives she touched, in her father's perceptive phrase, permanently mutilated.

IX

The Plastic Bread Crumb

The detective's question was routine. "When did your wife disappear?"

"Well," said the man, after a moment of mental calculation, "I'd say it was just about six and a half years ago."

"Why bother to tell us about it now?" asked the startled officer.

The husband had a ready answer. "Yesterday was our tenth anniversary, and I sort of got to wondering whatever became of her."

Every metropolitan Missing Persons Bureau includes a fable similar to this in its canon of folklore, which the police dutifully recite whenever an interviewer invades their paint-peeled sanctum in the precinct-house basement. Such anecdotes, the lawmen have discovered, usually send the writer contentedly on his way, without having penetrated the cover of a single confidential file or having caused the bureau personnel any special effort.

The labored parable cited above, for instance, is often disinterred to illustrate the police contention that wives are inclined to report missing spouses faster and with greater frequency than husbands are. The only supporting evidence for this assertion—the implications of which the police prefer not to explore—is the insistence of the police themselves and a certain logic in their proposition. Necessity more than sentiment hurries the wife to the station house; and if she is the mother of small children, an added element of desperation is evident in her plight.

But regardless of whether the husband or the wife is reported missing, the police reaction will be the same: if your spouse has voluntarily absented himself or herself, we have no jurisdiction. This response is frequently somewhat shocking, if only because of the belated realization that even the missing enjoy certain constitutional rights, and that among these rights is privacy. For the police arbitrarily to invade this lawful privacy and then to disclose that person's whereabouts indiscriminately, would expose the officers and the municipality they represent to legal retribution.

The basic statement of this restrictive policy—which, particularly in light of the recent decisions of the U.S. Supreme Court in regard to law enforcement, is now fairly uniform across the country—is contained in the New York City Police Department's Rules and Procedures, under the heading "Missing Persons Defined":

30.0 A missing person is one who is reported missing from a New York City residence and is:
  a. Under 18, or
  b. 18 or over, and:
    1. Mentally or physically affected to the extent that hospitalization may be required, or
    2. A possible victim of drowning, or
    3. Has indicated an intention of committing suicide, or
    4. Absent without any apparent reason under circumstances indicating involuntary disappearance.
30.1 The term "Missing Person" shall not include a person:
  a. For whom warrants have been issued
  b. Wanted for commission of a crime
  c. 18 or over, who voluntarily leave home because of domestic, financial or similar reasons.

Obviously, the wording of this definitive regulation gives the police maximum leeway to pursue anyone they wish to—

at least as far as the point where it becomes clear that the absentee is excluded from their purview. Sometimes the officer assigned to the case can determine beforehand, with a few carefully directed questions, whether his department has any legal basis for a search. More often, however, a preliminary investigation of sorts must be conducted merely to find out whether or not the police have any jurisdiction. This is particularly true when the possibility of accidental death is linked to the disappearance. When this happens, the police automatically become involved. It happened in 1957, when Larry Bader's boat was found washed up on the shore of Lake Erie; and again in 1959, when Edward B. Germain, a wealthy banker and former Assistant Secretary of the Navy, drove out of a Buffalo, N.Y., parking lot; and again in 1966, when William R. Cary waded out into the surf off Point Pleasant, N.J. At the various moments of their disappearances, only Germain was conceded much chance by the police investigators of being alive; in actuality, he was the only member of this trio of the missing who was dead.

The Bader investigation, conducted by the police in Lakewood, Ohio, with the active cooperation of the Akron department, concentrated of necessity on the background to his disappearance rather than on the boating incident. There were no witnesses to anything that occurred on the lake that night, nor was there any evidence ashore to indicate that someone had beached the craft and scampered away overland to parts unknown. Bader's recent activities, however, and especially his worsening financial situation, provided enough contradictions and possible motivations for the police to attach, at the end of a two-month investigation, a "suspicious" label to Bader's alleged death. But lacking any tangible evidence of the missing man's continued existence, the police conclusion remained a theory until Bader-Johnson was located eight years later at a sporting-goods show in Chicago.

Germain's departure was an entirely different proposition. He disappeared as abruptly and as inexplicably as Bader. Yet from the beginning the Buffalo police were suspicious, not of what the missing man might have done but of what might have happened to him the night of June 11, 1959. He had dined with friends that evening at a restaurant in the city, and had seemed in excellent spirits; he was last seen driving away in his own car. When he did not return home, an extensive police search was instituted. What the police were looking for was not a potential voluntary absentee but the possible victim of a crime. Germain, the former president of the Dunlop Tire and Rubber Company, was sixty-nine years old.

The investigation did not produce a single substantial clue. Neither did the $10,000 reward posted by Mrs. Germain for information concerning her husband's whereabouts. As the days and weeks passed, even the grim prospect of kidnapping for ransom faded. And as the months passed into years, without a trace of either the man or the car he was driving that night, so did the other theories about what might have happened to him. The police and his family were baffled.

It was not until September 4, 1963, that the mystery was finally unraveled. On that day a male torso was found on the banks of Buffalo's Squaw Island. It was decomposed beyond visual identification. But in what remained of the trousers was a wallet, and in the wallet was a tattered newspaper clipping of the 1958 obituary of Germain's sister, Mrs. Anne Germain Waterman of Boston. The wallet itself was subsequently identified by Germain's widow, Bettette, who was summoned by the police from her new home in Port Arthur, Texas. The case was officially closed the following week, when grappling operations near the site where the remains had surfaced led to the discovery of Germain's car, which had carried its driver, unobserved, to a watery grave more than four years before.

The Bader and Germain disappearances were eventually resolved by circumstances beyond the control or prophecy of the police. And it is worth noting that prior to the solution of these cases, it was equally possible that Bader, whom the

police suspected of having faked his death, might actually
have been drowned in Lake Erie, and that Germain, who the
police were convinced had been the victim of a crime or an
accident, could conceivably have absented himself. In both
instances, the police, unable to find any postdisappearance
evidence, arrived at reasonable premises that were based entirely on predisappearance information. But until Bader was
located and the body of Germain was found, these police
conclusions consisted of little more than informed speculation.

The last member of the trio was more considerate—at least
from the police perspective. Bader and Germain vanished at
night; each was alone; they provided no clues. William R.
Cary, a thirty-eight-year-old "buildings engineer mechanic"
with the New Jersey Bell Telephone Company, disappeared
in mid-afternoon in view of hundreds of uninterested witnesses. The date was August 19, 1966. Cary, his wife, and
their six children had driven from their Trenton home to
Point Pleasant for a day on the beach. Shortly before 4 P.M.,
Cary entered the water and began swimming seaward. When
he did not return, his family, thinking that he had come out
of the water further down the beach, finally asked to have
him paged over the loudspeaker system. He did not answer
the amplified summons, and at 6:30 the alarm was sounded.
The lifeguards searched the surf, but there was no trace of
Cary.

Early the next morning, Saturday, the police scoured the
beach area, two boats maneuvered just beyond the foam of
the breakers, and a helicopter from the Lakehurst Naval Air
Station examined the offshore waters. Like Bader, Cary was
considered a strong swimmer; moreover, although he was last
seen by one of his children "quite a distance" from the shore,
the lifeguards had observed no one in trouble, and there had
been no shouts for help.

What first made the police suspicious of the entire incident, however, was something that Cary, a Navy veteran,
apparently had forgotten to take into consideration: the tide.

The beach in question is located half a mile south of Manas-quan Inlet and is swept by the powerful currents that surge back and forth through the inlet. The moment Cary chose for his departure came during the waning minutes of the ebb tide, after which the ocean pours back into the recesses of the estuary. Therefore, the police reasoned, the body of anyone drowned off that particular beach at that particular time should have been carried back into the Manasquan River. The inlet and the river were carefully watched, without results.

The first indication that the police were dubious about Cary's disappearance came six days later, when his photograph was released to the press; he was described as "missing" rather than "lost at sea." The focus of the investigation shifted to his home area of Trenton, where the authorities were openly skeptical, for reasons they preferred not to discuss. But the reporters assigned to the story soon learned that Cary, shortly before he vanished, had taken out a "rather large" policy with the Prudential Life Insurance Company, against which that company flatly refused to consider any death claim. Further probing turned up hints from sources in the police department that Cary had telephoned his home several times after his disappearance and attempted to speak with his children. This led, on December 17, to the official announcement that Cary had been traced—although the po-lice refused to say exactly how—to Richmond, Va., where he was living under an assumed name with another woman. The couple had fled when they learned that the police were making inquiries about them, but their landlady had posi-tively identified Cary from a photograph.

A few months later, Cary was indicted in absentia by a Mercer County, N.J., grand jury for the neglect and aban-donment of his children and the desertion of his wife, Pa-tricia. And on May 23, 1967, Mercer County Judge A. Jerome Moore issued a warrant for his arrest. Two years later, the warrant remains outstanding. The police had dem-onstrated that Cary had not drowned; in the process, charges were brought against the man, which means that legally he is now a fugitive, not a missing person. But until and unless the warrant is served, he is still very definitely missing.

Issuing a warrant, of course, is much less difficult than serving one. And it is at this juncture that a certain ambivalence on the part of the police is most noticeable. For if it is true—and it is—that police interest in missing persons *per se* starts to flag once the potential ingredient of homicide in the case dissolves, then it is more apparent that the police are simply too busy, despite public protestations to the contrary, to spend much time or effort searching for errant husbands, even when these men are under indictment for abandonment and nonsupport. "We don't have much respect for people who run off on their husbands or wives, especially when children are involved," a police captain told me. "But when you think about it, it doesn't rank very high in the order of crimes against society."*

Most of the arrests made by the police of absentees who have changed their names come about in nonrelated circumstances. Occasionally these circumstances are of a sensational nature. When the Madeira Beach, Fla., police arrested Robert Coleman Johnson on August 21, 1966, they were unaware that they actually had locked up two men. Johnson, a fifty-six-year-old commercial fisherman and laborer for a local chemical firm, was taken into custody and charged with the murder of his wife, Phyllis, who had been found bludgeoned in the couple's three-room oceanfront cottage.

At the jail, Johnson added a strange twist to the tale he told his captors. His name was not Johnson; it was William Henry Waldron, Jr. He was not a laborer; he was a lawyer. It

---

* This apathy does not apply to the various district attorneys across the nation, who—with the gradual adoption by the various states since 1945 of a uniform support-of-dependents law that has simplified extradition procedures—have drastically increased their efforts in abandonment cases. Their investigators, moreover, are permitted access to the otherwise restricted files of the Social Security Administration and the Internal Revenue Service, especially when the deserted spouses are recipients of federal Aid to Families of Dependent Children funds.

did not take the authorities long to confirm their prisoner's story. In the process, they learned that Waldron-Johnson had been a prominent attorney in Huntingon, W. Va., with a wife and two children. One day in 1950, he had been seen getting out of a taxi at a local club, where he was a member. Then he vanished.

"It was just very sudden," Mrs. Waldron remembered. "The day after Christmas he just didn't come home. He had never stayed out all night and by the next day I called for help." Four days later she received a letter from Waldron, deeding her their Huntington home; the envelope was post-marked San Diego. The following week the missing lawyer was indicted for fraudulently withdrawing $7,000 from a West Virginia bank. Later the family made restitution, and the embezzlement charge was eventually dropped, after a federal court judge finally decided that Waldron would never be found. As far as the family and the courts were concerned, Attorney Waldron had joined the ranks of the permanently vanished. There he remained for sixteen years, until the Florida police found the battered, decomposing corpse of a fisherman's wife.*

The resolution of a missing-persons case through a charge of murder is obviously the exception. Most identity switches come to light procedurally, in the aftermath of a routine ID check in connection with some trivial offense. This is what occurred when Verne Hansen, the intellectual paint grinder in Chapter VI, was picked up for driving while intoxicated. The majority of police departments do not fingerprint persons arrested for such misdemeanors; but a few do. Rockford, Ill., happens to be one of them. When Hansen's prints were routinely forwarded to Washington, the FBI discovered that they were identical with the ones belonging to a missing

---

* The lawyer-turned-fisherman was charged with second-degree murder, found guilty by a jury in Clearwater, Fla., and, on February 2, 1967, was sentenced to twenty years in the state prison at Raiford.

Syracuse University professor, Carl Vernon Holmberg, and it so notified the Syracuse police.

The Federal Bureau of Investigation will, in Director Hoover's words:

> post a "missing person notice" in its Identification Division files when a request is made by an authorized law enforcement agency or by an immediate relative of the individual whose location is sought. For the notice to be placed in our files the individual must be missing for a period of less than seven years. If no fingerprints of the person being sought are on file, the notice will be posted only by name and description. Upon receipt of pertinent information regarding the whereabouts of the missing individual, the interested party is advised immediately. We do not furnish such data to business firms. All incoming fingerprint cards are checked against our active name and fingerprint searching files, which includes the missing person "stop" notices.

This is a polite way of saying that, in 1967, the names and/or fingerprints of more than six thousand missing Americans were intermixed in the bureau's active search file of fugitive criminals. Hoover explained that these "stop notices" on missing persons are kept up to date every three years by sending a letter to "the interested parties" asking whether the person has been located and whether said parties want the bureau to continue its search. Despite the passive nature of the FBI's efforts, this service constitutes a much more flexible interpretation of the laws guaranteeing a citizen's privacy than most law-enforcement agencies are willing to make. It also represents a freedom from disclosure restrictions that is not shared by any other agency of the federal government. It is thus less than comforting to learn that, as of January 3, 1967, this sacrosanct bureau of the Department of Justice had on file the fingerprints of 79,825,137 Americans.

Hoover's agents have even less authority to conduct an active search for a voluntary absentee than the local police, who have none whatsoever. Where then do the abandoned turn for aid? One answer is frequently provided by an exasperated police officer who has been trying repeatedly to explain the legal reasons why his department's hands are tied: "Have you considered getting a private detective?"

The suggestion is not without merit. For the private detective is an entrepreneur, largely immune from the lawful responsibilities and restraints that accompany access to privileged data. He manufactures a product, which happens to be information. He violates no professional-client relationship in the process, since his client is the pursuer, not the pursued. That he often acquires information by deception and misrepresentation and guile is peculiarly a matter for his own conscience. What he does and the way he does it are, for the most part, carefully within the letter if not the spirit of the law, meaning that he maintains parity with such other honorable trades as real-estate brokers, parking-lot operators, and advertising-copy writers.

This is not meant to denigrate private investigators collectively, although anyone who would take and keep such a position may be said to have already demonstrated a marked lack of concern for his self-respect. Obviously, some private detectives are better than others. Some, for instance, disdain to participate in the messy routine of collecting photographic evidence of adultery in divorce cases. Others prefer not to get involved in situations of industrial and commercial espionage. There are probably even a handful who would not consider rifling someone else's personal belongings. But it seems valid to generalize that these private investigatory agencies—whether or not the search for missing persons is a major or minor function of their activities—are actively engaged in the continuous and flagrant violation of privacy. If they were not, they would be less defensive when it came to discussing their methods.

Consider first, however, the rather basic question of their fees. Ask a private detective, and he will tell you that it all depends on the particular case. Ask two, and you will receive the same answer twice. Part of the reason is that private de-

tectives work on a retainer-plus-expenses basis—a legal requirement in many states and a common practice in the rest.
But it is equally true that while you are inquiring how much
the detective's services will cost, he is trying to determine
how much you are able and willing to pay. "It's the same
thing that happens every time the doctor walks over and
pulls down the blind in his examination room," one of the
more candid operatives explained. "He simply wants to take
a look at the kind of car you're driving, so he'll know how
much to charge."

This answer pretty much sums up the *modus vivendi* of
this industry. To test this hypothesis and simultaneously
establish some sort of monetary range, identical letters were
sent in February 1967 to eight firms, selected from their ad-
vertisements in the classified section of the Manhattan telephone directory. The envelopes bore the postmark of a town
in the Adirondacks, and the letters declared that the writer's
husband had left eleven months before on a business trip to
Chicago and never returned. The only subsequent word from
him had consisted of a postcard from New York City to his
"business partner." The missing husband was described by
height, weight, and color of hair and eyes; his birth date and
Social Security number were included. "I am sure that my
husband has been involved in some kind of accident that has
left him mentally disturbed, as there was absolutely no reason
for him to disappear like this," the writer added. "All of his
accounts are in order, his home life was extremely happy, and
he enjoyed his work [which was otherwise not specified] so
much. He has never done anything like this before and he
does not drink excessively. Needless to say, there has never
been any hint of another woman or anything like that."

As fatuous as this letter might sound, it nevertheless re-
produces in tone and content a fair sampling of the type of
correspondence received daily by these firms. The proof of
this is that, within the week, seven of the firms responded, in
varying degrees of grammatical competence. Their prices
ranged from $200 to $1,000, plus expenses estimated from

"very minimal" to "not to exceed $500." The most intriguing offer by far came from George Kauder of the United Service Detective Bureau, 160 Broadway, who explained that his firm charged fifty dollars a day and then asked the prospective client to decide how long she wanted him to work on the case. Having unabashedly braced his prospective client for an estimate of her financial determination, Kauder promised to commence the search as soon as a check for the decided amount of time was received.

The replies offered some other interesting, though scarcely reassuring, insights into the agency mentalities. For instance, A. J. Woolston-Smith, Agent in Charge of the Confidential Investigation Bureau Inc., 441 Lexington Avenue, whose services were listed at $500, asked specifically for a recent photograph and the names of the hotels that the inquirer's husband frequented on his business trips; he also suggested that she carefully examine the missing man's expense vouchers for any evidence of padding. John J. Lannig, manager of the William J. Burns International Detective Agency, Inc., 235 East Forty-second Street, inquired, despite well-known disclosure restrictions to the contrary, whether the writer had attempted to have the police in her town or the FBI find out from Social Security if her husband was still working under his old Social Security number. Lannig calculated the price of his agency's services at seven dollars an hour, allotted less than four days to the pursuit, and asked for a $200 retainer. Lannig's answer was mailed from New York, despite the fact that the stationery of this "international" firm lists a representative in the same town where the query originated.

The most resourceful proposal came from James B. Nolan, president of the company at 331 Madison Avenue, that bears his name. Nolan, a former deputy police commissioner in New York, promised to press his investigation in both Chicago and New York for only $200, plus minimal expenses. But he wondered frankly about how much her husband's partner might actually know about the disappearance. Delivered of this suspicious perception, he recommended in a postscript that her husband's firm, inferred from the mention of a business partner, underwrite the cost of his services. Under the circumstances, the suggestion stands as an ingenuous *beau geste,* since Nolan apparently intended to start by investigating the "partner" at company expense.

Only one firm, Tracers Company of America, Inc., 515 Madison Avenue, asked for and received additional information before quoting its fee. First the wife was asked to fill out a detailed questionnaire, covering her missing husband's vital statistics, his appearance, tastes, hobbies, education, military service, associations, jewelry, talents, past and present marital history, relatives, medical record, legal entanglements, and—inevitably—whether he had ever expressed an urge to reside somewhere else on this planet. After these personal data, complete with photographs and a handwriting sample, had been submitted to Tracers, that agency's Philip Gordon (whose own signature changed drastically in the course of the correspondence) asked for a summary of the search activities already undertaken by the wife. After analyzing all this information, Tracers offered to conduct the search for $1,000, with expenses not to exceed $500.

Tracers' bid was double the next highest and five times the lowest. Yet of the seven, it was the only one based on an extensive biographical profile and a detailed review of the investigative efforts already undertaken. Considering the longitude and latitude of the services these firms appear to promise, with their far-flung "networks of agents" and exhaustive attention to documented detail, Tracers' figure seems clearly the most reasonable estimate. After all, none of these agencies is philanthropic or intentionally nonprofit; their net gain consists of their retainers, minus operating costs.

On the other hand, six other firms, which claim "solution" percentages similar to Tracers, seemed to feel that they could do the same job for much less—and still have enough left over to keep the staff supplied with Mickey Spillane novels. As with Tracers, none of the other agencies promised any certainty of finding the mythical missing husband. In fairness to these others, however, they all expressed a need for more information before they could launch their searches. The principal difference, then, except for the prices quoted, between Tracers and the other six is that the competition felt competent and confident enough to set their fees solely on the basis of name, bank, and Social Security number. The reason gradually becomes apparent as one begins to explore the activities and methods of this singular industry.

For public consumption, these private agencies prefer to talk about two items: their numerical record of cases "solved" and the flight patterns of missing persons. As there is absolutely no way of verifying solution statistics, one can either accept or reject the percentages they offer (invariably between eighty and ninety percent). This choice is simplified somewhat by the knowledge that such confidence-boosting figures must be listed prominently on any inventory of agency assets.

When I asked the general manager of one firm how he had arrived at the previous year's solution rate, he ran his finger down the column listing the number of different types of cases (missing husbands, wives, debtors, stockholders, heirs, lease breakers, alumni, etc.) that his firm had "successfully concluded" during that period. When I pointed out that there was no mention of the number of unsolved cases in the various categories, he announced that those figures were unavailable. "Then how did you strike the percentage?" He looked puzzled for a moment, then changed the subject. Later, however, he unwittingly provided a substantial clue. I had noticed in his firm's promotional literature that almost forty-six percent of the missing husbands located the preceding year had fled because of "mother-in-law trouble." This statistic puzzled me for several reasons, one of which was that I had yet to see any hint of in-law conflict in the prospective-client correspondence he had shown me. When I brought this up to him, he laughed, somewhat nervously I thought.

"Yeah, well, that was the idea of one of the guys over at the public-relations company [that prepared the brochure]. But I must say, that particular item did draw a lot of comment in the press, just like they promised."

As to the predictability of flight—Easterners flee to California and Florida, Westerners to New York, Southwesterners to Illinois, and so forth—it would appear that there is a certain predictability to the prediction. Absentees assuredly have a need and an impulse to increase the distance between themselves and their former habitats. But no such discernible pattern emerged from the cases inspected during the course of researching this study; if anything, the emphasis seemed to be on random opportunity ("Trailways bus at Gate 17, now loading for . . ."). There is, in short, every reason to consider flight patterns as another of the investigation industry's flights of fancy, suffused with undemonstrable logic.

Private detectives may or may not subscribe to their own predictability theory. It is impossible to determine whether they do. What is fairly certain is that the theory serves them well in their client relations. Like the high solution percentages they claim, flight patterns that presumably narrow the search area must have a reassuring effect on prospective clients. Properly presented, this theory can even be made to pass for methodology. And if there is one subject that a private eye is more loath to discuss than his fee, it is his methods.

This reluctance is not, as the detectives themselves piously insist, because of any disclosure of unique techniques or trade secrets. Nor is it, as the industry's many detractors firmly believe, because the procedures employed are illegal or excessively unethical. Rather it is because of the disarming simplicity with which these private gumshoes ply this facet of their inestimable trade.

Obviously, no private detective would want to jeopardize his livelihood by such an admission, but the clues—as these gentlemen might put it—abound. A significant insight is provided by those widely divergent bids on the nonexistent missing husband. Six of the seven firms (which, one must assume, represent a fair sampling of this industry) estimated their fees and, by definition, their profits with only the skimpiest of information about their prospective quarry. That they all insisted they would need more information before their investigations could commence was irrelevant. Why? Because the additional data were, in a very real sense, unnecessary. Otherwise, there would be no way to explain why only three of the agencies bothered to ask for a photograph of the missing man.

All a detective really requires is the name of the person being sought and the date of disappearance.

Incredible as it may seem, the fundamental techniques of these private agencies are geared to the practical, though rather limited, assumption that the missing person will continue to use his or her own name. ("It's very difficult to change your name," one detective insisted, when I asked him to show me an example of a successful case that involved a person hiding under a fictitious name.) Armed with these two crucial bits of information and allowing a proper interval for the hunted person to establish some documented roots—estimates vary from six months to a year—a private detective can then turn loose his alleged vast network of agents and "contacts," most of whom, it develops, operate under such unlikely "covers" as postmen, government clerks, and credit-agency employees.

To oversimplify for the purpose of demonstration, let us suppose that John Larson Humbolt did not return home from the monthly gathering of the Improved and Benevolent Order of Ball-Bearing Manufacturers the night of August 12, 1968. In due course, Mrs. Humbolt finds her way to the office of a private detective, whom we may as well call Spade McPherson. His fee is agreeable, and a contractual letter is drawn up and signed; the wife's personal check does not bounce.

Spade now leads Mrs. Humbolt through an exhaustive survey of her missing husband's life, his habits, preferences, eccentricities, and associations, remote and recent. He probes the most intimate minutiae of their marital relationship, and demands an exacting physical description of Mr. Humbolt, down to the last mole and hangnail. He also collects such trivia as the expiration date of Humbolt's driver's license. Though she intuitively questions the usefulness of some of the information she is asked to provide, Mrs. Humbolt leaves Spade's office deeply impressed by his attention to detail.

Spade now swings into action, but not, as one might be tempted to suppose, by strapping on his .38-caliber automatic and beating the pavements. What he does is to write letters to the state motor-vehicle bureaus in the area to which he thinks Humbolt might have gone. What these letters ask is, quite simply, has your bureau issued a license to anyone named John L. Humbolt or J. Larson Humbolt or John Larson *since* August 12, 1968? That is all. Attached to the letter is Spade's check or a money order for the fee these bureaus charge to search their files and reply to such requests. These charges average $1.50, and Spade tries to avoid Texas, which has the highest (five dollars); he routinely queries the handful of states which offer this service gratis, even if they are not in the designated area. The detective next writes to Mrs. Humbolt, explaining prolixly how he and his far-flung staff have saturated the target area with bulletins, circulars, posters, and letters of inquiry to a plethora of public and private agencies and institutions that might have knowledge of her husband's whereabouts. Then he sits back to wait for the motor-vehicle responses.

Spade is hopeful that one of these licensing bureaus (some of which, to the dismay of the uninitiated, auction off their records annually to the highest direct-mail bidder) will solve the Humbolt case for him. But he will not be overly disappointed if they do not. For he has not begun to tap the largest and most important private source of alphabetized information on American citizens, the country's massive interconnected system of credit bureaus.

These bureaus, together with the credit departments of their customers, currently employ an estimated 1.5 million Americans. In 1968, the Associated Credit Bureaus of America numbered 2,068 such bureaus, which freely exchanged among themselves and their 365,000 customers the approximately 120,000,000 reports on individual consumers that repose in their supposedly confidential files. The biggest firm in this field is the Retail Credit Company (a representative of which, in Chapter VI, informed the diarist that he was too intelligent to become one of its employees). This Atlanta-based outfit, with 6,000 salaried employees in 1,500 offices scattered about this country and Canada, alone maintains dossiers on some 42,000,000 people, and all of this information is readily available to any of its 38,000 customers.

The sum of this information, which is considered "privileged" and thus safe from libel, is theoretically collected for the primary purpose of determining an individual's credit rating. A society that prefers to pay later, as ours does, would be hard pressed to function without this kind of service. But the reality is that this mass of information is frequently used, particularly by investigators from the FBI and the Internal Revenue Service, for purposes other than a test of the subject's financial stability. One of these purposes is the location of missing persons. Since this obviously infringes on the use of information gathered for the express purpose of assisting "credit-granting" businesses and organizations, the credit industry will deny that it supplies information to private detectives.*

---

* The subject of private detectives did not come up during the three-day hearings conducted by the House Subcommittee on Invasion of Privacy in March 1968, but considerable attention was given to the extensive use of credit-industry files by the FBI and IRS, neither of which, as Representative Cornelius E. Gallagher (D.–N.J.) correctly pointed out, could be charitably defined as a credit grantor. In addition, the president of one firm, Dr. Harry C. Jordon of the Credit Data Corporation, testified that Internal Revenue has filed two legal

The process works much the same way that the motor-vehicle check does. Spade McPherson writes to the regional or district offices of the credit bureau or bureaus he uses, and he encloses the fee (about $1.50 per request). This time the file check is made by name and the date of disappearance.

Now, suppose that the credit bureau answers that its files do indeed include a John Humbolt; in fact, three such names are contained in its files—and there are numerous ways of getting one's name into the bureau's records besides a credit application for some type of insurance. Assuming that these names have appeared subsequent to Humbolt's disappearance, Spade is now prepared to narrow the search further through a comparison of birth dates, or, if a substantial element of doubt still exists, by the expedient of paying a small honorarium to a credit-bureau inspector in the area to make a visual confirmation.

If the system functions correctly, McPherson and his trusty postal meter will have successfully resolved another intensive and complicated investigation—provided, of course, that Spade guessed where Humbolt was heading and that Humbolt did not radically change his name to, say, John Hunt. The utter simplicity of this procedure does not necessarily imply either lassitude or incompetence on the part of the private detective, although many of this breed are frequently guilty of both. If the person he is seeking has not taken a different name, and if the detective is resourceful and determined and well paid, the chances are excellent that the investigator will eventually locate that person.

Especially if that person wants to be found. Which is precisely what happens in the majority of the missing-persons cases solved by private detectives. Nevertheless, they spend an inordinate amount of time regaling the press and magazine writers about the chop suey devotee they traced by staking out all the Chinese restaurants in San Francisco (by informal

---

actions against his company because it refused to open its files to the tax agents for "fishing expeditions."

count, this hypothetical personage has been located twenty-seven times by the police and 142 times by private agencies).
But in real life the detective's best friend is not the maître d'hôtel but the missing man himself. Consciously or not, an absentee with a compulsion to be found will somehow make his whereabouts known. He will communicate with relatives or friends; he will use a credit card or make a long-distance telephone call; he will leave a trail of plastic bread crumbs.

When this happens, the investigation becomes no more difficult than, as one cynical police inspector described it, "catching a wild boar in a phone booth with a stool pigeon."

X

Ensuring the Past

Larry Bader's last act before leaving Akron the afternoon of May 15, 1957, was the payment of a $45.85 quarterly life-insurance premium. This premium was the last installment he paid on his wager with the insurance company, with that firm taking the mildly usurious position that he would out-live the amortization of his policy's face value. Symbolically, then, the money was a parting gesture by a man about to win that bet.

By the time the funds reached the coffers of the New York Life Insurance Company on Madison Avenue, the company was aware that its client had rather mysteriously vanished off or into the choppy waters of Lake Erie. In anticipation of the inevitable death claim, the company routinely routed the file jacket containing Policy No. 25 624 079 to its legal division for inspection. What the lawyers found was this: on February 8, 1956, fifteen months before his disappearance, Bader had signed up for a twenty-year, $7,000 ordinary life-insurance policy, which provided for the payment of a double indemnity in the event of accidental death. In addition, the policy provided reducing term mortgage protection, which meant that New York Life would pay off the family's outstanding mortgage debt should the insured die within the period of coverage.

Actually there was nothing in the policy jacket to cause

undue anxiety among the company's decision makers in New York. The length of time the policy had been in effect considerably narrowed the likelihood of fraud, as did the relatively small amount of life protection. Bader's application, moreover, indicated that he possessed another $7,000 straight-life policy with the Aetna Insurance Company; the combined benefits represented the minimum protection that a salesman with a large mortgage and a growing family should have. The fact that the New York Life policy had been sold to Bader by his brother-in-law, Robert Knapp,* was of no special consequence. All insurance companies expect their agents to sell to their relatives. This practice, in fact, has proved quite lucrative, in view of the tremendous personnel turnover in the industry, which continues to collect the premiums long after the would-be agents have gone back to selling shoes or widgets.

What was highly unusual, however, was the manner in which New York Life handled the death claim, duly submitted by the sole beneficiary, Mrs. Mary Lou Knapp Bader, after a long investigation by police and private detectives had not located any trace of her missing husband. New York Life promptly paid it!

The key word here is "promptly." As noted in Chapter III, the multibillion-dollar life-insurance industry, based on a projection of the 1966 experience of Prudential, annually receives about 1,500 death claims a year based on legal declarations of presumed death. These declarations mean that some court has decided there is reason to concede the demise of an individual, even though no corpse has been found. The average age of these claims, according to one industry survey, is *twelve* years from the date of disappearance. Even then, the

---

* Knapp's placement did not come anywhere near the company record for time elapsed between the sale of a policy and the date of a death claim. Another enterprising New York Life agent "closed" a $40,000 double-indemnity policy on Herman Clutter eight hours before he and his family were murdered, as Truman Capote described it, *In Cold Blood*.

companies involved have settled these claims only after con-
ducting extensive and thorough investigations of their own.
But despite this industry-wide practice, and despite, as will
soon be evident, its own tradition in this field, New York Life
handed Mrs. Bader a check for $24,579.14 ($14,000 in
double indemnity, $10,031 for the commuted value of her
mortgage, and $548.14 for interest and premium adjust-
ment) on May 22, 1958—just one year and one week after her
husband had vanished.

By contrast, Aetna absolutely refused to pay anything. Its
agents, of course, could find no trace of the company's missing policyholder, and its claims division still harbored deep
misgivings about the whole affair. It was not until Mrs. Bader
filed suit against the company in a U.S. District Court in
Cleveland that Aetna agreed to settle. Under the terms
agreed to, Aetna paid Mrs. Bader periodic interest on the
$14,000 double-indemnity claim for a period of seven years,
or until May 15, 1964, at which time that company paid her
the full amount, with no strings attached. This meant that,
nine months later when Bader-Johnson was uncovered,
Aetna had no legal grounds for the possible recovery of its
money.

New York Life, despite its unprecedented haste in settling
the Bader claim, took adequate precautions to safeguard its
money. Before Mrs. Bader received the settlement, she was
required to pay $750 to the Fidelity & Deposit Company of
Maryland for a $25,000 surety bond against the reappearance
of her husband. This she was happy to do, and this practice is,
again, standard procedure throughout the insurance industry. But it does not begin to explain why New York Life
rushed to pay Mrs. Bader or why it was even willing to
consider a claim two years before her husband was legally
declared dead.

Was it because the beneficiary was the sister of a New York
Life agent? New York Life refuses to say. In fact and in
practice, New York Life does not like to talk at all. When the
Bader-Johnson case burst into the nation's headlines in Feb-

ruary 1965, the company's New York officials quickly became upset about the apparent willingness of its Akron representatives to discuss the case with the press. A memorandum was dispatched to Ohio, to the effect that all future media inquiries regarding Bader were to be referred to the public-relations office in New York. Then a copy of the memo was sent downstairs to the public-relations director, with a notation explaining that all such press inquiries were to be answered the same way: No comment.

The company's public position on such matters was spelled out in a letter, dated March 2, 1965, from Francis L. Cooper, then the assistant vice-president for public relations, to one of the company's field agents in Denver. He pointed out that Bader, as a client of the company, deserved the same confidential relationship that a patient expects from his doctor. Apparently attempting to minimize the impact of Bader's reappearance, Cooper added that during his two decades of service to New York Life, he knew of only one other such case.*

The second case referred to, but not specified, by Cooper came to public attention on November 4, 1953, when attorneys representing New York Life entered the superior court in Nashville, Tenn., and informed a startled judge that they had located a man thought to have been dead for twenty-two years. Specifically, the lawyers demanded the invalidation of an eleven-year-old declaration of presumed death, so that the company might repossess the $53,588.76 it had previously paid the man's "widow." Having made this request, the New York Life attorneys executed an unusual but quite legal maneuver. They did not leave their petition on file, explaining that this would jeopardize the privacy of their returned-from-the-dead policyholder.

---

* This is a rather amazing statement for a responsible official of the nation's third-largest insurance company to make. Twelve years before, his own office had issued a press release that began: "In a life insurance company as large as New York Life, which has over 3½ million policyholders, disappearance cases are by no means uncommon. . . ."

It was a futile stratagem. The missing policyholder had been a prominent member of the local aristocracy by name of Thomas Craighead Buntin. Prior to his sudden disappearance in 1931, he had been the manager of a Nashville insurance company founded by his grandfather. As soon as the newspapers learned of the sensational court action, they launched an intensive investigation on their own and, aided and abetted by some injudiciously dropped hints, soon located the long-lost Buntin in Texas.

The Buntin saga, one local wag pointed out, was the biggest piece of news to come out of Nashville since 1829. That was the year that Sam Houston, governor of Tennessee and newly married to the former Eliza Allen, abruptly quit his job after his wife left him, and departed permanently for Texas and a more familiar role in history. But in the barrage of publicity surrounding Buntin's exposure, only casual attention was given to New York Life's pertinacious pursuit. "The general public does not realize that, regardless of court decisions, we never give up an investigation into reported death cases until a body is identified as that of the missing person," a company sleuth was quoted as saying. "As far as the company is concerned, the case is never closed as long as the person is unaccounted for."

Even allowing for hyperbole on the part of the speaker, the quotation accurately depicts the determination of the majority of insurance companies when it comes to locating errant policyholders. The fact that one company had grounded an elusive client after more than two decades effectively illustrates why the insurance companies represent the greatest and most persistent threat to the total anonymity of the voluntary absentee. More so, obviously, than the private detective agencies. The reasons for this are apparent through comparison.

The private detective conducts his search in order to *make* money; the insurance company looks for the same man in order to *save* money. Hence, the private detective, whose retainer and expenses are set before the investigation begins, can only look so far before he begins spending his own money. The insurance company's resources are, for all practical purposes, limitless; if it wants to—and occasionally it does—it can even hire private detectives. And regardless of how large the detective agency's field staff is, it can never begin to match the resourceful organization that even an average-sized insurance company maintains throughout the country for general business purposes.

The most important distinction, however, is that the private detective seeks the missing person *for* a client, whereas the insurance company wants to find him *because* he is a client. When the detective locates his quarry, he passes along the information to the person who hired him. But the insurance company, unless forced to reveal its client's whereabouts by a court, simply uses the generalized evidence of continued existence to defeat any claims made against it by the would-be beneficiaries of the missing person.

This was precisely what the attorneys in Nashville tried to do when they refused to file with the court the petition containing the whereabouts of Buntin. This legal ploy to protect his privacy might have succeeded had not the Buntin name commanded so much attention in the community. In the majority of such cases, however, the drama of pursuit and recovery is acted out quietly and unobtrusively, behind the closed doors of a judge's chambers.

One representative example of this involved an Easterner who had retired on a partial-disability pension at the age of forty-six. After his disappearance three years later, his pension benefits gradually accumulated to more than $10,000. At the end of seven years his wife, the principal beneficiary of his group-insurance policy, succeeded in having him declared legally dead. Her lawyer next entered a claim for both the value of his policy and the undistributed pension payments.

Meanwhile, the insurance investigators had determined that their client had fled in company with a woman from the same town, whose married daughter lived in California.

More important, they knew that he had not changed his name. Through the name-checking services of regional credit agencies (the same technique used by private detectives in the previous chapter), they had tracked the man to a small town in Michigan. Arriving after the man had departed, they still had managed to secure photostatic copies of his employment and motor-vehicle applications, which, by handwriting comparison, would demonstrate that he was still alive. But stronger proof was needed, and there remained the problem of the mounting, undisbursed pension payments.

The company's investigation therefore centered on the daughter. Periodically, one of the company's regional managers in California was instructed by the home office to visit the woman, explain the situation, assure her in the most emphatic terms that the company had no intention of disclosing the whereabouts of its client, and plead with her to at least transmit this information to her mother's companion. The message was short and explicit: We won't tell where you are, but please collect your money. These visits continued despite the woman's insistence that she did not have the slightest idea where her mother was.

The man had been officially missing for eight and a half years when his wife announced her intention of suing for the death benefits and pension funds. At first the company merely acknowledged the letters from the wife's attorney, who became more and more demanding. The company's position had been made clear from the beginning: it could not pay any death benefits because its policyholder was alive. The turning point came when the wife's lawyer, using somewhat intemperate language, threatened to take the company to court and force it to reveal the man's location. The company announced that it would welcome such action, and a private meeting was scheduled with the judge who had issued the presumptive declaration, "in order that the integrity of the court's records might be preserved." But before a meeting took place, a man walked unannounced through the revolving doors of the company's Manhattan headquarters and said, "I hear you fellows have been trying to find me." For the next two hours, the man sat, sipping from the container of tea he had requested and chain-smoking imported cigarettes, while myriad questions were put to him by the company officials concerned about the legal implications of his situation. He consented to pose for a color Polaroid photograph of himself holding the current issue of *Life,* with the date quite visible in twenty-four-point type.

This photograph was shown the following Tuesday morning to a Superior Court judge, who immediately agreed to vacate the declaration of presumed death. At no point was any pressure brought upon the company by the court or the wife to disclose the whereabouts of its client. In return, the company lawyers volunteered the information that, just before he went off to collect his accumulated pension benefits, the husband had, almost by afterthought, removed his wife as beneficiary.*

From the industry's standpoint, the distinction between a missing disability pensioner and a vanished scion like Buntin is a minor one. Both are categorized as "lost policyholders," and the procedures for tracing them are essentially the same. Basically, two types of clients fall into the "lost" category, and every insurance company, including New York Life, has its share of each. The first type, which predominates, consists of people who, without notifying the companies, simply stop paying the premiums. Since many of their policies have accumulated dividends and cash values, the company is literally left holding the bag (i.e., undisbursed funds). Some policies provide for this contingency with a policy rider that automatically credits these cash balances against uncollected premiums, and the policy remains in force until the policyholder's equity is exhausted. These clients are obviously the

---

* As a token of appreciation to the claims investigators who had carefully protected his whereabouts, this policyholder has for the past several years included them on his Christmas-card list, and invariably signs his greeting, "The man you found by opening the door."

easiest to locate, since they are not in hiding; each year they and their beneficiaries are pleasantly surprised by the receipt of several millions of dollars in unclaimed benefits, courtesy of the resourceful initiative of the insurance industry.

The second and far more elusive type of "lost policy-holder" is the one who disappears. The industry tends to divide this group into two subcategories: fraud and potential fraud. This is the beginning premise of all insurance investigations of missing-persons cases; it is often the investigation that makes the final distinction.

Consider, for a moment, Norman H. Briggs and George F. Knoop. Briggs was an insurance salesman and builder in Troy, N.Y. He was married and had two children. He enjoyed scuba diving. Knoop lived in Las Vegas, Nev., where he worked as a machinist. He too was married and had two children. He also enjoyed scuba diving. On July 17, 1960, Briggs, then twenty-eight, drove his jeep to Tomhannock Reservoir outside Troy and vanished. On March 27, 1964, Knoop, thirty-one, drove his car to Lake Mead, on the outskirts of Las Vegas, and also vanished. Briggs was declared legally dead, his double-indemnity insurance policies were paid off, and his wife remarried. Knoop was declared legally dead, his double-indemnity insurance policies were paid off, and his wife also remarried. Norman H. Briggs was not dead, and neither was George F. Knoop.

But there the similarity ends abruptly.

The Troy police knew all along that Briggs was alive, but they could not prove it. Outwardly, his disappearance contained all the trappings, minus corpse, of an accidental drowning. Witnesses had seen Briggs moving around in the water about dusk, and later his glasses and trousers and empty wallet and car keys were found in the jeep. But when rescue teams of skin divers, including two state troopers who "walked" back and forth across the bottom of the reservoir, failed to find any trace of the man, the police became dubious about the whole incident. The recovery of Briggs' weighted yellow face mask up on the rocks of the highway causeway crossing the reservoir terminated the aqueous phase of the search.

What the police discovered on land at least confirmed their suspicions. First there was evidence that someone had spent the night in the hayloft of a nearby barn. Then there were reports that a man answering Briggs' description had been seen walking along the highway toward Troy early the next morning. Finally a pair of rolled-up socks belonging to the missing man were found by the side of the road.

The clincher, as far as the skeptical investigators were concerned, was a telephone call received by a Troy insurance company two days before the disappearance. The caller, who declined to reveal his identity, had inquired about the procedures involved in securing death benefits on his policy should he happen to drown and his body not be recovered. The questioner explained that he needed the information because his brother had recently drowned in a Colorado lake and his sister-in-law was destitute. The police already knew that Briggs had once lived in Colorado, and, after a teletype check with Colorado authorities disclosed that no such drowning had been reported, they were convinced that Briggs had been the caller.

The police reconstruction was now complete: Briggs had cashed a $500 check in preparation for flight, called the insurance firm to make sure that the staging of his "accidental death" would not abrogate the terms of his policies, driven to the reservoir and established his presence in the water with witnesses, then crept away unseen to the barn, slept in the hay, and walked off in the early dawn. Only one detail was left unaccounted for.

Where was Briggs?

His family did not know, his friends could not say, and the police and insurance investigators were unable to find out. About the only person still convinced that his body was in the reservoir was Roland Briggs, Norman's brother, who clung stubbornly to the presumption of accidental drowning. Roland even persuaded several volunteer scuba enthusiasts to continue the underwater search after the police divers had packed up their gear and pressed their inquiries in more promising directions. The amateurs found nothing either. But in the spring of 1962, twenty-one months after Briggs disappeared, something happened that made people wonder if Roland had been right all along.

On Easter Sunday, the police were forced to resurrect the reservoir theory when a scuba tank, its leather back straps rotted by long exposure in the water, floated to the surface. The oxygen supply in the tank was exhausted. It was found near the last location Briggs had been observed diving. And it was positively identified as the tank that the missing man had rented from a Troy sporting-goods store. "When the tank was found," his wife, Gail, later recalled, "I really thought he was dead."

So did the rest of the family, so did the courts, and so did the insurance company, which paid Mrs. Briggs about $117,000 in double indemnity and back interest on her husband's policies. Only the police remained skeptical, refusing to close the Briggs case. Rensselaer County Sheriff Harold H. Harriman, in particular, just could not forget the mysterious eleventh-hour phone call to the insurance company. "The coincidence was too much for me," the sheriff insisted. "I knew Briggs would turn up."

He did. In March 1965, a month after Bader-Johnson had been recognized in Chicago and widely publicized across the country, the press was informed that Briggs was working as a cowboy in Wyoming under the handle of Clayton (Clay) Hollister. Some newspapers went so far as to link the two cases, but the media had apparently been saturated with double-identity stories, and Briggs-Hollister faded quickly from the national headlines.

The bizarre turn of events was big news in Troy, of course. As the family lawyer, Pierce H. Russell, told it, Briggs had been unmasked by a teacher from Denver. She had met him at a Colorado ski resort, where he revealed his dual identity and even his college. "That got me to thinking," she said.

"I'm naturally inquisitive and I had to put the puzzle together." She managed to trace him through the alumni office of Cornell University. He had told her that he was employed on the Kenneth Adkins cattle ranch, about thirty-five miles southwest of Newcastle, Wyo. The teacher relayed this information to his parents, and his father, Hollis Briggs (from whose given name the son had compounded his new moniker), headed West for a visit.

Norman Briggs, it was subsequently learned, had unobtrusively returned to Troy to spend the Thanksgiving of 1964 with his parents. But it was not until February 16, 1965, that the police and his former wife were informed. Eight months before, Mrs. Briggs had become Mrs. Earl A. Koenig of North Greenbush, N.Y., having taken the precaution of obtaining an Alabama divorce. Now expecting her third child, she announced that she had "no desire for a reconciliation" with Briggs. Her attorney added, to the apparent satisfaction of everyone involved, that the insurance money would be refunded.

The reappearance of George Knoop, however, began badly and swiftly got worse. Instead of being turned in by a vacationing teacher, he was arrested on January 5, 1967, by the police, acting on a tip that he had staged his death. Nor was he in the process of acting out a Marlboro cigarette commercial; he was still a machinist. All that had changed was his location, El Segundo, Cal., and his name, now John L. Deviland. The police told the reporters that Knoop-Deviland was being held on a Nevada fugitive warrant for failing to return $150 worth of rented scuba gear that he was carrying when he took his "fatal" dive in Lake Mead three years before. But when the judge set bail at $15,000, the press sensed immediately that the plot was, as they say, thickening.

At first, Deviland would not admit that he was Knoop, although he readily acknowledged his mother and sister when they entered the jail. The women, convinced that their son and brother was dead, were shocked to learn that he had been living incognito five miles from their home. So was Mrs.

Brenda Deviland, a twenty-five-year-old brunette divorcee, with two children by a previous marriage, who had married Knoop-Deviland six days before the police took him away. She assured the authorities that she knew her husband only by his assumed name.

Knoop's first wife, Janice, may or may not have been shocked by his arrest, but she was hardly surprised. After his disappearance, she had returned to her hometown, Cedar Falls, Iowa, where she married a college teacher, Chester McNelly. But she knew all along what the police investigators, including agents of the FBI, were just finding out; namely, that Knoop had driven his car to the shores of Lake Mead, dropped his shoes and a towel on the sand, and conspicuously left a marked trail of footprints down to the water. After swimming some distance along the shore, he left the water and drove off in a second car registered in the name of John L. Deviland.

This other car eventually was what led the investigators to his El Segundo doorstep—once they were convinced, for reasons no one would discuss, that he had faked his death. The Nevada motor-vehicle records showed that Deviland had purchased the car from Knoop a few weeks before the disappearance. Having sold the car to himself under his new identity, Knoop-Deviland then drove from Lake Mead to the Los Angeles area, where he easily obtained a Social Security card in Deviland's name and began plying his old trade. When it became clear that all this was known by Mrs. McNelly, who had collected some $23,000 in insurance and Social Security benefits on the death of her first husband, she was also taken into custody. Four months later, they both pleaded guilty to conspiracy charges to defraud the government, and both received suspended sentences.

George Knoop and Norman Briggs vanished under identical circumstances. But in the end, Knoop-Deviland was convicted of a crime and placed on probation, whereas Briggs-Hollister vaulted into the saddle of his quarter horse and rode off into the proverbial sunset. Knoop and his wife, according to the police, perpetrated a fraud in an attempt to solve their marital and financial difficulties. Briggs, on the other hand, was not consciously defrauding anyone. His disappearance was not carried out with the knowledge or participation of any other person, and he could not and did not share in any of the proceeds that accrued from his "death." The problem that the insurance companies face, of course, is that the possibility of fraud in such cases cannot realistically be dismissed until an investigation is conducted. That fraud represents only a minor problem to the industry's claims personnel is a statistical tribute to the thoroughness and perseverance of its investigatory processes.

Naturally, fraud is anathema to any business. The insurance industry considers it a mortal enemy, for reasons that help explain, if they do not quite justify, why certain companies will occasionally expend more in the chase than the amount at stake. The nature of the life-insurance contract demands a viable atmosphere of trust. The policies must be written and *enforced* in a way that will guarantee that the policyholder's beneficiaries have more to gain by his living than by dying. The industry defines this as the "insurable interest," and what it simply means is that once an insurance contract begins to favor the beneficiary instead of the insurer or the insured, the potential of fraud becomes very strong. Thus, the unexplained disappearance of a policyholder is hardly an isolated annoyance to the insurance company, or an excuse for its claim department to play detective.

One major advantage that the men who do the investigating for the industry enjoy over their counterparts in the private detective agencies is, shall we say, a certain edge on the cooperation offered by local, state, and federal officials— particularly when it comes to tapping governmental sources of restricted or confidential information.

As previously indicated, the massive depositories of information in government custody, especially at the national level, are supposedly protected by law and in theory from outside perusal. In practice, however, all information is for sale, provided the price is right and the approach properly discreet. There are endless direct and indirect ways that a large insurance company, with assets in the billions of dollars, can secure meaningful data from the restricted federal vaults.

The assistance of highly placed government officials is the capstone of this process, as well as an indication of the powerful influence such corporations wield. One flagrant example should suffice. The State Department's Passport Office is, according to Title 22 of the Code of Federal Regulations, prohibited from releasing the confidential information it possesses except in four specific instances: when the applicant requests it, a court orders or subpoenas it, another government agency asks for it, or the Secretary of State authorizes it. This regulation, however, has not stopped the office's assistant director, Miss Frances G. Knight, whose operations have been a matter of public controversy on numerous occasions, from exceeding her authority in connection with requests from private institutions, including the insurance industry.

In 1952, for example, the Passport Office went so far as to withhold a passport from a lost policyholder who had been the subject of periodic inquiries from one of the largest companies. The office duly informed the company of the man's application and promised, although the company had asked only for information, not to issue the document until it heard from this *private* company. At about the time the company's astonished New York officials were digesting the message from the passport officials, an equally astonished branch manager in San Francisco was weathering a verbal assault from the man himself, who, unable to board a ship for Cape Town for lack of a passport, was now considering—at the top of his lungs—staying in this country instead for the express purpose of suing the company. The company reacted quickly and with considerably more intelligence than had Miss Knight's subordinates. One telephone call to Washington got the passport released posthaste; another to San Francisco instructed the anxious manager to apologize and simultaneously secure a photograph of and a notarized statement from the man, who until that moment was unaware that his wife, whom he had abandoned eight years before, had managed to have him declared legally dead.

Such abuses do not, one may hope, occur with much frequency. But they do provide a partial insight into the prestige a large insurance company can apply to its investigations. The real effectiveness, though, consists of its enormous field staff of agents and representatives, who can be diverted in the course of their business rounds for research assignments. One notable instance concerned a contractor-builder in the Southwest, who left his second wife a "suicide" note.

The wife submitted this letter in support of her claim for death benefits from the insurance company. But the company's investigators, noting that her husband had parked his car near the railroad station, would only concede that their forty-seven-year-old missing policyholder was, as he had promised in the note, far away.

The company never did locate the man. The case was closed nine years later when his sister mailed the company a copy of her brother's actual death certificate (on which three aliases were listed). During that time, however, the company had to defeat several legal maneuvers by the wife to collect, including her erroneous identification of a skeleton found on a farm about a hundred miles from the man's former home. Meanwhile, the company's search produced few tangible clues until a former business associate of the missing man notified the company that he had spotted him in the lobby of the El Cortez Hotel in San Diego. In his affidavit, the witness, who had been attending a convention, was able to provide the precise date of his visual encounter.

A list of the 237 persons registered at the hotel on that date was procured by the company, and the names and home addresses were sorted out into the regions and districts where its sales agents were stationed. These agents were then sent photographs of the missing client and instructed to drop by the homes on the pretense of having a little sales chat. On one point the orders from the home office were quite specific: there is to be no mention of the San Diego conclave, "in order to avoid any possible embarrassment, since we have only the word of the hotel registration blank that the wife of the man you will be interviewing was actually with him at the convention."

This elaborate stratagem failed, though hardly for want of resources, resourcefulness, and determination. Nor does it diminish the value of the advice to the voluntary absentee that was inadvertently offered by the chief inspector of one large claims department. "I think if I were going to try and disappear," he reflected, "I'd be inclined to save myself and the company a lot of trouble by cashing in my life insurance first."

The suggestion would certainly not have gone unheeded by Thomas C. Buntin, whose protruding left ear became a twenty-two-year obsession of the New York Life Insurance Company. Buntin was the grandson of a rich man. In 1931, he was twenty-eight, and he enjoyed a lot of things that not many others had at that depressing time. To begin with, he drew $300 a month as the general manager of the James E. Caldwell Insurance Company, a family business founded by and named after his maternal grandfather, the late president of Nashville's Fourth and First National Banks. To his salary was added a $200 allowance from his mother. The then munificent total was more than enough to provide his wife and three sons with all the creature comforts, including two cars. He also carried two $25,000 policies with New York Life.

Buntin possessed something else, something that money and family and social position could not compensate for. It was deep inside him, and it made him moody and frequently depressed. He drank wildly, and his moments of exhilaration were usually followed by dark, dangerous periods of depression, during which he often expressed a desire to kill himself, as his father had done in 1918. His wife later testified that she had awakened one night to find him holding a pistol to his head.

The breaking point came the afternoon of September 19, 1931, when Buntin, thoroughly drunk, was arrested after he had blundered into the home of two horrified spinsters, who summoned the police. Two days later he disappeared, and his friends assumed that the scandal surrounding his arrest had driven him to carry out the threat of self-destruction he had so often uttered. This feeling was strengthened a few days after he vanished, when his family received two wills mailed by Buntin from Saint Louis.

But six weeks later, the proponents of the suicide theory were shaken by the disappearance of Buntin's former secretary and bookkeeper, twenty-two-year-old Betty McCuddy. She had about fifty dollars with her when she left her home in Russellville, Ky., after telling her father that she was going to visit friends in Nashville. What really puzzled the investigators, however, was the fact that she abandoned approximately $37,000 in assorted bank deposits and trust funds. (After she was eventually declared dead in the early 1940's, her share of a million-dollar inheritance was awarded to a nephew.)

The combination of Miss McCuddy's departure and the very real possibility of a large death claim from Buntin's family was enough to start New York Life's investigative mills grinding. To head the search, the company selected a thirty-year-old investigator named Albert M. Alexander, who had once known Buntin socially. For the next two decades, the Buntin file remained on his desk, a constant reminder of the great unanswered question in Alexander's life. The search was intensive and exciting at first, for there were many leads and tips to run down and check out. In 1940, Alexander pursued one "sighting report" all the way to Panama, where he spent a futile month peering into strange faces and displaying his photographs of Buntin.

The bulk of the investigation was concentrated in the years

preceding the 1942 court decision that declared Buntin legally dead. From about 1943 to 1952, there were, by the company's own admission, no reports on the missing man. During these nine years, Alexander studied and restudied the voluminous dossier, trying to reason out the fading mystery he had been charged with solving. Periodically he would jog the memories of the company's field staff with more photographs, a description of how Buntin had probably aged, and the same admonition: be on the lookout for a tall man with the telltale protruding left ear. He also included pictures of Miss McCuddy, on the presumption that if Buntin were alive, she would be with him.

After Buntin had been located, estimates appeared in the press—which the company refused to either confirm or deny—that New York Life had spent in excess of $100,000 to find a man whose life had only been insured for $50,000. It was in this context that the company investigator, previously quoted, insisted that missing-persons cases are never closed until the body has been accounted for. "Our only object in the case," New York Life sanctimoniously explained, "is the recovery of funds which we feel belong to the Company and its mutual policyholders." The logic of expending a huge amount of money to recover a smaller amount is peculiarly a matter between the officers of this corporation and its acquiescent policyholders. But the duration of the company's costly search suggests another underlying reason, a reason explained by the decision of Grafton Green, the chief justice of the Tennessee Supreme Court.

In contesting its obligation to pay death benefits, the company went before Judge Green in 1942, arguing that there was no real evidence of Buntin's death, that there was every reason to believe he had run off with Miss McCuddy, and that, in any case, his policies with the company had lapsed. Not so, declared Green. Buntin, the judge ruled, was a "prodigal son," who was "incompetent" to support himself. In rendering his decision, Green noted the subsequent disappearance of Miss McCuddy, but he dismissed it as a determining factor on the ground that neither she nor Buntin had carried much money with them. If they were alive, why hadn't they tried to tap some of the considerable financial assets Miss McCuddy had abandoned?

Finally, Green buttressed his decision for a presumption of death by pointing out that Buntin, by reason of affluence and ill health and a proclivity to strong drink, was totally unsuited for unskilled work. Because of the Depression, there were few jobs available, and a surplus of unemployed skilled workers to fill them. Buntin, therefore, could not compete; and if he could not compete, then he could not survive for a period of, well, seventeen months.

And that, fellow litigant, was the stinger, the part that hurt New York Life right where it lives—in the pocketbook. For, as the company lawyers ruefully noted, that judge's seventeen-month estimate of how long Buntin could survive out in the cold, cold world just happened to coincide with the length of time his insurance policies had remained in effect after his disappearance.

Green's somewhat unorthodox mortality calculations cost New York Life more than $50,000, a figure that would be doubled and perhaps tripled before the company finally proved that the court had been wrong and it had been right. Buntin's file stayed on Alexander's desk. Grafton Green died. The case still remained open. The years passed.

They were not easy years for Tom Buntin and Betty McCuddy. She had joined him, as the company suspected, in Saint Louis, and, as Mr. and Mrs. Thomas D. Palmer, they had boarded a flight to New Orleans early in November, 1931. The flight was diverted by fog, and landed instead at Brownsville, Texas. The couple debarked on impulse.

The Palmers lived in Brownsville until 1948. The change of scenery had not cured Buntin of his alcoholism, which cost him one job after another—much in the manner that Judge Green had imagined. What the court had vastly underestimated was Buntin's resiliency and Betty's courage.

A very likable person—who was even admired, someone later pointed out, by the people who fired him—he kept bouncing back, even after severely injuring his hip in a fall. New jobs replaced the lost ones, and he gradually conquered his drinking problem. During the worst moments, Betty, who had also retained her given name, used her secretarial skills to make ends meet. The couple had six children.

The Palmers had been gone from Brownsville more than four years when Alexander's bloodhounds reached that Texas town, guided by some specific information, the source of which the company still refuses to reveal. Once the investigators learned Buntin's new alias, it was a simple matter to locate the elusive couple.

The necessary affidavits were quickly secured, in return for which the company promised to protect the real identities and location of the Palmers. The next step was up to the company, and it consisted of recovering what was left of its original insurance payment to Mrs. Buntin, who had since married Lewis Phillips, president of the Broadway National Bank of Nashville. This amounted to approximately $31,000 in trust funds for her three sons, which, in November 1953, the company succeeded in freezing with a court injunction.

The court action proved to be the beginning of the end of the Palmers' privacy. One of the company's attorneys in Chattanooga let it slip that Buntin was living in a "citrus" city in Texas. This was apparently enough of a clue for Silliman Evans, the publisher of the Nashville *Tennessean,* who promptly dispatched a photographer and a young reporter, John Seigenthaler (the *Tennessean*'s present editor), to search for the missing couple. Twenty-two days later, the *Tennessean* announced that it had located Thomas Buntin and Betty McCuddy, although Seigenthaler ascribed a large dose of luck to his discovery. He was driving down the main street of Orange, Texas, he claimed, when his photographer, Jimmy Holt, spotted a likely-looking man with a jutting left ear getting off a bus. The reporter was disappointed at first, because the man had a pronounced limp, but they followed him to his home at 1001 Orange Street. After a couple of days of observation and some more checking, Seigenthaler entered the courthouse in Beaumont, twenty-four miles away, and approached Betty Palmer, who was employed there as a court reporter.

"You're Betty McCuddy, aren't you?" he said.

As he later described the confrontation, Betty stared at him for a moment, paled slightly, and began to tremble. Then she admitted that she was indeed Betty McCuddy.

She and Seigenthaler drove to a nearby television-appliance shop where her husband worked. She got out of the *Tennessean* reporter's car and went in to tell Tom that what they had both feared would happen ever since the insurance company had located them had actually occurred: they were about to reenter a world they had abandoned twenty-two years before. Outside, conversing in the car, Seigenthaler offered them, on behalf of the *Tennessean,* a thousand dollars for their story. Betty McCuddy Palmer answered a number of questions with her refusal: "If money had meant anything to us, we wouldn't have done what we did. We were in love." Seigenthaler quoted her explanation in his copyrighted story the next day. He neglected to mention his financial offer that had prompted her candid response.

After the national press was done with the story, two families were left to sort out and reassemble the inevitable debris that floats to the surface of every exposé. The publicity had obviated any need for Buntin-Palmer to return to Nashville for the subsequent court hearings (which might explain the "hints" that launched the *Tennessean*'s haystack jaunt to Texas), though he did return later to visit his aged mother. Betty Palmer talked with her father by telephone and learned that her mother had died shortly after her disappearance and her only brother had been killed in an airplane crash. Mrs. Phillips, the first Mrs. Buntin, remained in uncommunicative seclusion, while New York Life pressed its claim to her sons' trust funds. On April 27, 1956, the Tennessee Supreme Court, which fourteen years earlier had declared

Buntin incompetent to survive, ordered the remaining monies refunded to the hound that had so patiently run its hare into the ground. The court split, three to two, on the decision.

A more fitting epilogue, in a sense, to this unusual case had already been written. Ten months after Buntin's existence became known, Albert M. Alexander, who had been in charge of the investigation for practically his entire career with the company, died in his sleep at the age of fifty-two in his Memphis home. The man he had sought so diligently would survive him by a dozen years. It is difficult to resist comparison of Alexander with Javert, the police inspector who relentlessly pursued Jean Valjean through the pages of *Les Misérables*, only to end his life upon learning his quarry's worth. The long search was over. The file marked "Buntin" was closed.

XI

A Rational Presumption

In the lobby of the imposing building that houses the U.S. Department of Commerce in our nation's capital is an electronic gadget which, by simultaneously adding each birth and subtracting every death, registers a second-by-second estimate of the burgeoning population in this country. Whatever the purpose of this demographic nightmare, it has the effect of reinforcing the mistaken public impression of an omniscient government, one that knows with computer certainty where all its citizens are. Provided that those citizens keep their government informed of their whereabouts and activities, it does. This information is carefully recorded by the government, which tries to keep it as up to date as possible.

This immense filing system, which extends from the lowest to the highest levels of government, is not infallible. From time to time, at unexpected places, singular people casting thin shadows slip unnoticed through the coroner's files. Some are the victims of unaccused assassins, others the casualties of unwitnessed accidents.

Many vanish.

When this happens, society can wonder, and it can speculate, and it can doubt. It can and does launch exhaustive searches for its missing members. But if no evidence is found that they passed this way or that, only one thing is left for society to do, and that is to presume. What society presumes, of course, is that its unaccounted number is dead.

Mrs. Mary Lou Bader made such a presumption in May 1957, after her husband disappeared from a small fishing boat on Lake Erie. "I had to accept the fact that he was dead," she explained. "I always have come to the conclusion that the man was positively dead; that was the only conclusion that I ever came to."

She is not a lawyer. The "fact" that she felt obligated to accept, in the tenuous wake of her husband's unverified death, is considered by the law as a rational presumption, supported in the main by a lack of contradictory evidence. Convincing a court, she soon discovered, proved considerably more difficult than collecting her husband's insurance death benefits from New York Life.

The reason, for all its complexity, was simple. No one, not the police or the insurance investigators or the private detectives hired by the Bader family, could produce any proof that Larry Bader had survived the storm swirling across the lake that last night. Nevertheless, there were too many possible reasons why it would have been to his distinct advantage to absent himself voluntarily. These ranged from his growing financial predicament, aggravated by his failure to file his income-tax reports, to the unelaborated suggestion by the Lakewood, Ohio, police chief that the missing man had "family problems."

The mechanics of his disappearance—a substantial amount of cash, a small suitcase full of clothing, a determined disregard for the worsening weather conditions on the lake—also detracted from the credibility of the death presumption. The cumulative implications prompted the Social Security Administration to reject Mrs. Bader's first application for survivor benefits for herself and her four children (her third son, Timothy, was born in September 1957, four months after his father had disappeared) .

The defeat was a double blow. It denied the "widow"

necessary financial aid, and it also reinvoked all of the anxious questions surrounding the Lake Erie episode. Her family and in-laws had eased the initial burden of expenses, and the proceeds of a thousand-dollar group-insurance policy had helped. But clearly a steady source of income would be required to maintain a pleasant home and provide the daily necessities needed by a young and growing family. This pressure increased the year after Bader vanished, when the Internal Revenue Service filed a lien against the missing man's family for $3,789 in undeclared and unpaid taxes.

Accordingly, Mary Lou Bader appealed the Social Security ruling, specifically on the ground that a series of exhaustive investigations had failed to find any trace of her husband. The full weight of this absence of evidence supporting his continued existence was placed before a Social Security referee during a protracted hearing in 1959. The government countered by questioning the basic validity of her claim to any benefits whatsoever, inasmuch as Bader, by neglecting to pay any federal income tax on his sales commissions between 1952 and 1957, had likewise failed to make his required contribution to the Social Security program.

Ultimately the argument was resolved in favor of Mrs. Bader, who would henceforth receive regular survivor payments of $254 from Social Security. This monthly sum would have been larger, except that a predetermined amount was deducted from each payment to satisfy the tax lien that was secured, in the old "company store" tradition, by Internal Revenue.

This particular arrangement is worth noting. More than one woman, doubting somehow the actuality of her missing husband's death, has attempted to enlist the federal government in the search by refusing to pay any personal tax owed by the absent spouse. "When the government finds out that he hasn't filed for last year," one irate housewife announced to an insurance-company sleuth, "the FBI will go looking for him, and save me the time and money." Nonsense. Internal Revenue, amoral to a fault, will merely wait until the abandoned family has settled with Social Security and then garnishee a portion of the benefits. The tax men do not always get their man, but they usually get their money—even if they must strip his widow in the process.

The one sour note in Social Security's reversal of its initial position on Bader's disappearance was the particle of doubt that lingered in the mind of the government referee. "There does remain, of course," he wrote in his decision to pay Mrs. Bader the monthly benefits, "the remotest possibility that [Bader] may have voluntarily absented himself for reasons known only to himself." The remark constituted Washington's final suspicious needling; the only personal consolation it provided the family was that it specifically absolved them of any complicity in the disappearance.

The legal consolation was more tangible. Armed with the favorable ruling from Social Security, Mrs. Bader now approached the local probate court in Akron for the document upon which she, a Roman Catholic widow, would begin erecting a new life. Social Security's skeptical seal of approval was adjudged sufficient proof, and a declaration of presumed death was finally granted and Bader's estate opened to probate by Superior Court Judge Vincent Zurz on May 26, 1960—three years and eleven days after Bader had headed the boat into the unpredictable waters of Lake Erie.

The precedent for Judge Zurz's action was established back in 1604, when a Bigamy Act was added to English common law. This statute excluded from prosecution anyone who remarried after his or her spouse had been overseas or incommunicado for more than seven years. In 1667 the logic of this act was extended to include the estates and legal contracts of the missing person, so that eventually the common-law protection came to be interpreted thus:

If it is proved that for a period of not less than seven years no news of a person has been received by those who would naturally hear of him if he were alive, and that such inquiries and searches as the circumstances naturally suggest have been made, there arises a legal presumption that he is dead.

In the seventeenth century the extreme hazards of travel, especially on the high seas, obviously justified the enactment of such a legal concept. It is, if anything, even more necessary today. We move faster and with greater safety over longer distances than before, to be sure; but as we have reduced the dangers of mass mobility, we have multiplied the number of societal contracts required by the functions of a modern industrial world—all of which, whether mortgages or installment credit or life insurance or compulsory health and welfare programs, place a premium on documentation.

To oversimplify: when we arrive in this world, we are automatically issued a certificate attesting our birth. This entry notice becomes the cornerstone of the documentary edifice we construct over the years. When we depart, we are expected and required to reciprocate by verifying our leave-taking with a certificate of death. The only qualification for the final affidavit is a corpse. The penalty for passing away *corpus in absentia,* as it were, is the mass of legal briefs that society extracts from our relatives and beneficiaries and creditors. It obtains them by freezing our assets in an administrative limbo for a period, in an era of supersonic flight, equal to twice the longest sailing voyage during the reign of Elizabeth I.

The year after the Virgin Queen's demise, the English jurists decided that seven years was the reasonable length of time for a presumption of death. Today it is the unreasonable interval still required in thirty-nine of these somewhat United States—when the intention of said declaration is to secure possession of the missing person's property. Arkansas, Indiana, and Vermont require five years; Minnesota, incredibly enough, asks a mere three months; no specific time limit is defined in Maine, Maryland, Massachusetts, New York, Tennessee, Washington, and Wisconsin. In an effort to modernize and standardize the probate procedure, the

National Conference of Commissioners on Uniform State Laws drew up in 1939 a "Uniform Absence as Evidence of Death and Absentee's Property Act." This proposed law incorporates many of the humane ideas set forth by the late John H. Wigmore, dean of the faculty of law at Northwestern University, who argued that the common-law requirement of seven years' absence was arbitrary, unrealistic, legally obstructive, and absurdly long. His recommendation was that the disposition of property be governed by definite statute, "regardless of the period of absence and without regard to whether the absentee be living or dead." He believed that insurance policies, with percentage premiums established by law, could be used to cover the risk of reappearance. By 1963, only Maryland, Tennessee, and Wisconsin had enacted this model statute.

These presumptive laws, designed primarily for the regulation of property probate, have generated a considerable amount of misapprehension about the so-called Enoch Arden divorce, named for Lord Tennyson's shipwrecked sailor who returned after a decade of silence to find his wife remarried to his best friend. This misapprehension is quite simply resolved: there is no such thing. What is often termed "Enoch Arden divorce" is in reality an exemption from prosecution for bigamy, in the event that the missing spouse returns after a prescribed period of time.

This waiting period varies from state to state. The maximum is, of course, the old common-law rule of seven years. The majority of the states, however, subscribe to a period of five years; a handful are convinced that three years is long enough; Pennsylvania holds that the abandoned spouse may remarry with impunity, provided that the missing partner has been gone for at least twenty-four months.

But protection from prosecution for bigamy is hardly the same as divorce. The common law provided for the dissolution of the *second* marriage if the missing spouse returned, regardless of the length of time that had passed. This is currently the general rule in most of the United States, particularly in those states where abandonment is considered adequate ground for divorce; in several of these states, the law even permits the returning spouse to sue for damages. On the other hand, some states either recognize the validity of the second marriage (if undertaken after the stipulated length of time) or offer the returned spouse the option of having the first marriage declared null and void; a few states automatically dissolve the first marriage after the time limit has expired. In every instance, the children of the second marriage are considered legitimate as long as one spouse has acted in good faith.

Faced with such a shifting thicket of geographical interpretation, many deserted spouses understandably take the added precaution of divorcing their missing mates, even when these absentees have been previously declared dead by the courts.

As Mrs. Bader discovered, the courts are sometimes hard to convince. Unexplained absence is merely one of the elements needed to prove to a judge that a fatal presumption exists. The emphasis, moreover, must be on the unexplainable. A healthy young man, for instance, who packs his belongings in a suitcase and leaves in search of opportunity, or even, for that matter, a middle-aged man or woman who stalks off with the expressed purpose of improving his or her circumstances —these people are obviously not prime candidates for probate, unless it can be effectively argued that their lives were imperiled at some point. The rule of thumb in such instances is that the fewer the reasons a person had for absenting himself, the more reason to presume that that person is dead.

Under the common-law tradition, the duration of the absence and the lack of personal contact during that period would suffice. But the trend in recent years has been toward evidence of active and systematic search. The abandoned wife who tells the judge that neither she nor her relatives and friends have heard from or of her missing husband has not made as strong a presentation as the woman whose petition includes a detailed report of the unsuccessful investigation by a private detective agency. Naturally the wife's case is further strengthened before the court when a government agency has officially awarded her death benefits, as Social Security did for Mary Lou Bader.

It was not the Social Security decision itself that enabled Mrs. Bader to have her husband declared dead in less than half the time that common law and the sovereign State of Ohio require. Rather it was the ominous added element of "specific peril" involved in Bader's disappearance. Specific peril means just that. It is used to characterize disappearances under such disparate circumstances as Edward F. Nelson's amid the fire and destruction of the San Francisco earthquake in 1906, aviatrix Amelia Earhart's over the Pacific in 1937, and Lawrence J. Bader's on the turbulent waters of Lake Erie in 1957. When the disappearances occur in situations as specifically perilous as these three random examples, the driving implications of "specific peril" can be and are used to circumvent the legal time requirements.

More importantly perhaps, specific peril has the effect of choking off the legal debate over the actual time of "death," a factor that figured prominently in the case of Thomas C. Buntin in the previous chapter. What irritated the insurance company was not the legal determination that Buntin was no longer alive but the judge's insistence on arbitrarily conclud- ing that the missing man had succumbed within seventeen months. In the Buntin case, the calendar was crucial. Had the court decreed that Buntin could have survived eighteen months, the insurance policies would have lapsed and Mrs. Buntin would not have received any death benefits. Over the years, the insurance industry has successfully maintained in thousands of cases that declarations of death presume the demise of the policyholder at the end, not the beginning, of the legal waiting period. Lawyers refer to this theory as "the English rule," which in practice places the burden on the plaintiff to prove otherwise.

Many judges, however, particularly at the lower levels of our judicial system, have sharply criticized this approach as creating an artificial twilight zone of existence, during which the missing person is presumed neither dead nor alive. The inconvenience that ensues from placing estate and property in a legal limbo during this lengthy period has been described, in decisions handed down by these judges, as unjust and impractical.

"Court opinions often recite facts which are not essential or even material to the issue of life or death," W. Calvin Wells, Jr., complained to the 1963 American Life Convention in Chicago, "and it is sometimes difficult to ascertain what a particular court considers material facts. In most jurisdictions there must be more than proof of absence and lack of tidings." Wells, the associate general counsel of the Lamar Life Insurance Company in Jackson, Mississippi, went on to list a series of "concurring facts" that he maintained are generally sufficient to justify a declaration of presumed death. The first was, obviously enough, an unusual absence over an extended period of time. Next came proof that people who would normally be expected to hear from the missing person had not received any information from or about the absentee. "Diligent inquiry and search" also constitutes evidence, and so does a recital of the circumstances of the disappearance which would indicate that the absentee "can only be accounted for upon the hypothesis that death has intervened."

Aware that his audience, composed of insurance attorneys like himself, was equally interested in how to defeat these presumptive declarations, Wells proceeded to spell out defensive maneuvers, ostensibly in descending order of importance. Logically, proof that the missing person had returned was mentioned first, followed by evidence that the absentee had been seen or heard from. "Evidence of financial condition, unhappy family relationships, that the absentee was a fugitive from justice or left to avoid prosecution" would be acceptable in some instances, as would any demonstration that the missing person had a "substantial" motive for vanishing.

By way of illustration, Wells recounted the disappearance

in 1907 of Lex Brame, Jr., a lawyer from Jackson, Mississippi, who was last seen sitting on the bank of the Mississippi below a hotel in Vicksburg, reading a copy of Eugène Sue's *The Wandering Jew*. This evocative but misleading title was permitted into evidence—completely irrelevantly, Wells insisted—when in 1916 the family was forced to go to court to collect its death benefits from New York Life. To win the case, the Brame heirs had to demonstrate that their missing relative had no reason for voluntarily absenting himself. "In his mid-thirties," Wells stated, "the scion of a distinguished and respected family, a successful lawyer, [Brame] enjoyed good health, affectionate family relations, and the warmth of a large circle of friends." The court believed Brame's relatives, and New York Life was required to pay the death benefits.*

In a case where the missing person is last seen near a waterfront, however, lack of motive is only one reason for the introduction of substantial testimony to stable character. Another reason is to avoid the conceivable rebuttal of self-destruction. Wells did not touch on this sensitive subject in his speech, possibly because of the bewildering array of legal precedents concerning implications of suicide in disappearance cases.

There was no precedent whatsoever for the case that attorney William P. Hindman, Jr., described to the American Bar Association in 1965. "The insured was a well-to-do young New Yorker," Hindman explained. "He was last seen alone in a small boat off Atlantic City on a calm September day. The following morning his boat was found adrift, empty and with a revolver and expended shell on the flooring. The family received suicide notes, citing recurrence of kidney

---

* This particular policyholder was in all probability a murder victim. The Vicksburg police suspected several men of the killing, but lacked the evidence to charge them. Years later, in 1937, an unidentifiable skeleton, presumed to be the missing Lex Brame, was disinterred on the site of the former residence of one of the suspects.

pains for which the insured had been hospitalized recently. The insured's body was never recovered, however."

What really complicated the issue, according to Hindman, was the fact that the policyholder, at the time of his disappearance, was still within the two-year limited-benefit period of the suicide clause in his policy. Under New York State law, this meant that the insurance company need only return the premiums paid if it could prove that the insured had killed himself. Nevertheless, the wife-beneficiary sued to collect both the face value of her husband's insurance *and* double-indemnity payments. Her claim was based on the novel assumption that her husband had accidentally drowned while staging a suicide hoax to frighten her.

"The suspicion of hoax was not without foundation," Hindman conceded. "There had been a marital spat, after which the insured made his way to Atlantic City, concealing his tracks by alias hotel registrations over a three-day period and shaving off his mustache. But through either carelessness or desire to be traceable, he had a car rented in his true name left at the boat pier and had made himself memorable to an Atlantic City bellhop by giving him a penny tip. Yet assuming a hoax, how could accidental death be found instead of successful completion of the hoax and deliberate disappearance by the insured?"

Hindman carefully avoided any mention of the name of the missing man in his speech, but the disturbing question he raised explains why the New York Police Department still refuses to close its investigation into the mysterious disappearance of James Laurence Barber, a ranking officer of the Barber Steamship Lines in New York City. The shipping company was founded in 1883 by two brothers, one of whom was his grandfather. Barber became a director of the firm in July 1953, at the same time that his brother, Edward J. Barber, Jr., was elected president. Four years later James was named to a vice-presidency of the Barber Lines, the American West African Lines, and other affiliates.

He left on September 24, 1959. Specifically, he left his wife of nine years, he left his eight-year-old son and six-year-old twin daughters, he left his fashionable residence at 320 East Seventy-second Street, and he left a suicide note on his desk, attached to a pile of unpaid bills. The thirty-five-year-old executive spent the day at his office. It was his last completely normal act. Instead of going home that night, he stayed at the Westbury Hotel, a few blocks from his family. Returning to his office the next morning, he withdrew $500 on account, then went to the Statler Hilton, where he registered in his own name.

That same afternoon, he checked out. A few hours later, he walked into the lobby of the Hotel Claridge in Atlantic City and signed the register as Mr. John L. Birch of Pittsburgh. The bellboy who lugged his bag up to the room remembered him distinctly and still carries the penny he received. No one knows just how or with whom Birch spent his first night in that New Jersey resort. What is known is that he paid his bill right after breakfast the next day and moved to the nearby Flamingo Motel, where he signed in as Mr. and Mrs. Henry Markwalter.

The same day, Saturday, September 26, he let Hertz put him in the driver's seat under his real name and drove the few miles to Brigantine, where he reserved a small fishing boat for the morrow. At 10 A.M. on Sunday, he left the dock and, revving up the outboard motor, headed out into the Atlantic. He neglected to take a pole or fishing tackle with him.

During the afternoon he was spotted, moving about in his drifting boat, by the captains of two charter boats trolling in the area. One of them, Michael Boutross, skipper of the *Afyah II*, later testified that he had kept Barber's boat under surveillance for some twenty minutes, as the craft was much too small to be so far out in the ocean. But Boutross continued on his way when the man gave no sign that he needed assistance.

The proprietor of the fishing station where Barber had rented the boat sounded the alarm at sunset. A Coast Guard rescue vessel finally located the boat about three miles off-shore the following afternoon. On the floor of the boat were a .45-caliber automatic and one shell casing; missing were the gasoline can, some rope, a makeshift anchor, and Barber.

Barber's wife, Jacqueline, had been summoned by the police to Atlantic City on Sunday night, after the fishing boat had been reported overdue and the missing man's true identity (he had signed for the boat as "W. Rogers") had been secured through a car check with Hertz. She informed the police that her husband had recently under gone major surgery for kidney trouble. He had, in fact, spent a total of twenty-nine days on three occasions in New York's Roosevelt Hospital during the previous seven months. On Monday, while the sea search was in progress, Mrs. Barber learned by telephone about the suicide letter he had left on his desk. Barber had mailed a similar message to his brother on the day he disappeared.

Under the circumstances, the press coverage of this remarkable incident was almost nonexistent. *The New York Times* devoted only four paragraphs back on page 30 to the disappearance, with the subdued heading "MISSING EXECUTIVE FEARED A SUICIDE." The rest of Manhattan's press establishment, which has never been accused of imitating the *Times*'s lofty disdain for sensationalism, printed not a line about Barber, for reasons that perhaps could best be explained by their advertising directors. And despite the plethora of unanswered questions raised by the disappearance—not the least of which was the absence of any bloodstains on the rented boat or whether there was a Mrs. Markwalter—no New York City newspaper published any follow-up stories.

But there was a follow-up, and it occurred in the U.S. District Court for the Southern District of New York. Which is where and when William Hindman, the Bar Association speaker, became involved. Hindman, a member of the New York firm of Townley, Updike, Carter & Rodgers, was seated at the defense table on May 5, 1964, when the district court prepared to hear *Jacqueline Barber* v. *John Hancock Mutual Life Insurance Co.* To John Hancock, Barber was more familiarly known as policyholder No. 6574304. This policy, dated November 18, 1957, provided for twenty years of term insurance amounting to $32,500 and an additional $13,000 in straight life insurance.* Thus, if Barber could be demonstrated to have died accidentally, the double-indemnity provision on the straight-life amount would increase the total death benefits to $58,500—the precise figure for which Mrs. Barber was suing John Hancock.

Mrs. Barber's lawyer, Eli B. Levy, spelled out his client's position in a pretrial memorandum. She was entitled to the death benefits, he insisted, because her husband had gone to Atlantic City "with an intent to commit a hoax upon her, specifically, to disappear under circumstances creating the appearance of suicide and thereafter to reappear." In the execution of this unusual stratagem, he was unexplainably killed, Levy concluded.

The company position, as set forth by Hindman, was simply that Barber was either alive or had taken his own life. If he was alive, the company could not pay any death benefits; if he had killed himself, then all the company owed, because of the unexpired terms of the suicide clause in the policy, was the total premiums paid to date. Apparently Hindman was hopeful that the district-court action might clear up some of the legal confusion surrounding the element of suicide in disappearance litigation. "The jury's essential task was to decide what had happened to the insured," he told the American Bar Association convention. "No innocent explanation, consistent with 'the experience of mankind,' was available. Even the theory of suicide hoax, compounded with the beneficiary's assumption that her husband had intended eventually to return home, was too radical a departure from standard conduct to permit reliance upon presumptions

---

* The ubiquitous New York Life Insurance Company also held *three* $25,000 policies on Barber's life.

based on accepted norms. The best chance of getting a fair decision from the jury lay in presenting all the circumstantial evidence, unencumbered by artificial and confusing presumptions."

Hindman was not permitted that chance. On May 12, 1964, the sixth day of the trial, Judge Frederick vanPelt Bryan dismissed the complaint with prejudice and without cost to either party. He also dismissed the jury, explaining that a settlement had been reached. Although the judge did not reveal the terms, he gave the jury a strong hint by announcing that, because of the difficulties in ascertaining what had really happened to Barber, "the insurance company no longer presses its contention that there was suicide in this case. . . ."

Today only the New York City police publicly persist in believing that James Laurence Barber is alive. This does not mean that the police are smarter or more obstinate than the courts and the insurance companies. It is just that the police, who have adequate precedent for their skepticism, labor under no obligation to resolve the legal morass that inevitably envelops the administration of a missing person's estate.

This confusion is slightly abated when no immediate relatives and beneficiaries are involved. An example would be the unusual borough-hall-on-stilts in Spotswood, N.J. Finding this Middlesex County settlement is a task in itself; securing a cogent explanation of how the town came into possession of the cross-shaped, blue-paneled, plastic-decorated $250,000 architectural mélange mounted on twelve-foot columns is considerably more difficult. But eventually an answer of sorts emerges, and it revolves around the shadowy figure of Bernard M. Bueche, M.D.

Nobody in Spotswood knows very much about Dr. Bueche. Apparently nobody in or out of Spotswood has the slightest idea where he is now. This includes Spotswood's six-member constabulary, the construction company that held his mortgage, the Federal Bureau of Investigation, and the American

Medical Association, which continues to list him as a member but with "address unknown." His whereabouts, however, is only one of the many unanswered questions about this mysterious general practitioner.

Bueche was a graduate of the University of Michigan Medical School. His residency training was spent in New York City. In 1955 he appeared in Spotswood and, through the uncommon expedient these days of being willing to see a patient at any hour of the day or night, quickly established a "healthy practice" in the community. He also gained a reputation as a moody, distrait man, who kept his own counsel and who was difficult to reach in conversation. He seemed at times self-obsessed, a loner. The townspeople frequently observed him strolling aimlessly about the surrounding fields, his red hair covered by a coonskin cap. But his availability and willingness to serve more than balanced any doubts they might have had about his habits. His medical practice continued to prosper. Gradually he began to accumulate the funds he needed to translate a dream into a reality.

Bueche wanted his own hospital.

He selected and purchased the location—a one-acre tract on Summerhill Road. He tore down a building that stood there and carted away the debris in a rented truck. He laboriously removed the trees on the site. The locals watched in awed dismay, as the short, bespectacled doctor cleared the land with his own skilled hands.

Robert J. O'Neill, a Perth Amboy architect, did not believe Bueche the first time the doctor casually asked him to draw up some plans for a nineteen-room private hospital. "I didn't think he was serious, so I forgot about it," O'Neill recalled. But two weeks later, Bueche called and demanded the rough sketches. "So I worked late that night and drew up this crazy thing on stilts—and he loved it. It was built without one change in the original rough sketches." As a down payment on his fee, O'Neill received a brown paper bag full of cash.

The doctor may have loved it, but the bankers—who

dream, when they dream, of rising interest rates and chattel mortgages in default—were unmoved. Attempting to secure the necessary financing, Bueche dropped his idea of a private hospital and converted his quiet vision into a medical office building. The bank still refused to provide a mortgage. The project seemed doomed until the contractor agreed to put up the money. In 1959 the "house on stilts" was finished. Inside were Bueche's offices and living quarters, and facilities for two other doctors and a dentist. More than one motorist who passed it during the next five years was startled by the sight of a short figure in a coonskin hat, perched motionless on the roof of the strange buiding, staring vacantly off toward the horizon.

Early in July 1964, Bueche called a dentist tenant, Robert Rosen, and told him that he would not be in his office that day. He did not give any reason. Nor did he take anything with him except for a few clothes. The rest of his personal belongings, his medical equipment, and his car remained at the cherished building he was abandoning. "I didn't think anything of it," Rosen recalled. "It wasn't the first time he abruptly went off somewhere." But it was, as far as Spotswood is concerned, the last time. The local police declared the forty-year-old physician missing on July 14 and the New Jersey State Police on August 4; the FBI entered the investigation somewhat later, although it refuses to say when or why. "His file is marked confidential, and that's all I can say about it," explained a bureau spokesman, who did admit that the FBI has given up looking for Bueche.

Naturally the disappearance of one of Spotswood's four doctors caused a great deal of speculation. Some folk insist that he succumbed to wanderlust and is probably practicing medicine in some foreign country. Others, who did not know that Bueche was divorced, are convinced that the doctor has returned to a family he had abandoned somewhere nine years before. At least one wag is convinced that the doctor was some kind of secret agent. Practically everyone in Spotswood regularly watched "The Fugitive" on television.

But while the residents were trying to figure out what happened to Bueche, the town officials were debating what to do about the "house on stilts." Ultimately their solution was to buy it from the mortgagor early in 1966 for $65,000. It was large enough, they reasoned, to house all the borough offices and the local police department. Mayor Russell B. Kane called it a great bargain. It was, but a majority of Spotswood's voters considered it a "blue-and-white elephant" and turned Kane out of office at the next election.

Still, there was little they could do about their new borough hall, which was eventually forgotten in the heat of a spirited and successful community campaign to block the establishment of a pool parlor in Spotswood. The new mayor, Donald Brundage, summed it all up—the doctor, the building, even Spotswood itself—when he said: "No one cares. Certainly I don't. Why should anyone care about Dr. Bueche?"

Why, indeed?

Society labors steadfastly to keep track of all its various parts. It counts them, measures them, weighs them, averages them, categorizes them. But all systems are imperfect, and every so often one of the innumerable digits—Bader, Buntin, Brame, Barber, Bueche—is lost. When this happens, society wonders, it speculates, it doubts, it looks. If the missing part cannot be located, society exercises its prerogative and makes a rational presumption.

And life goes on.

XII

Some Sweet
Oblivious Antidote

Life goes on a lot more smoothly if the missing and presumed dead stay presumably dead and missing. Their continued absence is no solution to the riddle of their disappearance. But neither, as it sometimes happens, is their reappearance. If anything, the convolutions of circumstance become darker and more devious.

Bader-Johnson is a case in point. He disappeared from the surface of Lake Erie on May 15, 1957. He was declared legally dead in Akron three years later. He was spotted by a former classmate at the National Sporting Goods Show in Chicago at about 10 A.M. on February 2, 1965. Missing, presumed dead, relocated. "It's an old plot for storytellers," observed the Akron *Beacon Journal*.

Perhaps. But this old plot contained some bizarre detours. The man who had vanished in 1957 was a Roman Catholic named Bader; he was a kitchenware salesman, with a wife and three children, a fourth on the way. The Unitarian at the sportsman show in Chicago was named Johnson; he was a television announcer, with a wife and two children.

Bader and Johnson had both been in the Navy; they were expert archers and tropical-fish enthusiasts; they were approximately the same age; they looked and sounded alike, and the Federal Bureau of Investigation said they had the same fingerprints. There was, in other words, no question about Bader being Johnson. But was Johnson Bader?

The question is not as rhetorical as it might seem. The coincidences, the evidence, the testimony of knowledgeable witnesses, including one Omahan* who claimed to have known Bader in Akron *and* Johnson in Omaha, all pointed to the continued existence of Larry Bader. The only factor unresolved was that Johnson would not or could not admit that he was indeed the missing Bader. He, John Francis "Fritz" Johnson, had no recollection of anyone named Lawrence J. Bader, had never been in Akron, and, to the best of his knowledge, was an orphan.

Fritz explained this to the woman who came to view him at the sports show and said she was his niece; he told the Bader brothers the same story when they accosted him the next day; and he repeated it to Chicago Police Lieutenant Emil Giese, after the officer had fingerprinted him at his own request. It was a tale that Fritz would never alter, even after he himself was convinced by the incontrovertible evidence that he and Bader were one and the same.

This evidence piled up quickly in the days following his telephone conversation with Giese on February 6, during which the lieutenant read him the FBI findings and suggested he get a lawyer. "It was like a physical shock," Bader-Johnson told the inquiring reporters. "Up until that moment, I had no doubt that I was *not* Larry Bader. But when I heard that, it was like a door had slammed and somebody had hit me right in the face."

---

* Walt McCourt, the owner of McCourt Enterprises, Inc., in Omaha, told the press that he was a childhood neighbor of Mrs. Bader's, had known Larry Bader, and had noticed the resemblance between the missing man and Johnson when he met the latter in Omaha in 1957. But, he explained, he had dismissed the possibility of Bader and Johnson being the same person as too incredible. The newspapers adopted a similar attitude toward McCourt's tale and did not give it much currency.

Bader-Johnson spent the next day, Sunday, under sedation and in seclusion, but only after he had persuaded the Omaha police to run another comparison of his fingerprints through the FBI identification files. Newsmen who hurried out to the couple's $11,000 home at 3314 Howard Street learned only that the man they had come to interview was resting quietly. With him were his wife, Nancy, and their two children, Krista, five, whom he had adopted, and John, two. A very brief statement on Bader-Johnson's behalf was read by a friend at a press conference that afternoon in a downtown hotel. He began by saying that Fritz still considered himself the victim of an incredible coincidence. "If you give him the benefit of getting the information in the proper perspective," the friend added rather cryptically, "you will find that our faith in him is not badly taken." Exactly what this meant, the press was unable to learn. The spokesman would not elaborate, and he refused to comment when asked if Bader-Johnson would submit to a lie-detector test.

Part of the confusion was cleared up on Monday. Fritz and Nancy met the press in the office of their attorney, Harry J. Farnham. The couple sat silently, holding hands, while Farnham read a prepared statement. His client was now ready to admit, on the basis of the evidence, that he must be the missing Ohioan, Farnham announced, "but he has absolutely no recollection of this portion of his life. I want to emphasize that Fritz and Nancy are an extremely devoted couple, with two children, and you must remember that he has no recollections of any previous family and he is therefore primarily interested in maintaining this marriage—and come what may, his wife, Nancy, is one hundred per cent behind him. Next, Fritz has instructed me that no matter what happens, and no matter what he does not remember, he has no intention or desire in any way to shirk any legal or moral obligation that he might have. Therefore, if Fritz is Larry Bader, and he has absolutely no recollection of so being, we must come to the conclusion that there has to be a medical reason to explain this."

Farnham revealed that in an effort to learn this medical explanation, Bader-Johnson would enter Saint Joseph's Hospital the following morning to undergo a series of "exhaustive physical, neurological, and neuropsychiatric tests." The lawyer hinted that there might possibly be some connection between the memory loss and the tumor that had been removed from his client's head the year before. After the statement was read, Nancy burst into tears and threw her arms around her husband.

Farnham then departed for the airport and a Tuesday meeting in Chicago with the Bader brothers, John and Richard, and the missing man's brother-in-law and insurance agent, Robert Knapp. What this get-together accomplished is not clear, although one of the agenda items undoubtedly involved the support payments that Bader-Johnson would henceforth make to Mrs. Mary Lou Bader.

After the conference at the Continental Plaza Hotel, Farnham repeated the statements he had made the day before in Omaha, adding only that he and the Baders had not had enough time to discuss such problems as the two wives or the death benefits paid to Bader's "widow" by the insurance companies and the Social Security Administration. The Bader brothers were already convinced that Fritz had drawn a complete blank on his past. During their two-hour confrontation the previous week at the sporting-goods show and later at Chicago police headquarters, Bader-Johnson's attitude and manner and conduct had apparently demonstrated to them that their missing brother had not recognized them. "He doesn't believe he is Lawrence Bader," John told the press. "We feel very sorry for him and for everyone at home."

One of the people at home, of course, was Mary Lou Bader. Her brother, Robert Knapp, informed the reporters that his sister had been quite shocked to discover that her husband was alive. "She is concerned in seeing that Larry gets proper medical attention." Mary Lou's children had not been informed of the news, he said, because "they are not really old enough to realize what it means." Knapp made no reference to the insurance policy with his company, New York Life, that some newspapers were claiming—erroneously —had been sold to Bader two days before the disappearance.

Three days later, Farnham called a second press conference at his Omaha law office. The purpose was to announce that his client, still under observation in the hospital, had decided to give up his second wife, at least temporarily. The lawyer said that Fritz and the twenty-four-year-old Nancy were "proceeding under the general assumption that he is still legally married to Mrs. Mary Lou Bader of Akron, Ohio. Therefore Fritz and Nancy will not live together as man and wife until this matter is resolved."

At this point, both families and their legal spokesmen retreated from the headlines to await the results of the hospital tests that would presumably prove whether Bader-Johnson was, as the Akron *Beacon Journal* phrased it, either "a colossal liar and a superb actor or he really had suffered one of those rare mental transitions." The newspaper did not bother to clarify just what these rare mental transitions might consist of, but the implied note of cautious skepticism typified the general press reaction—outside of Omaha, that is. Thus, *Life* informed its readers:

A special team of psychologists and one neurologist—hired by Fritz's lawyer—examined him for 10 days, and concluded that they could find "no indication that Mr. Johnson has any recollection of his life as Larry Bader—nor did [we] find any neurotic and/or psychotic tendencies to explain this loss of memory." Larry Bader may indeed have suffered some calamity in that fishing boat which might have obliterated all his previous memory. To fill that void he may have reconstructed an elaborate but completely false past and then accepted it without question as being completely true. There is, on the other hand, considerable argument in support of the hoax theory. The psychiatrists used hypnosis on Fritz during the examination, but because of his agitated state, they did not administer sodium pentothal (the so-called "truth serum"), which might have provided some indication whether or not he was lying about his past.

Life tarnished this otherwise fairly balanced attempt to analyze Bader-Johnson's memory lapse with its suspicious shaft at a medical team "hired by Fritz's lawyer." The effect of this less than innocent aside was to undermine in advance the doctors' conclusions, by implying that the underlying motive for the hospital examination was legal rather than medical. Every magazine is entitled to its own bias, though not at the expense of accuracy. The medical consultants who tested Fritz were not hired by his lawyer. Instead, they were selected and supervised by Dr. Lee C. Bevilacqua, who had been the Johnson family physician for three years. Bevilacqua issued a typewritten statement on February 18:

> I asked Mr. Donald Fauth, Staff Psychologist at St. Joseph's Hospital, to make extensive psychological evaluation. I also asked an Omaha neurologist to make a complete neurological examination, and I personally conducted a thorough physical examination. I further requested two Omaha psychiatrists to make separate and independent psychiatric evaluations.
>
> After consultation with these men, the following conclusions have been reached:
>
> Mr. Fauth stated that Mr. Johnson was completely within the range of normal, both in his test response and test reaction to test stimuli.
>
> The neurologist performed a complete neurological evaluation, and reported that he found no neurological abnormalities except the absence of the left eye.
>
> As attending physician I performed additional examinations, and found Fritz to be in good physical condition at this time. My findings, and those of the neurologist, were particularly encouraging in view of the fact that a cancer, specifically a malignant melanoma, was removed from the back wall of Mr. Johnson's left eye on March 17, 1964, by an Omaha oculist. This necessitated the permanent removal of his left eye.
>
> Both psychiatrists [converted to "a special team of psychologists" by *Life*], after their separate psychiatric evaluations,

advise me that they could find no indication that Mr. Johnson
has any recollection of his life as Larry Bader—nor did they
find any neurotic and/or psychotic tendencies to explain this
loss of memory. Therefore, at this time it would be mere conjecture to ascribe specific reasons for such a loss of memory.

It should be noted that this hospitalization was only for the
purpose of testing, and not for treatment. In fact, at this time
further testing or treatment would not be advisable because of
Mr. Johnson's emotional state.

The inability to recall such an extensive and vital period of
a person's life obviously represents a deepseated psychiatric
problem. Fritz is very desirous of commencing psycho-therapy,
and both psychiatrists advise me that it would take an indefinite period of such treatment to ascertain the exact nature
of such a problem. Hence, Fritz will commence this treatment
as soon as is practicable—which should be in a very few days.

Bevilacqua's statement offered few specific points with
which the skeptics could begin rebutting the report's tentative conclusion, but this did not prevent them from trying.
Overnight the Akron *Beacon Journal* managed to find two
local psychiatrists, who, enlightened by skimpy news reports
from Omaha, stated that the medical team's evaluation contained "obvious discrepancies." There was no elaboration of
these discrepancies—perhaps because, one is left to assume,
they were so "obvious" to the newspaper's informants.
Nevertheless, the unnamed Akron psychiatrists insisted on
describing the Omaha report as "paradoxical" and replete
with "good language to avoid getting into legal entanglements."

About the only defense that can be made for this type of
pseudomedical journalism is to recognize that ample reasons
existed for Bader-Johnson's attorney to have given final form
to the medical statement. The legal entanglements were
multiplying faster than Fritz's prolific tropical fish, as a
battery of lawyers explored the judicial quicksands of desertion, abandonment, income-tax violations, potential fraud,
misrepresentation, and bigamy.

In Cleveland, Lawrence Cotleur, the man who had rented
Bader the fishing boat eight years before, filed a $1,250 suit
against Bader-Johnson for damages to the craft. In Akron,
Probate Judge Nathan Koplin announced that, since Larry
Bader had not died in Lake Erie, he intended to take action
to "expunge the earlier judgment [the 1960 declaration of
presumed death] from our record and set our files straight."

And in Omaha, Bader-Johnson was released from the hospital and returned to his job on television station KETV,
although he would not again appear on camera. One of his
columnist friends on the Omaha *Evening World-Herald* described him in print as a "minister of the gospel of good
cheer" and promised that his friends would support him
through the coming ordeal. He had been living with one of
these friends for about a week when the press learned that
Nancy Johnson was seeking an annulment of her marriage.

Still calling himself Fritz, Bader-Johnson gradually began
to adjust to a third identity—that of a man whose actual past
was apparently forgotten and whose remembered past had
never existed. He was quite willing to talk about anything
that had happened since his arrival in Omaha in 1957, but he
declined to discuss the Bader years. "I'm very sorry," he told
an interviewer, "but my doctors have warned me not to try to
figure it out by myself. They say it might hurt me."

Captain John H. Ayers, in case the reader has forgotten,
was the founding chief of the New York Police Department's
Missing Persons Bureau. In the fall of 1925, after he had
been on the job for seven years, he granted an interview to a
writer named John K. Winkler. The results were published
on November 21 in *Collier's*, under the provocative title
"Where Are They Now?"

If Captain Ayers was to be believed, the answer was that all
but a handful were back home. The main reason for this
happy outcome seemed to be that Johnny Ayers was extremely proficient at his job, which often consisted not only
in finding the missing but also of convincing them that they

would be better off back in the familial fold. Sometimes this job of persuasion presented a problem. But Ayers was portrayed as a very resourceful cop. He had a foolproof solution, and that solution was for the absentee to claim that he or she had been suffering from amnesia, or, as Ayers preferred to call it, aphasia (which does not mean loss of memory but rather the inability to communicate).

The captain prefaced this rather incredible suggestion by stating that genuine amnesia is quite rare. But by submitting the following anecdote for publication, he was clearly suggesting that, as long as the returned absentee stuck to his story, nobody could really disprove it:

A season or two ago the wife of a Chicago broker, returning to the city with her two children after a vacation in Michigan, found her apartment empty, her husband gone. There were no clues. She rushed to the head of a private detective bureau. Three days and nights of investigation produced nothing. The broker's affairs were in splendid shape, his life was well ordered, his home surroundings were good.

Finally the detective got a hunch.

"Tom," he instructed a bright young operative, "our man was a companionable sort of bird. Find out where he lunched and with whom he talked. Maybe he dropped a hint to a waiter or a friend."

Tom was back in three hours, a grin aproning his countenance.

"Boss," he reported, "McMissing is registered under an assumed name at a hotel on the lake. He went away with a soubrette—one of those sudden infatuations. Met her through a man he lunched with almost daily in a Loop restaurant. While Mrs. McMissing was away they played foursomes, Mc-Missing, the soubrette, her girl chum and the other man.

"The chum and her beau got a phone message last night. They say our man is worried silly over the only foolish thing he ever did in his life."

Two hours later the detective walked into the resort hotel room and introduced himself to a man who sat alone, head in hands. A brief interval of futile denial, then the missing man broke down, verified the whole story and moaned:

"I regretted this mad act from the first. The girl has gone away. God, old man, what can I do? I can't face my wife."

His grief was so genuine that even the hard-boiled detective was touched. He asked, "Do you really want me to pull you out of this mess?"

"Oh, yes."

"Well, then, listen to me. You didn't run away of your own volition. You have been rambling around under an attack of aphasia."

"But what shall I tell my wife?"

"You haven't anything to tell. You didn't even recall your name until I talked to you. You have not the slightest recollection of what you have been doing."

That evening a touching reconciliation was staged at the broker's home. To this day the wife is none the wiser. But the broker is—and the detective swears he has never been tempted to repeat his experiment.

One can only hope that the broker's wife was not a subscriber to *Collier's*, not because she might have learned the "truth" about her husband's post-Victorian interlude but because it would have spared her this God-old-man-what-can-I-do? dose of Dink Stover melodrama. Obviously Ayers had no mercy when it came to pricking the credulity of an unsuspecting, gullible public. The anecdote, from conception to execution, is patently contrived; what insight it might contain consists of the way it illustrates a general misapprehension about the mnemonic processes. Ayers could not fathom it in 1925; his successors still do not understand it; and given the minimal penetration that scientists have thus far made into the vast electrochemical labyrinth of the human mind, this confusion will, probably, persist long after the memory of what's-his-name has faded.

The word "amnesia" is derived from the Greek prefix *a*, meaning *not*, and the verb *mnasthai*, meaning *to remember*. That is precisely what it means, and ever since the word was coined, men have been trying to learn why—why, as Cicero lamented, "I remember things I do not wish to remember, but I cannot forget things I wish to forget." Thousands of years later, we still do not know, despite all the available theories about how the axon in the neuron communicates with the dendrite through the synaptic knob.

The human mind is far too complex for the human mind to comprehend. It operates around the clock, controlling and stimulating and regulating the numerous body organs, constantly maintaining an extremely delicate chemical balance and rigorously adjusting the temperature all over the body. Simultaneously it is receiving and disbursing reflex orders, registering and reacting to the stimuli of sensation, thinking, calculating, reasoning, deciding, rejecting, imagining, and—central to its entire function—remembering as many as a million billion (1,000,000,000,000,000) "bits" of information in a lifetime. The entire electronic computer industry, with all its sophisticated hardware and exaggerated estimates of what its blinking machinery is capable of, will never begin to approximate this mental capacity.

The comparison is valid up to a point. For the brain alone is an elaborate and gigantic computer, composed of some ten billion nerve cells or neurons, which in turn are sheathed in about one hundred billion glial or interstitial cells. It is the dazzling and lightninglike interaction of the molecules in these cells (which also have thousands of individual interconnections) that, scientists now believe, accounts for the infinitely varied subtleties that characterize the human mind. But just how this electrochemical miracle is transformed into memory and consciousness and learning remains an inscrutable mystery.

Memory in particular has proved especially elusive to the physiologists, who have otherwise succeeded in localizing a number of mental functions—such as hearing, speech, sensory perception, muscle coordination, heartbeat, and vision—in specific areas of the cerebrum, cerebellum, and medulla oblongata. But information storage and analysis and retrieval has defied the best efforts of the laboratory researchers, beyond the general observation that memory appears to be dispersed over the entire cerebral cortex. Which is the equivalent of saying that we have located the meadow but not the haystack where the needle is hidden.

Ignorance of the workings of this fibrous maze, however, has not prevented the psychologists from attempting to theorize the matter of mind from external evidence. One of the inductive conclusions they now agree upon is that memory is a multilevel proposition. The most common level is the short-term, which consists of the thousands and thousands of sensory impulses recorded by the brain every waking second and just as promptly discarded. The second or medium-term level, characterized by a seldom-used telephone number or the ZIP code of one's mother-in-law, has a retention period of anywhere from a few minutes to forty-eight hours. Students operate at this level when they try to absorb the knowledge of an entire semester on the night before a final examination. So do people with dental appointments.

The third and most important level is the long-term. This information is deeply embedded on both the conscious and unconscious mental strata. It is obviously the data that, because of significance and vividness and interest and permanence and function, the cerebral cortex has elected to preserve. That vast areas of individual experience are permanently fixed in the less accessible regions of the brain has been graphically demonstrated by researchers, who have produced total recall of childhood incidents from patients whose cortexes have been "short-circuited" by electronic probes.

Agreement on the levels of memory and the mechanics of reception, retention, and recall serve only as theoretical road maps to the workings of this unique system. Nor is this understanding much increased by the knowledge that the mind adjusts and distorts memory for the express purpose of making the individual more adaptive to his environment. In other words, if the memory of something or other is interfering with the daily performance of a person, that person's mind either changes the contour of that memory or, in extreme cases, drives it from the realm of consciousness.

Even Macbeth would consider that some sweet oblivious antidote, indeed!

This last insight derives from the pursuit of abnormal psychology, and brings us to the point so casually oversimplified by Captain Ayers and anyone else who posits memory loss on an either/or basis. There are essentially three types of memory disorders: *hypermnesia,* which is abnormally pronounced memory; *amnesia,* which is the loss of memory; and *paramnesia,* which is the falsification of memory. Each of us suffers, in varying degrees, from all three.

Hypermnesia is usually associated with mania of some sort, and it simply means that a certain event or experience or interest is indelibly engraved in one's memory and can be recalled with unusually vivid intensity. The range of this phenomenon obviously stretches to the outermost limits of human activity, and could be as varied as the recollection of an electrocution, of a first tentative kiss, of a distant tornado, of a glowing campfire at lakeside. Why the mind has singled out a particular memory for such conscious detail is often not so apparent, but psychologists and psychiatrists have found these high points to be extremely useful clues, particularly in the treatment of paranoia.

Obviously, hypermnesia could be defined as the polarity of amnesia. And again, just as a few things stand out in extreme relief in everyone's memories, so certain other things fade from consciousness. It is merely a matter of degree whether we forget someone else's name or our own; both omissions are examples of amnesia, and everyone—creditor and debtor alike—feels its annoying sting on occasion. There are two basic medical causes of amnesia: organic and psychogenic. Organic amnesia is the physical disruption of the neuron cells in the brain in such a way as to interfere with the transmission system. This could happen because of a clout on the head, a dietary deficiency, or, most commonly, the degenerative processes of age. Psychogenic amnesia is the inhibition of memory for reasons of deep-seated psychological need.

When Oscar Frank Barnhart wandered into the Boone County, Mo., sheriff's office in March 1953 and informed the police that he had been an amnesiac for the previous twenty-one months, he neglected to specify whether he had been a victim of organic or psychogenic amnesia. The police did not bother to ask, either.

They had been waiting for Barnhart to reappear ever since June 26, 1951, when the Electrolux salesman did not return from a routine business trip. His wife reported him missing the next morning, but a police search of the area surrounding Barnhart's hometown of Columbia, Mo., turned up no clues. Then, on August 8, an airmail letter postmarked two days before in Portland, Ore., was delivered to Mrs. Barnhart. The annals of crime contain nothing to compare with its unrepentant message:

> I am only doing this letter to you to ease my conshun. Your husban begged me to write so I am tipewriting it to you. I hiched a ride in his car as he was going east from Boonvil but when I shoved my 45 automat in his side he made a quik turnaround and headed west as I told him to. I was suprized at the amount of of money he had better than a grank. He beged me not to take the money as he had to meet a company inventory. Then he ast me to at lease write yoy. Imade him get out west of Boonvil at a brdg–he ast me to let him get a sack and coat but he started shootin out of the sack but not be fore I kissed him with my 45 and he fell down the bank into the water I wood have got his gun but I didnt have any shells in my 45 so I droveoff in a hurry I wnt you to know I didnt kill him unless he droned in the water. I left the car about 2 blocks west or north of the greyhound bus depo in K.C.M. Its onaslope prached at angle oon a deadend street. He had a lot of boxes in the back, but I didnt bother them. This fills my promise to write.
>
> A hich hiker with a conshun

At the request of the Columbia authorities, the Kansas City police located Barnhart's 1941 black Buick sedan parked outside 743 Locust Street, well within the area indicated by the "hich hiker with a conshun." Inside the car were an Electrolux sweeper with attachments, a briefcase containing "miscellaneous papers," a few receipt pads, and a bankbook covered with brown stains that might have been dried blood.

The bankbook was sent to the police laboratory for analysis, and a teletype alert was dispatched from Kansas City to "STATES SURROUNDING MISSOURI: MISSING FROM COLUMBIA MO SINCE JUNE 27 OSCAR FRANK BARNHART 43 5-8 200 LIGHT BROWN HAIR BLUE EYES WAS DRIVING BLACK 41 BUICK SEDAN MO 749855 HAS NO BAD HABITS WAS INVESTIGATING SHORTAGE OF FUNDS FOR ELECTROLUX CO FOUL PLAY FEARED ELECTROLUX SALES OFFICE IN KANSAS CITY."

This message did not mean that the police had accepted the theory of foul play. To begin with, the car had been parked at the Kansas City location indicated by the "hich hiker" for only two days before it was found, according to witnesses in the neighborhood. Since the letter had been mailed from Portland, Ore., *three* days previously, there was obviously a second person involved. The police had reasons for believing that the extra participant might be Barnhart himself.

The letter was the foundation for this skepticism. As Lieutenant Harry Nesbitt, the chief of the Kansas City Homicide Bureau explained, the author displayed an inordinate concern for his "victim's" obligations to his employer—a concern marked by his sudden improvement in spelling and syntax when he reached the phrase "to take the money as he had to meet a company *inventory.*" The spots on the bankbook turned out to be human blood, but, as Nesbitt pointed out, they consisted of just a few drops and could have been caused by a cut finger.

Three days after the car was discovered, a pile of business cards and personal papers belonging to Barnhart, including his membership card in the National Rifle Association, was found in a gutter a block away. This cache merely made the police more suspicious; the papers were not stained, despite the fact that it had rained hard during the previous seventy-two hours. Someone, it was now clear, had returned to the scene, after the car had been towed away by the police, and planted the documents.

But who that someone was remained a mystery. And so did the whereabouts of Barnhart—until the afternoon of March 25, 1953, when he entered the sheriff's office and identified himself. He told the authorities that he had "awakened" to his real identity the day before as he walked along a street in Kansas City. In his pocket were a billfold bearing the name "J. K. Anderson," some cash, and a key to a room in the local YMCA. His first realization of the passage of time, he claimed, was his discovery that Dwight D. Eisenhower and not Harry S Truman was President of the United States.

Barnhart insisted that the last thing he remembered was being hit on the head with a gun held by a young hitchhiker whom he had picked up just outside Midway, Mo.* He did not recall asking his conscience-stricken assailant to drop his widow a line explaining where the inventory items could be located. He also claimed to have no recollection of what he had been doing the past twenty-one months, although he did admit that he had somehow acquired a considerable skill in laying tile bricks. He even invited the dubious investigators who sought him out at his Columbia home to inspect the tile walls he had installed in the bathroom since his miraculous return.

A thorough physical examination of Barnhart did not

---

* If that elusive marvel, the "hich hiker with a conshun," did not exist, the .45-caliber automatic mentioned in his letter certainly did. It was next seen in the hand of Oscar F. Barnhart at 2:57 P.M. on November 24, 1954, as he fled with $289 from the Household Finance Company in downtown Jefferson City, Mo. The vacuum-cleaner salesman was arrested three minutes later, pleaded guilty to armed robbery, and was sentenced on March 16, 1955, to ten years in prison. Forty-three months later, he was released on parole, from which he was discharged on September 16, 1962.

uncover any medical explanation to support his claim of memory loss; nor could the doctors find any evidence of a wound that might have resulted from a severe blow on the head. His weight was the same as it was when he disappeared, and Barnhart himself stated that he could feel no ill effects from the entire experience, except for a brief headache about the time he remembered who he was. The various police departments involved simply canceled their missing persons bulletins and considered the episode closed.

Technically, what Barnhart was describing—whether or not he actually did believe he was a tile setter named J. K. Anderson during his long sabbatical from being Barnhart—was not amnesia but paramnesia. Such memory falsification and distortion does not, however, result from organic causes like head injuries. Instead, it is completely psychogenic, a mental device that serves to protect a person from intolerable anxieties. Most commonly, it takes the form of retrospective alteration, which means that afterwards we have the tendency to remember only the facts of an experience that please us and embroider or make up the rest.

This phenomenon is frequently observed in former servicemen who, consciously or not, have gradually revised their military experiences in the retelling over the years. This often takes the form of increasing and exaggerating their combat exploits. A collective instance might be the famous Battle of the Bulge that began during the closing days of 1944; if every American who now claims to have fought in this battle had been in or around Bastogne at the time, the Germans would have been vastly outnumbered. An individual instance might be a former Navy corpsman named Bader, who never went past a secure stateside hospital billet, but who later, as Fritz Johnson, claimed to have been wounded when his ship's magazine exploded during a submarine attack outside the English Channel.

When such distortion reaches the extreme where an actual identity transformation occurs, the paramnesiac is said to have entered a process called confabulation, during which the breaches in his memory structure have been filled by fabrications. This new biographical information, although groundless in fact, soon assumes the dimensions of reality. How real depends upon the depth of the psychological need that occasioned the metamorphosis in the first place. Hence, in the absence of a neurological explanation for memory loss, "a deep seated psychiatric problem," as Bader-Johnson's physician phrased it, would seem indicated. To which he might have appended the penetrating observation somebody once made that "Remembrances embellish life but forgetfulness alone makes it possible."

XIII

The Mourning After

A broken clock does not retard the flow of time, and a person who abandons his place in the magnetic chain of humanity risks losing it forever. The links of the chain reknit, with a new strength that sometimes exceeds the sum of its fewer parts. After a very, very brief interval, reentry becomes difficult, almost impossible, to accomplish.

"No one seemed overjoyed on my return," the quixotic hero of Samuel Butler's *Erewhon* observed at the end of his satirical flight from the mean contradictions of nineteenth-century industrial England, "and I soon discovered that when a man's relations have once mourned for him as dead, they seldom like the prospect of having to mourn for him a second time."

The man who shattered—accidentally and instinctively and irretrievably—the anonymity of Lawrence Bader-Fritz Johnson then refused to reciprocate. He had gone to school with Bader in Akron; he was familiar with the mysterious "accident" on Lake Erie that had presumably taken Bader's life; and when he spotted Fritz at the sporting-goods show in Chicago, he rushed to tell the Bader family that he had found its missing son and brother and husband. But having identified Johnson as Bader, this harbinger of unresolved memories refused to identify himself.

222 "If I had it to do over again . . ."

Nor would he say why. He had been in Chicago on business. The morning of February 2, 1965, he had happened to be visiting the show in McCormick Place. That was the extent of his explanation. Just keep my name out of it, he asked.

Why?

What was his own anonymity worth? Was he merely being shy or did he have a more pressing reason? Was he concerned about somehow becoming "involved," or was he instead worried about disconnected repercussions? Did he feel that his employer would resent his having been at a sports show during working hours? Was he even supposed to have been in Chicago that day?

No one will say, but the questions are worth raising. Irony, when it exists, is found not on the surface of events but deep within the unexpected fabric of experience. It would have been ironic indeed if the man who converted the fantasy of Fritz Johnson into the legal and moral and emotional quagmire of Bader-Johnson had in turn been somewhere he was not supposed to be—had, in fact, himself been acting out a tiny and momentary escape dream at the precise moment he came upon the missing man.

For the people whose lives were rudely jolted by the exposure of Fritz Johnson and the documented reappearance of Larry Bader, however, there was no irony; only shock and disbelief and uncertain agony. In Omaha a marriage was dissolved, and a young woman was separated from the man she loved, the man who had fathered her infant son and adopted her daughter, the man she had known as Fritz but who now had another name and a past she could not share. Their son was legitimate. The law provides for that, as long as one parent at least is unaware that a bigamous relationship exists. But Nancy Johnson no longer had a husband and a father for her children, and the person she had previously considered both did not, in a sense, even exist.

Omaha's loss, moreover, could hardly be considered Akron's gain, for Bader-Johnson could or would only admit that he was not Johnson; he had mainly the word of the Federal Bureau of Investigation that he was Bader. The Bader family seemed equally convinced that its missing member had no recollection of his life in Akron. For them, his reappearance served only to still any lingering doubts about whether he had actually drowned in Lake Erie. For them, there would be no bittersweet joy of homecoming.

The full weight of this strange revelation fell on Mrs. Mary Lou Bader. "I just wish it wasn't true," was her initial reaction. "We had become adjusted, we had adapted to and accepted his 'death.' It was just . . . well . . . *wrong* that this had to happen." The press pictured her as forlorn and dejected, waiting helplessly by an unlisted telephone for the call from Omaha that would never come. Published speculation that she had recently accepted a marriage proposal was vigorously denied by her attorney, Charles F. Scanlon.

Six days after Bader-Johnson had faced the press in Omaha, Mary Lou also appeared in her lawyer's office for a session with reporters. But whereas her husband had remained silent while his legal spokesman read a prepared statement, Mrs. Bader, flanked by her two brothers, candidly responded to a wide range of questions put to her by staffers of the Akron *Beacon Journal.* This copyrighted exclusive interview, which effectively outlined her position—personally *and* legally— toward Bader-Johnson, dominated the front page of that newspaper on February 14, 1965:

Q—Now that he has reappeared, do the circumstances lead you to any conclusion about why he left?

A—I've been thinking about this. I can't seem to think very clearly about all these things. I seem to—well, first of all it was such a shock to me when I heard this [the discovery Bader was alive]—it was something very unreal. It was sort of like a numbness. It wasn't an emptiness like I felt when I thought he was drowned. But it was something else that I just couldn't explain. I haven't been able to think clearly since then.

Q—But did you reach any conclusion about what happened eight years ago?

A—I couldn't come to any conclusion about that. . . .

Q—What happened a week ago [Bader's reappearance] is the first thing . . .?

A—That is the first thing that has come up, yes. As I said, it was a very unreal thing. It's hard to believe. The rest of the family was the same way. It was a very emotional thing . . . and it was a very frightening thing, very frightening.

Q—What was your first reaction upon hearing this—upon finding out that there was a possibility that he was alive?

A—I was very stunned and frightened, at first. But then I decided it just couldn't be true . . . that this could not be possible.

Q—What first convinced you that it was true?

A—I suppose the fingerprints. I don't really understand the whole thing. . . .

Q—Have you been able to stand up pretty well under the strain of this?

A—Yes, I think so. I'm used to this. I've stood up under many things in the past eight years.

Q—How have you been able to get along financially in these eight years? Has it been a strain on you?

A—At the beginning, yes. But I can't say that I've ever been destitute.

Q—You have not worked regularly, have you?

A—No. I did some substitute teaching. (Mrs. Bader now is studying at Akron University for a teaching certificate.)

Q—How have the children reacted to this situation?

A—I think the children have been pretty wonderful, considering everything.

Q—Some of them would not have actually known him, would they?

A—That's true. But of course we've talked about him through the years and that's almost the same as knowing a person.

Q—What seems to be the children's feeling about it now?

A—I don't know. I sort of dread to think of what will come out of this as far as they're concerned. I don't know what problems I'll have in the future; that's something I'm going to work out when they come up.

Q—As you see Larry Bader now from a distance, as you hear

or see him through what's in the press and these other descriptions, does he seem like the same person to you? Or does he seem different, and in what way?

A—Well . . . it's hard to answer that. I'm sure his looks have changed because he never wore a mustache and I haven't seen him with long hair for a long time. He was a clean-cut good looking young man when I knew him.

Q—From these descriptions you've had about his life in Omaha, which seems to be the opposite of conservative, does it seem strange to you?

A—It seems fantastic to me.

Q—He was not the kind of person to do anything like this when you knew him?

A—I certainly can't say that he could have been that kind of person.

Q—Were there any other differences apparent to you?

A—From what my brothers-in-law said, who talked to him for a couple of hours, they claim he has the very same mannerisms, the very same gestures, the very same build.

Q—As things stand now, what is your paramount interest in this situation? Is it your children?

A—Yes, of course.

Q—In other words, whatever comes of this, your primary concern is how they come out of it?

A—Yes, that's right. That's my primary concern.

Q—It was suggested earlier that you were not interested in prosecuting Larry Bader. However, from what you say about the children, if prosecution becomes necessary as a matter of serving their interests properly, would you proceed with it?

A—Yes, I probably would have to.

Q—Are you somewhat hurt by the fact that you haven't heard anything (from him)?

A—Yes, somewhat.

While Mrs. Bader endured the probing of her interviewer, the *Beacon Journal*'s women's editor, Betty Jaycox, was quietly analyzing

. . . this stylish young woman whose husband, Lawrence Bader, took on a new life, a new religion, a new name, a new

wife and another family in Omaha, Neb., either through a
mental quirk or through deliberate intent. "How could any
man in his right mind desert such a woman," I said to myself
as I looked at her, "let alone abandon his children?" . . . She
sat straight with pretty legs crossed in their sheer stockings and
neat black pumps. She sat quiet and serene, with the only clue
to possible nervousness hidden by the strained expression on
her pretty face.

Her figure, as slim and shapely as a high school girl, was
outlined softly with a black and white herringbone dress
trimmed in black leather buttons and a black fringed ascot.
You would have thought she had faced cameras and interview
questions most of her life from the poise with which she held
her chin high and her head higher.

The physiognomical difficulties of such a position did not
prevent Mrs. Bader from expressing her adverse views on the
single maneuver that might have provided a legal resolution
to at least part of the troubles ahead.

Q—Mr. Bader's lawyer in Omaha has suggested that their
plan of action might be to seek an annulment of his marriage
in Omaha, and a divorce of your marriage and then a remarriage in Omaha. Are there any circumstances under which you
would divorce your husband or would consent to him divorcing you?

A—That question is too much for me. I think that the
people who know me would know the answer to that.

Q—Can you give us a hint for those people who don't know
you?

A— (Laughing) Well, I'm a woman, too, you know.

Q—Have you had any social life since your husband has
been gone? Have you been able to make a personal life for
yourself?

A—Yes.

Q—Were you ever able to get over this thing enough to start
dating?

A—Yes.

Q—Were there any occasions during this eight years when
you might have remarried?

A—Oh, yes.

Q—Is there any particular reason why you didn't?

A—I don't wish to answer that.

Q—One of the reasons I asked the questions was that I wondered whether at any time the question of remarriage was in front of you and yet you had any kind of a feeling at all that your husband might still be alive.

A—No, I don't think so. No.

Q—You were free to remarry?

A—Yes.

Q—In the future, if both the legal and the religious obstacles were not present, do you think it is possible you might remarry?

A—Well, I can't answer that. (Mrs. Bader's lawyers explained that remarriage would have been possible prior to Bader's reappearance, but that they do not believe she can be remarried now, even with a civil divorce, as a Roman Catholic.)

Q—Is it possible for you to form any future plans for yourself and your family? Do you have any distinct plans?

A—No, I don't. I couldn't begin to think of what I would do first. The only thing I know of is to try to live as normally as possible for now and try to fit these pieces together and form a future for my children. My lawyers have advised me to live from day to day.

The interview was drawing to a close, and the staff photographer had finished snapping the "candid" pictures of Mary Lou that would appear scattered about the text of the article. There were a few more questions about when and where Mrs. Bader might be united with her husband. Then the reporter asked what more and more people had begun to wonder:

Q—Are you sorry he showed up?

A—Well, at the beginning I'm sure I was so numbed that I wasn't sure how I felt, and now I don't know how I feel—it's too involved.

Q—Could you describe what your feelings right now are about him?

A—About Larry? I can't say that right now.

Q—Do you even know how you feel?

A—Well, I'm not sure whether I know, I guess.

Q—Do you feel that he should be punished in any way for this?

A—I can't say that, because I don't know whether the things he's done are true or not—I only know what I read in the paper.

Q—Do you mean that you don't know whether he knew what he was doing?

A—I just don't know. I don't understand the whole thing.

As the group prepared to leave the office, Women's Editor Jaycox noticed that Mrs. Bader's left ring finger was bare. Naturally, she inquired about it:

"When," I asked her, "did you take off your wedding ring, Mary Lou?" The question seemed to startle her, and she looked at the finger in surprise. "I don't know," she said, seeming somewhat fussed as she flicked her lighter. "I don't exactly remember. I still wear my engagement ring but on my right hand."

At no point in the interview, possibly at the prior insistence of Mrs. Bader's lawyers, was she asked anything about the disposition of the approximately $40,000 she had received—and, according to sources close to the family, had spent on the balance of the mortgage on her home, among other things—in death benefits from the insurance companies. Bader-Johnson's position concerning this money was curt and to the point: "I didn't receive any of it," he was quoted as saying in Omaha.

From a legal standpoint, the crux of his statement was that it was made in Omaha, which is where he intended to stay. His lawyer, Harry Farnham, made this quite clear when he emphasized that his client would meet with anyone who wanted to come to Omaha but that Bader-Johnson had no plans to travel to Akron. This meant that if anyone wanted to prosecute him in Ohio for abandonment and nonsupport, he would have to be extradited by Nebraska. And the possibilities of extraditing someone who does not remember who he is and then convicting him of something he disclaims any memory of did not begin to balance the regular support payments that Bader-Johnson had volunteered to make.

Even without the blurring complication of memory loss, there is a decided tendency not to prosecute in situations where the absentee has been missing for many years and his or her "survivors" have adjusted to new circumstances. This is almost always the case when the wife, having collected the insurance benefits, has herself remarried. If she refunds this money to the company, as Norman Briggs's ex-wife did in Chapter X, the matter is usually considered of no further interest to the police or to the wife herself. Atypically, she greeted her missing spouse's reappearance as a Wyoming cowboy named Clay Hollister with the announcement that she had "no desire for a reconciliation."

Briggs, to recapitulate, had vanished in 1960, after telling his wife that he was going scuba diving in the Tomhannock Reservoir outside Troy, N.Y. A thorough police search of the reservoir indicated that he might have staged his death. But when some of his equipment floated to the surface two years later, his wife convinced the insurance company that he was indeed dead. She collected about $117,000 in benefits.

Mrs. Briggs had been Mrs. Earl Koenig for eight months when the news that Briggs-Hollister was living in Wyoming was made public in March 1965. The reporters who went out to the Kenneth Adkins ranch to talk with the cowboy succeeded only in learning that the former salesman had little trouble making the transition from the order pad to the saddle. Owner Adkins made it plain to the press that his employee's life was strictly his employee's own business (which is not, in practice, a statement that many employers in this country could honestly make) .

About the only person who was not willing to forget the Briggs case was Rensselaer County (N.Y.) District Attorney M. Andrew Dwyer, Jr. While the New York State Police, who had originally conducted the search of the reservoir, were in the process of closing their four-and-a-half-year investigation, Dwyer was just starting his. He began by announcing that he had subpoenaed thirteen persons, including Briggs' father, brother, and former wife, for a hearing at which he would preside in the county courthouse. The district attorney stated that Briggs and his wife had discussed divorce on more than one occasion; he hinted darkly that the benefits paid by the insurance company appeared to him "suspicious"; and he insisted that he would probe into the ownership of an apartment house that Briggs-Hollister had built prior to his disappearance. After the hearing, Dwyer planned to fly to Wyoming to question the missing man.

What followed over the next sixteen months was an inconclusive legal gun battle that did not enhance the reputations of any of the participants. District Attorney Dwyer did manage to have his man indicted in May 1965, on counts of abandonment and insurance fraud by a grand jury, the foreman of which, Briggs fired back through his lawyer, was his former wife's grandmother's first cousin. But when Dwyer tried to drag the suspect back to Troy for arraignment, the cowboy temporarily slipped the noose when the Wyoming Supreme Court intervened just as Briggs-Hollister was being taken from the Newcastle jail. Then, after the district attorney had finally arraigned his quarry, a Troy judge let him return to the ranch on $5,000 bail.

The same county judge, John T. Casey, threw out both indictments on July 22, 1966. His decision, he announced after a careful study of the preliminary testimony, was based on the fact that "the grand jury can receive none but legal evidence." He characterized some of this testimony as "patent hearsay" and most of the rest as irrelevant and prejudicial to the defendant. But the foundation of his dismissal rested on his belief that the charges themselves were self-contradictory. Specifically, the judge informed the district attorney that it was improper to accuse someone of leaving his family destitute and, at the same time, of defrauding the insurance company in order to provide for his family:

> The charges contained in the indictments, at least under the facts as revealed by the grand jury minutes, cannot coexist for they are mutually repugnant, each to the other. It is undisputed the defendant himself never realized any financial gain from his pretense. If the motivation of his deception was the hope of pecuniary gain for his wife and children (and this is well within the realm of foreseeability and a material and determinative element necessary for the validity of the insurance indictment), then it is difficult, if not impossible, to conclude that he willfully abandoned his children in destitute circumstances, proof of which is vital to the abandonment indictment.
>
> For, if the effect of his disappearance was to deprive his children of the fruits of his paternal labors, then equally, the result of such disappearance also was to provide them with the gain effected by his deception. The record is devoid of any objective proof that the children were left in destitute circumstances. Without a showing of actual, objective destitution (defined as being, or likely to be, a public charge), there can be no basis for legal abandonment. While morality would certainly dictate no such requirement, the law mandates it.

Having dismissed the abandonment indictment *because* of the insurance-fraud charge, Judge Casey then proceeded to throw out the other indictment "for the insufficiency of proof," although he did grant leave to the district attorney to resubmit "to a different grand jury either, or both, cases on competent and legal evidence." Dwyer did not accept the judge's polite challenge. The Troy *Record* had begun estimating that the prosecution had already cost the County of Rensselaer about $20,000. Moreover, seven weeks before the indictments had been dismissed, Briggs-Hollister had gone before a justice of the peace in Cheyenne and married up with the former Joy Chittim. The State of New York decided to rest on its saddle sores.

Whatever the logic of dismissing Indictment A because of Indictment B and then throwing out B for insufficient evidence, the judge's decision merits further consideration as an example of the peculiar difficulties of establishing motive and intent in situations where absentees have simulated their "deaths." There was no question but that Briggs had done just that; and when he was located more than four years later, he did not claim or pretend that he could not remember his life as Norman Briggs. Judge Casey took note of this in his written decision when he pointed out: "The main thrust of the evidence underlying both indictments demonstrates that on July 17, 1960, the defendant staged, produced and directed a monodrama complete in every respect, save fiction, and purposely designed to convince his family, the authorities and the public that he had met death accidentally while scuba-diving in the reservoir and, as a result, his wife was caused, without apparent knowledge of his deception, to file claims on his life insurance policies, as beneficiary, and thus to collect the substantial proceeds thereof."

But was this evidence "legal"? Briggs-Hollister would not appear before a grand jury and confess that he had staged his death in the reservoir—rather than just telling his wife good-bye and heading west—so that a fraudulent claim for life insurance could be made, so as to provide money for the support of his abandoned family. Even if this were the reason he did what he did, he has a constitutional right not to incriminate himself.

Such proof, obviously, must come from the testimony of others. In this instance, "others" meant specifically the insurance agent who, two days before Briggs disappeared, had received a telephone call from an unidentified man inquiring about the procedures for collecting death benefits in situations where the insured had drowned accidentally but the body had not been recovered. At the time of the disappearance, this telephone incident was enough to convince the police investigators that Briggs was not in the reservoir. But could it be used five years later against him in court?

Judge Casey ruled in the negative. "One witness," he pointed out, "was permitted to testify to the contents of a telephone call made by an anonymous caller, who, shortly before the defendant's departure, inquired about the insurance requirements in case of a disappearance. No effort was made to connect the defendant to this conversation and its contents constituted illegal evidence before the grand jury." For the purposes of investigation, the nameless caller may logically have been presumed to have been Briggs, but in a court of law he must remain simply anonymous. Unless proved otherwise, this type of testimony is inadmissible hearsay.

Actually, the judge spelled out his reasonable test of admissibility when he described Briggs' act as a "monodrama," staged and produced and directed by the missing man. It would have been redundant for him to have added that the cast of any monodrama also consists of one person. It is rare in the theater and rarer still in real life for the actor to break the aesthetic distance that separates us, his audience, by stepping over the footlights and explaining his performance. But unless and until he does, the action must perforce be inferred and interpreted from the hints contained in the script. This inference might satisfy a critic but not a judge.

The third act of the Bader-Johnson story, in this sense, opened to a bare stage. It was no longer, had not been for some time, a monodrama. The problem was that the central character had forgotten most of his lines and a good part of the cast. There would be no reunion, only reintroductions.

The first to make the memory pilgrimage was his mother, Mrs. Stephen Bader. She flew from Akron to Omaha on March 24, 1965, a month and a half after her son's existence had become known. She was met at the airport by attorney Farnham, who drove the sixty-nine-year-old woman to meet the son she had not seen in eight years. They had a pleasant visit that evening, despite the discovery by the press that she was in town. Back in Akron her second son, Richard, dismissed the inquiries of persistent reporters with one sentence: "She said she just wanted to see him."

Although the couple had been corresponding ever since his February exposure, the initial meeting between Bader-Johnson and his first wife did not take place until the last weekend in July, a month after an Omaha court had granted an annulment to Mrs. Nancy Johnson. He would not come to Akron, and Omaha obviously would have been inappropriate to the purpose. To discuss his future they decided to meet in Chicago, where his past had caught up with his present.

"I was surprised to see him," Mary Lou confided to the *Beacon Journal.* "He looked the same to me as when he disappeared, except for his mustache and eye patch."

Among the items discussed by the couple was a second meeting in the near future with their four children. It was agreed that it would also be held in Chicago and that it would not be discussed publicly in advance. Mrs. Bader, at least, hoped that this family gathering might be the first step toward a permanent resolution of the mystery that continued to envelop the man called Bader by some and Johnson by others.

On Saturday, August 28, she packed her four children—Elizabeth, twelve, Lawrence Jr., ten, Stephen, nine, and Timothy, seven—and some luggage in her station wagon and headed for Chicago. He was not due to arrive until the following day, so she and the children had a chance to get settled at the motel they had selected for the meeting. "We picked him up at Union Station in Chicago on Sunday and spent Sunday and Monday together," she said afterwards.

It was a particularly exciting experience for the children. Mrs. Bader remembered how her missing husband had moved quickly, almost instinctively, into the role of the father from the outset. "He was trying to organize things, so I just stood back and watched, and it was a circus." The two days were spent swimming or lounging around the motel pool, sightseeing, and talking. Mainly talking. "The children told him of experiences with him that they recall. They warmed up to him right away. Larry looked at his father like he worshipped him. On the way back to Akron, I asked the children if they liked him and they said: 'Oh, yes! He's nice.' "

Mary Lou admitted to the press that she had also enjoyed the two-day reunion. "He was just wonderful with all of us. He treated the children like he had known them all their lives." The trouble was that he still insisted he had not. "He's convinced himself," said Mrs. Bader, "that he doesn't recognize anybody. I think he is sincere in thinking he doesn't remember, but I don't see how he can go along with two lives forever."

Of this second life there was very little mention at the Chicago meeting. Bader-Johnson told her that he had left his sportscasting job at television station KETV and was again working at Ross's Steakhouse, where he had started in 1957 as a bartender. She told him that she had completed her course work at the University of Akron for a teaching certificate and was about to begin her practice teaching. When they parted, it was still indefinite when or whether he would visit Akron.

Bader-Johnson refused to discuss the Chicago weekend with the press in Omaha, except to confirm that it had taken place and to describe the Bader children as "wonderful." Farnham, his lawyer, added that his client was working very hard to fulfill his commitments to two wives and two families. "He has three jobs and works seven days a week. He works days as a bartender and nights as a janitor at Ross's Steakhouse and part time as a ring announcer at wrestling matches." The little bit of money left over after the weekly support payments went toward the rent for his room at the local YMCA. "But he doesn't complain," said Farnham.

On October 15, 1965, the Fidelity & Deposit Company of Maryland was finally convinced that Fritz Johnson of Omaha was, in fact if not in memory, one and the same as Lawrence Bader of Akron, and did therefore cause to be delivered to the New York Life Insurance Company its corporate check for $25,000. The transaction, which was unpublicized, was in fulfillment of the surety bond executed in May 1958 by Mary Lou Bader.

The press knew all about this surety bond. It was a matter of public knowledge that she had to pay a $750 premium to Fidelity & Deposit, an amount equal to three percent of the face value of the bond held by New York Life against the reappearance of her husband. It was also widely known that she had used most of the money paid her by New York Life to pay off the $17,000 mortgage held by the First National Bank of Akron.

What was not known was that the Maryland company had, in addition to its premium, required Mrs. Bader to hand over to it the mortgage deed on her home for a period of five years. If her husband did not reappear during that time, meaning between May 14, 1958, and May 14, 1963, then Fidelity agreed that the mortgage would be satisfied of record. Quite true, admitted Fidelity, after repaying New York Life. But when the five-year period had expired, Mrs. Bader had neither asked for return of the deed nor requested any cancellation of the mortgage. Thus the deed was still in the possession of Fidelity. In addition, Fidelity announced to a startled Mrs. Bader that it had acquired the mortgage note from the bank that she thought she had paid off. Henceforth, warned Fidelity, she would have to pay that company the monthly sums ($110.78) called for in the original mortgage note or risk foreclosure proceedings against her home.

The Akron judge who had declared Larry Bader dead in 1960 was himself dead. Nathan Koplin, the new judge on the Probate Court bench of Summit County, Ohio, was determined to expunge the court record of this life-and-death, or death-and-life, inaccuracy. Accordingly, he ordered Mrs. Bader to submit a petition requesting that the earlier declaration of presumed death be vacated. As evidence, she presented duplicate fingerprint cards of Bader and Johnson, supplied by the FBI, and the receipt for a registered letter, signed "L. Bader," that she had mailed to her husband in Omaha. After a fifteen-minute hearing before Koplin, the judge pronounced Bader alive again. The date was February 18, 1966.

It proved a futile gesture.

XIV

The Mass of Men

At 10:55 A.M. on September 16, 1966—seven months after he
had been legally restored to the ranks of the living by an
Akron judge—the man called Fritz died in Saint Joseph's
Hospital, Omaha. The news of his passing brought sorrow to
many; others received it with a sense of relief; a few were
actually glad. But no one was surprised, including Bader-
Johnson, who had named six honorary pallbearers for his
funeral.

His terminal cancer had been disclosed in May. During the
final three weeks, Bader's wife and two brothers visited him
in the hospital. The night before he succumbed, Johnson's
former wife maintained a bedside vigil. To the end Bader-
Johnson insisted that he had no recollection of Akron, Ohio.

The man was gone. The basic question remained—unanswered.

Were this man merely a literary invention, we might be
justified in arbitrarily assigning motivations and intent to his
actions, in forcing extra words and sentences into his reluctant mouth, in pressing unproved meaning from his example.
But the license of fiction is unavailable and inappropriate in
this instance. Bader-Johnson was an actual person. He lived
in specific places at specified times; he passed this way and

that; he did such-and-such; his needs were immediate and personal. He existed.

On the other hand, it could be argued with considerable accuracy that the fictional actually overwhelmed the factual in Bader-Johnson. At a minimum, one quarter of this man's life was a figment of imagination—his own—from which sprung full blown the conception and character of John "Fritz" Johnson. This delightful, carefree product of a Massachusetts orphanage and the U.S. Navy was an imaginative feat of the first order, and Bader-Johnson proved it by openly enjoying the impersonation all the way to the grave. The literary flavor was provided by the fact that Fritz was an adult characterization without known antecedent.

Literature can seldom make that boast. Authors draw heavily from experience and personal fantasy, which is why John Stockton, the groping protagonist of Sherwood Anderson's 1925 best seller, *Dark Laughter,* has a special pertinence to our purpose. Stockton had been a newspaper reporter in Chicago, married unsatisfactorily to a nascent *littérateur* who typed away at short stories on the kitchen table after dinner each night.

At the beginning of the novel, Stockton was wandering about a small town in Illinois, on his way from New Orleans to his boyhood home in Old Harbor, Ind. He had abruptly abandoned his distracted wife after "a sort of wordless quarrel," and had spent several months drifting down the Mississippi, trying to reinvoke the primordial Mark Twain and listening incredulously to the mocking, unrepressed laughter of the "niggers," as yet unspoiled by industrial sterility.

Along the way, impulsively, Stockton changed his name:

He had just walked along the main street of the town and had seen two signs over two stores, "Bruce, Smart and Feeble—Hardware" and "Dudley Brothers—Grocery."

It was like being a criminal. Perhaps he was a kind of criminal, had suddenly become one. It might well be that a criminal was but a man like himself who had suddenly stepped a little out of the beaten path most all men travel. Criminals took other people's lives or took goods that did not belong to them and he had taken—what? Himself? It might very well be put that way.

"Slave, do you think your own life belongs to you? Hocus, Pocus, now you see it and now you don't. Why not Bruce Dudley?"

. . . The name Bruce Dudley had a kind of something in it. It suggested solidity and respectability and Bruce had got an hour's amusement, while waiting for the train up to Old Harbor by walking about the streets of an Illinois town and trying to think of other possible Bruce Dudleys of the world. "Captain Bruce Dudley of the American Army, Bruce Dudley, Minister of the First Presbyterian Church of Hartford, Connecticut." But why Hartford? He, John Stockton, had never been to Hartford, Connecticut. Why had the place come into his mind? It stood for something, didn't it? Very likely it was because Mark Twain lived there for a long time. . . .

The man who had been John Stockton and who suddenly, by a whim, became Bruce Dudley, had been thinking a lot about Mark Twain during the six months before he took the new name. Being near the river and on the river had made him think. It wasn't strange after all that he chanced to think of Hartford, Connecticut, too. "He did get all crusted up, that boy," he whispered to himself that day when he went about the streets of the Illinois town bearing for the first time the name Bruce Dudley.

Anderson was not musing about the phonetic impact of his character's name. He was establishing the central theme of *Dark Laughter,* in which the simplicity and promise of youth is dissipated by the effete sophistication of urban existence:

. . . When he left Chicago and his wife he had cut out to a place called La Salle in Illinois and had started down the Illinois River in an open boat. Later he lost the boat and spent nearly two months, . . . in getting down river to New Orleans. It was a little trick he had always wanted to do. Since he was a kid and had read Huckleberry Finn, he had kept some notion in mind. Nearly every man who lived long in the Mississippi Valley had that notion tucked away in him somewhere.

The great river, lonely and empty now, was, in some queer way, like a lost river. It had come to represent the lost youth of Middle America perhaps. Song, laughter, profanity, the smell of goods, dancing niggers—life everywhere! Great gaudy boats on a river, lumber rafts floating down, voices across the silent nights, song, an empire unloading its wealth on the face of the waters of a river! When the Civil War came on, the Middle West got up and fought like the Old Harry because it didn't want its river taken away. In its youth the Middle West had breathed with the breathing of a river.

"The factory men were pretty smart, weren't they? First thing they did when they got the chance was to choke off the river, take the romance out of commerce. They may not have intended anything of the sort, romance and commerce were just natural enemies. They made the river as dead as a door-nail with their railroads and it has been that way ever since."

Big river, silent now. Creeping slowly down past mud banks, miserable little towns, the river as powerful as ever, strange as ever, but silent now, forgotten, neglected. A few tugs with strings of barges. No more gaudy boats, profanity, song, gamblers, excitement, life.

When he was working his way down river, Bruce Dudley had thought that Mark Twain, when he went back to visit the river after the railroads had choked to death the river life, that Mark might have written an epic then. He might have written of song killed, of laughter killed, of men herded into a new age of speed, of factories, of swift, fast-running trains. Instead of which he filled the book mostly with statistics, wrote stale jokes. Oh, well! You can't always be offending someone, can you, brother scribblers?

In a desperate and not quite convincing attempt to reverse this emasculating process, Stockton deserted the "elevated" world of metropolitan journalism and, as Stockton-Dudley, became a laborer in the varnishing room of the Grey Wheel Company in his native town.

In truth, many other writers have explored this alien territory with more finesse and greater artistic success. Yet in this instance, Anderson's insights have a unique propriety that adds a distinct element of authenticity to his voice. This special authority to examine the private nature of middle-age despair was his own experience. Before he became a novelist, before he was thrust into the vanguard of literary realism in America, he too was apprenticed to the bitch goddess, who rewarded (and punished) him with a narrow reputation as a resourceful businessman.

It was in this capacity that he started dictating a letter to one of his customers the afternoon of November 27, 1912. He broke off in midsentence and, after a moment's hesitation, walked out the door of his factory office.

And disappeared.

Anderson was thirty-six years old, married, the father of three. His life to that point had been a self-conscious struggle to overcome an impoverished boyhood in bucolic Clyde, Ohio, through accomplishment in the world of business. A rather promising, though personally disturbing beginning had been achieved during the early days of advertising in Chicago, after which Anderson had plunged into the "presidency" of a mail-order concern in Cleveland. But despite his demonstrated skill at preparing direct-mail sales literature, this venture had collapsed in 1907 when the incubators Anderson had been promoting failed to incubate.

For the next five years, Anderson struggled halfheartedly to peddle by mail an inferior brand of paint called Roof Fix. He organized his own firm, induced other businessmen and bankers to finance it, and established his own factory in Elyria. That he was initially successful is apparent. During his second year of operation, he was able to purchase the company that manufactured his paint.

But Anderson was already beginning to march, in Thoreau's metaphor, to a different drummer, and his hours at the factory soon became annoying interludes between absorbing hours at his desk in the attic of his home. He wanted to be a writer. Considering his limited education, his age, and his family and financial responsibilities, it seemed a quite impossible dream. When the dream became an obsession, everything (and everyone) suffered. The first tangible signs of this enervating conflict between aspiration and obligation showed up in his business. His autobiographical description of his leave-taking, published a dozen years after the fact, constitutes a strangely eloquent testimony of a man contemplating the ragged edges of his former promise:

There was a door leading out from my office to the street. How many steps to the door? I counted them, "five, six, seven." "Suppose," I asked myself, "I could take those five, six, seven steps to the door, pass out at the door, go along that railroad track out there, disappear into the far horizon beyond. Where was I to go? In the town where my factory was located I had still the reputation of being a bright young business man. In my first years there I had been filled with shrewd vast schemes. I had been admired, looked up to. Since that time I had gone down and down as a bright young man but no one knew how far I had gone. I was still respected in the town, my word was still good at the bank. I was a respectable man.

Did I want to do something not respectable, not decent? I am trying to give you the history of a moment and as a tale-teller I have come to think the true history of life is but a history of moments. It is only at rare moments we live. I wanted to walk out at a door and go away into the distance. The American is still a wanderer, a migrating bird not yet ready to build a nest. All our cities are built temporarily as are the houses in which we live. We are on the way—toward what? There have been other times in the history of the world when many strange peoples came together in a new strange land. To assume that we have made an America, even materially, seems to me now but telling ourselves fairy tales in the night. We have not even made it materially yet and the American man has only gone in for money-making on a large scale to quiet his own restlessness, as the monk of old days was given the Regula of Augustine to quiet him and still the lusts in himself. For the monk, kept occupied with the saying of prayers and the doing of many little sacred offices, there was no time for lusts of the world to enter in and for the American to be perpetually busy with his affairs, with his automobiles, with his movies, there is no time for unquiet thoughts.

On that day in the office at my factory I looked at myself and laughed. The whole struggle I am trying to describe and that I am confident will be closer to the understanding of most Americans than anything else I have ever written was accompanied by a kind of mocking laughter at myself and my own seriousness about it all.

Very well, then, I wanted to go out of the door and never come back. How many Americans want to go—but where do they want to go? I wanted to accept for myself all the little restless thoughts of which myself and the others had been so afraid and you, who are Americans, will understand the necessity of my continually laughing at myself and at all things dear to me. I must laugh at the thing I love the more intensely because of my love. Any American will understand that.

It was a trying moment for me. There was the woman, my secretary, now looking at me. What did she represent? What did she not represent? Would I dare be honest with her? It was quite apparent to me I would not. I had got to my feet and we stood looking at each other. "It is now or never," I said to myself, and I remember that I kept smiling. I had stopped dictating to her in the midst of a sentence. "The goods about which you have inquired are the best of their kind made in the—"

I stood and she sat and we were looking at each other intently. "What's the matter?" she asked. She was an intelligent woman, more intelligent I am sure than myself, just because she was a woman and good, while I have never been good, do not know how to be good. Could I explain all to her? The words of a fancied explanation marched through my mind: "My dear young woman, it is all very silly but I have decided to no longer concern myself with this buying and selling. It may be all right for others but for me it is poison. There is this factory. You may have it if it please you. It is of little value I dare say. Perhaps it is money ahead and then again it may well be it is money behind. I am uncertain about it all and now I am going away. Now, at this moment, with the letter I have been dictating, with the very sentence you have been writing left unfinished, I am going out that door and never come back. What am I going to do? Well now, that I don't know. I am going to wander about. I am going to sit with people, listen to words, tell tales of people, what they are thinking, what they are feeling. The devil! It may even be I am going forth in search of myself."

The woman was looking into my eyes the while I looked into hers. Perhaps I had grown a little pale and now she grew pale. "You're sick," she said and her words gave me an idea. There was wanted a justification of myself, not to myself but to the others. A crafty thought came. Was the thought crafty or was I, at the moment, a little insane, a "nut," as every American so loves to say of every man who does something a little out of the groove.

I had grown pale and it may be I was ill but nevertheless I was laughing—the American laugh. Had I suddenly become a little insane? What a comfort that thought would be, not to myself but to the others. My leaving the place I was then in would tear up the roots that had gone down a little into the ground. The ground I did not think would support the tree that was myself and that I thought wanted to grow.

My mind dwelt on the matter of roots and I looked at my feet. The whole question with which I was at the moment concerned became a matter of feet. I had two feet that could take me out of the life I was then in and that, to do so, would need but take three or four steps to a door. When I had reached the door and had stepped out of my little factory office everything would be quite simplified, I was sure. I had to lift myself out. Others would have to tackle the job of getting me back, once I had stepped over that threshold.

Whether at the moment I merely became shrewd and crafty or whether I really became temporarily insane I shall never quite know. What I did was to step very close to the woman and looking directly into her eyes I laughed gayly. Others besides herself would, I knew, hear the words I was now speaking. I looked at my feet. "I have been wading in a long river and my feet are wet," I said.

Again I laughed as I walked lightly toward the door and out of a long and tangled phase of my life, out of the door of buying and selling, out of the door of affairs.

"They want me to be a 'nut,' will love to think of me as a 'nut,' and why not? It may just be that's what I am," I thought gayly and at the same time turned and said a final confusing sentence to the woman who now stared at me in speechless amazement. "My feet are cold wet and heavy from long wading in a river. Now I shall go walk on dry land," I said, and as I passed out at the door a delicious thought came. "Oh, you little tricky words, you are my brothers. It is you, not myself, have lifted me over this threshold. It is you who have dared give me a hand. For the rest of my life I will be a servant to you," I whispered to myself as I went along a spur of railroad track, over a bridge, out of a town and out of that phase of my life.

He did not stay missing long. On December 2, 1912, the Cleveland *Leader* reported:

Wandering gypsy-like about the countryside after disappearing from his home in Elyria four days ago, walking almost incessantly save for a few hours of sleep snatched in thickets and all the while unconscious of his identity, Sherwood Anderson . . . was discovered late yesterday afternoon in a drug store at E. 152 St. . . .

Anderson was found by a physician to be suffering from the effects of some severe mental strain and was taken by friends to Huron Road hospital.

What had happened during those crucial four days? How had Anderson, who claimed to have had only five or six dollars when he left, traversed the forty miles of frozen terrain between Elyria and Cleveland through a bleak Ohio winter? And what was his real purpose in fleeing?

His biographers categorically reject Anderson's post facto assertion that he somehow "feigned" a mental breakdown to ease his guilt and his transition from the world of business to the universe of art, "that if men thought me a little insane they would forgive me if I lit out." They spurn this version for a variety of reasons, not the least of which was Anderson's inability or refusal to tell his own story the same way twice. In his *Memoirs* (published posthumously), he not only changed his parting quote to "My feet are cold and wet. I have been walking too long on the bed of a river," but he completely reworked the circumstances of fact:

> When I had left my factory, walking down the railroad track that day in 1910 [*sic*], I had kept on walking until I got to the city of Cleveland. It was summer [*sic*] and I slept for two nights out of doors. One night in a lumber yard and another night in an open field. In Cleveland I had borrowed a little money from a friend, Mr. Edwin Baxter, now I believe an official in one of Cleveland's larger banks, and had returned to Chicago.

Despite Anderson's prefatory admonition that "When I deal in facts, at once I begin to lie. I can't help it. I am by nature a story teller. . . . Besides, men do not exist in facts. They exist in dreams," such blatant distortion has obviously provoked the scholarly ire of his biographers, whose mission, after all, is partly to impose form where previously there had only been meaning.

But the rejection of this explanation of the watershed incident in the Anderson mythology does not justify the substitution of an oversimplification to the effect that Anderson's four-day hiatus was merely, as one biographer summed it, a nervous collapse "quickened by business worries, immediately provoked by an inability to choose a consistent course of life, and based on a fundamental psychic maladjustment in his private life." Such compression has the advantage of sounding perceptive and inclusive. Its chief disadvantage is that it tends to contradict the same biographer's previous observation that Anderson's brief disappearance is only "a legend that has sunk deeply into the American imagination, [because] it is profoundly relevant to the emotional climate of American life, to the half-suppressed yearnings with which so many Americans wear out their lives."

Anderson continuously addressed himself to those "half-suppressed yearnings" in his writing and in his life. It would be quite consistent to view his abrupt departure from the factory as the enactment of a special yearning that could no longer be suppressed. There was certainly ample precedent in his behavior. Before and after his break in November 1912, he was constantly "losing" himself on brief, unpremeditated excursions to strange towns and other cities, for a day, a night, a night and two days. He could and did retreat into his own thoughts anywhere, at any time. Compulsively, he gathered the experiences of others, sounded out their unfamiliar tales in strange taverns and along isolated rural roads.

Much later, as he tried to reconstruct the reality of his agonizing decision to devote himself to literature, he understandably rationalized:

> . . . "I might be able to do it," I found myself saying to myself. . . . afterwards when I did become a writer and began telling tales it was said of me by critics that all my tales were of one sort . . . they were stories of escape . . .
> . . . it must have seemed to me then, as for that matter it does yet, that the real tale of American lives is as yet just that.
> . . . eternal fleeing from something.
> . . . "I will. I won't. I will. I won't." . . .
> . . . "it is the fault of this woman. I will flee from her" . . .
> . . . "I can do nothing in this town" . . .
> . . . "city life may save me" . . .
> . . . "no. It is not that. I will flee from the city to the town, from the town to the country . . ."

"The mass of men lead lives of quiet desperation," Thoreau had pronounced, almost a century before. "What is called resignation is confirmed desperation. From the desperate city you go into the desperate country, and have to console yourself with the bravery of minks and muskrats. A stereotyped but unconscious despair is concealed even under what are called the games and amusements of mankind. There is no play in them, for this comes after work. But it is a characteristic of wisdom not to do desperate things."

Anderson was not a Transcendentalist philosopher; he did desperate things, and his eternal fleeing from something never really ceased. From the day he took those fateful steps toward the door of his factory, he remained in uneasy flight. That he intended to renounce commerce for literature had been apparent prior to his disappearance. He confirmed this in a newspaper interview a few days after he was located. "Sherwood Anderson Will Write Book on His Experience as 'Nomad,'" the Elyria *Evening Telegram* informed its readers, adding that, during the four days he was missing, "He knew his identity but could not disclose it; he wanted to return home but could tell no person of his desires."*

Curiously, Anderson avoided any written explanation of his ninety-six-hour absence, although he scribbled a great deal about his life and experiences before and after this episode. The omission neither means nor proves that he did not remember what had happened. Even if he had forgotten, his imaginative artistry has obviously filled many another memory chasm. And the incident would appear tailor-made to a compulsive storyteller like Anderson, the voluntary nomad, wandering unhailed and unrecognized the streets of Cleveland.

But whatever it was that he glimpsed, that he sensed, that he did those four days, he would not discuss. It was his secret. It accompanied him to the grave.

One of the potentially revealing answers that died with Anderson was whether or not he actually intended to return once he had disappeared. He probably considered the question unnecessary. During the decade after his disappearance, he completely changed his life, his location, his vocation; his marriage was dissolved. His new identity emerged gradually through the force of his own personal will. Through the vehicle of his writing, Anderson made it seem both natural and logical:

---

* When the world-famous author of that American classic, *Winesburg, Ohio,* died in 1941, the Elyria *Chronicle-Telegram* headlined his obituary "SHERWOOD ANDERSON, FORMER ELYRIA MANUFACTURER, DIES." Elyria, it would seem, is a city that does not easily condone the sins of its sons.

Anderson knew who he was and, more important, who he wasn't.

This distinction does not apply to the mass of men. It was particularly inapplicable to Bader-Johnson, whose death presented a curious problem. When one man with two names and two documented existences dies for the second time, where and how should he be buried?

On Sunday afternoon, September 18, 1966, a memorial service was conducted for Johnson in Omaha's First Methodist Church. Beside the coffin stood the six men selected by Fritz. One was a local sports editor, another was a wrestling promoter; the television and radio stations that had employed him were represented, as was the steakhouse where he tended bar; the last man was an archer.

In a brief eulogy, the Reverend Robert Naylor referred only to John F. Johnson, not to Bader. "We will remember Fritz for his sparkling personality, his beautiful voice, his deep capacity for friendship, his vitality, his integrity and his unswerving devotion to truth. We who know him well," he emphasized, "know that when he spoke he spoke the truth."

The next day, attended by Mrs. Bader and her four children, the body of Lawrence Bader was taken to the Holy Cross Cemetery in Akron for interment in the Bader family plot.

Under the circumstances, the newspapers understandably reacted parochially. The Omaha *World-Herald,* which divides life into Morning and Evening editions, headlined the death of Fritz Johnson. The Akron *Beacon Journal* announced the demise of Larry Bader. The Omaha press put Johnson's age at thirty-nine, which was Bader's actual age, whereas the Akron paper incorrectly listed Bader as forty, which the records indicate was Johnson's assumed age.

A more serious error, subscribed to generally by the press, from *The New York Times* to the *Eagle-Tribune* in Lawrence, Mass., was the posthumous stress on the "duality" of Bader-Johnson, whether by "double life" or "twin identity" or "dual role." Even if, as such phrases imply, Johnson had been aware of Bader, at no time did the two existences overlap or interweave, not even in the final days. A minor technical mistake, to be sure, but one that helps explain the media's difficulties in handling the Bader-Johnson story.

Otherwise, the press coverage was predictable. Nationally, the story of his death was played much as the story of his life had been—with an air of detached curiosity. Locally, the Omaha media were the more inclined to quiet compassion, partially because they were mourning a fellow resident, primarily because so many of the men who staff Omaha's press facilities had come to know Fritz, to marvel at his unusual personality, to bask in his effortless cheer, and later, to be impressed by his dignity in time of stress. They told the story of his death straight, without embellishment, unapologetically.

What little public agonizing Omaha permitted itself was carried on intermittently the following three weeks in the *World-Herald's* letters-to-the-editor column, "The Public Pulse." Mrs. L. B. Riley entered the first plea: "Although beset by insurmountable troubles compounded by an incurable illness, this courageous man never wavered in his attempt to do right for both of his families. We lost an honorable man, an outstanding personality." Someone with the pen name of Maggie then was moved to expound the rationalization most of the community preferred to accept: "It seems ridiculous that any one in his right mind could doubt Fritz Johnson's story that he did not remember his former life, wife and children. Had he secretly known all along about his other family, he would also remember that he was an archery champion and well known. He would not have gone to Chicago, where he was bound to run into some one who knew him. Nor would he have gotten the type of job he did, meeting the public on every hand." There the defense rested, until Erma Clinchard added a final fillip to the Omaha discussion: "Some things in life we never understand, but must accept or reject at face value. A case in point was

that of the man known as Fritz Johnson. No one will know
what happened to split a life in half. But to people who knew
him in Omaha, he was a good and gentle man with a rare gift
of friendship."

The official attitude of Omaha—or at least of those closest
to Bader-Johnson in that city—had been articulated more
than eighteen months before by Wally Provost, the *World-
Herald* sports editor, in his column of February 12, 1965:

> Three weeks ago, the head table at the Night of Champions
> banquet was graced by a National Football League coach, a
> World Series hero, a Hall of Fame member and other athletes
> of considerable prominence.
>
> Opening remarks were made to the overflow crowd of five
> hundred by the outgoing president of the sponsoring Omaha
> Sportscasters Association—a guy named Fritz.
>
> He was applauded with enthusiasm. Later there were many
> handshakes for the man who found great popularity in this
> city, and whose closest friendships amount to a cult.
>
> Last week end, authorities reported—on evidence he also
> accepted—that Fritz is the solid reincarnation of Lawrence
> Bader, an Ohioan who disappeared in May of 1957.
>
> The cult was shaken but not shattered.
>
> Fritz said he had no knowledge of the earlier life. Content to
> judge only the man it has known, the cult clings to a yet
> undefined theory of conversion in the twilight zone of psy-
> chogenesis.

For Provost and his cult colleagues in Omaha, the entire
affair amounted to a mysterious malfunction in the central
nervous system. How had this happened? Omaha wanted to
know, with an admixture of curiosity and affection. The
stranger in its midst was clearly Bader, not Johnson.

The priorities were different in Akron. There the paramount question was Why? The city's necessity paralleled, in
a sense, the experience of the Bader family itself—rejected,
deserted, and finally spurned.

The Akron *Beacon Journal* wasted no time in establishing
this perspective. Twelve days before Bader-Johnson's death,

253 The Mass of Men

the newspaper carried a front-page exclusive on the man dying in Room 333 of Saint Joseph's Hospital. The staff writer began by describing the pain-killing drugs injected every three hours, then came quickly to the thrust of his report:

> And while he sleeps, this once-handsome man whose face has become gaunt, the deadly mass within him grows—the cancer which, nine years ago, may first have attacked his brain . . . then, in 1964, took his left eye and now assaults his liver.
>
> . . . The demise of Fritz Johnson-Larry Bader, however, will not end what may be one of the most intriguing psychiatric puzzlers of the century. Was Bader truly a victim of amnesia, who did not recall his past life as a $10,000-per-year appliance salesman in Akron and the wife and four children he left behind? Or was he simply a liar, a gambler, a magnificent actor who was willing to die in the role he created for himself as one of Omaha's most popular and respected citizens?

This was the same theme the *Beacon Journal* had maintained from the day Bader-Johnson had been spotted in Chicago. The skepticism is carefully veiled, but it can be extracted easily enough by weighing "a victim of amnesia" against "a liar, a gambler, a magnificent actor." This geographical prejudice was even more apparent in the obituaries. Akron announced flatly that Bader died "without changing his version," in contrast to the less tendentious report from Omaha that "Fritz . . . never wavered in saying that he did not remember anything of his life in Akron."

Not that the *Beacon Journal* refused to consider other possibilities. It dutifully quoted Bader-Johnson's physician, Lee C. Bevilacqua, when the doctor suggested that "It is quite likely the cancer which is now killing him and which took his eye, first manifested itself as a brain tumor. This tumor may have caused the amnesia. We will not know for certain unless we perform an autopsy."*

---

* Bader-Johnson authorized such an autopsy in his will, and it was performed at Saint Joseph's shortly after his death. According to

254 "If I had it to do over again . . ."

No explanation seemed too absurd for the Akron news-paper to share with its avid readers. "The hand of God has revealed itself in this tragic situation," someone described as a friend of the Bader family told the *Beacon Journal.* "Why else would He have allowed Larry to be found, only to die?"

But mainly the *Beacon Journal* doubted. It utilized the occasion of Bader-Johnson's death to resurrect all of the previously voiced suspicions. It began by reinvoking that anonymous panel of Akron psychiatrists that, a year before, had questioned the "obvious discrepancies" in the report issued by a medical team that had examined the missing Akronite in Omaha. This panel, which had been two in number but which was now expanded to "several" psychia-trists, complained initially that the Omaha authorities had not provided enough real information on Bader-Johnson's mental condition. In the posthumous version, the *Beacon Journal* had one of its unnamed medical sources insisting that the mental and physical "causes of amnesia are rea-sonably determinable—yet none was found at the time of the examination. The psychiatrist added that it was possible Bader may have been able to hang onto his loss-of-memory story for the benefit of the examiners."

The Akron paper climaxed its incredulous report with the recollections, delivered *cum grano salis,* of one Jack Fitz-gibbons, the news director at WAKR-TV in Akron. He was, he claimed, a close friend of Larry Bader for several years prior to his disappearance. During that time, "Bader con-stantly questioned him about radio and how to be a success as an announcer." Fitzgibbons went on to suggest that Bader-Johnson might have borrowed his name (John Fitzgibbons to John "Fritz" Johnson) and his place of birth (Fitzgibbons had been born in Massachusetts; Johnson claimed to have been raised in a Massachusetts orphanage) .

Bevilacqua, the results are confidential and will not be released. The embargo is, however, irrelevant. Most medical authorities agree that melanoma does not affect the brain and therefore could not possibly have had any effects on the victim's memory processes.

Having delivered itself of these final misgivings, the *Beacon Journal* heaved an editorial sigh and intoned: "It's all over now; there is no tomorrow for the man who claimed to recall no past. All that remains is the mystery."

And the speculation, of course.

Was Bader-Johnson telling the truth? Those who thought not seized on the circumstantial evidence that Bader had deliberately "staged" his death on Lake Erie in 1957. They pointed to his financial difficulties at the time, to his failure to file any income-tax returns for five years, to the hints of marital discord, to the unusually large sum of money he was carrying the day he vanished, to the milk company's threat to cancel deliveries, to his wife's fourth pregnancy.

The advocates of the "faked amnesia" theory were also fascinated by the obvious contrasts between Larry Bader, the hustling, debt-ridden kitchenware salesman, overwhelmed by the responsibilities of a growing family and a large mortgage, and the flamboyant, carefree Fritz Johnson. This viewpoint was summarized, though with minimal regard for the medical probabilities involved, in a memorandum written by one of the ranking officers of the New York Life Insurance Company. Dated a few days after the company's long-lost policyholder had been located in 1965, the memo speculated that, assuming Bader-Johnson was a liar and a neurotic personality, "public pressure" would soon force him to "regain" his memory. "On the other hand," the official hypothesized, "he may be suffering from a true psychosis. Perhaps the modern-day schizophrenic, instead of becoming 'Napoleon' or 'God' becomes the swinging tv announcer, sportsman, flagpole sitter and general bon vivant."

Many people, including most of the Bader family in Akron, were convinced that Bader-Johnson was telling the truth, that he was a bona fide amnesiac. This position, they insisted, was supported by the same evidence offered by the skeptics who believed that the entire caper was, in *Life's* phrase, "just an ingenious seven-year hoax by a man who wanted a change." They argued that Bader had been under tremendous stress the afternoon he rented the fishing boat; either his mind "short-circuited" or he was somehow injured during the storm on Lake Erie; after wandering around "dazed and memory-less" for a few days, he invented a new identity and background and came to Omaha.

Otherwise, his supporters reasoned, why would he have permitted himself to become a public figure? Fugitives do not solicit photographs and stories about themselves in newspapers, and they do not work before television cameras. Nor do they pursue former hobbies like archery, which might put them in contact during championship competition with former acquaintances. Besides, how could he have tricked not only a medical team but his relatives in Akron into believing he did not remember them? And, if he knew he was really Bader, why would he have volunteered to be fingerprinted in Chicago?

The basic problem with the "amnesia vs. hoax" debate is that it seriously and unnecessarily limits the range of alternatives. To begin with, there is no need to date specifically the onset of memory loss. What is clearly involved here is paramnesia, not amnesia. Paramnesia is the falsification of memory; it is not the result of abrupt organic causes like head injuries but is instead a mental device that protects a person from extreme anxieties, and it is usually a gradual process.

In other words, it would have been quite possible, medically, for Larry Bader to have deliberately beached his boat west of Cleveland, made his way to Chicago, acquired the props he might need to pass himself off as a recently discharged sailor, and then taken a bus to Omaha—all the while consciously constructing the outlines of a new identity. By the same reasoning, this new identity, his own creation, could conceivably have assumed larger and larger dimensions, until it finally took full possession of him, thereby destroying any functional relationship to Bader. This means simply that if he was not Johnson when he arrived in Omaha in 1957, he also was not Bader when he left in 1966.

In short, there is sufficient reason to believe that Bader had staged his death. It is equally reasonable to accept Johnson's belief that he was raised in a Massachusetts orphanage, a conviction that led him confidently to submit to fingerprint comparison. Psychologically, this is certainly feasible, and there is more than enough factual overlap in the biographical experience of Bader and Johnson to strongly suggest it. This approach has the advantage of reconciling the seeming contradictions between the proponents of amnesia and the advocates of hoax.

One point that both sides have overlooked or misunderstood is the nature of Bader-Johnson's "celebrity" in Omaha. The publicity, the outrageous stunts, the affectations of media exposure—all this has been cited by his supporters as "proof" that he did not remember Akron and by his detractors as "evidence" that he was merely bored with his previous, humdrum suburban existence. But the fact is that the Fritz Johnson who arrived in Omaha had no intention of becoming a "swinging tv announcer, sportsman, flagpole sitter and general bon vivant." He set out to become a bartender, a "nocturnal bachelor" in pursuit of the "sweet and uncomplicated" life. Nothing more. And during his early months in Omaha, that is what he did and that is what he was.

Bader may or may not have quizzed a friend back in Akron about broadcasting, as Fitzgibbons later insisted. The reality of his transition from mixing drinks at Ross's Steakhouse to spinning records on KBON was something else. Bader-Johnson did not apply for the announcing job. One of his customers, attracted by his voice and manner, suggested that he audition. *Fritz turned him down.* The man persisted, and finally—perhaps even reluctantly—Fritz accepted the offer and got the job, thereby exposing his voice, not his face, to the public. It was not until six years after his disappearance and one year after his marriage that he made the switch from radio to television. It was also about this time that he started to receive extensive newspaper publicity, complete with photographs.

This gradual identity conversion is only a theory. Obviously, it cannot be proved. But there is more logic in this interpretation than in all the assertions of the pro-amnesia adherents and all the insinuations of pro-hoax observers. It becomes even more plausible when we consider the most crucial oversight of all: the cancer that took the life of Bader-Johnson.

The press frequently mentioned this malignancy, both at the time the missing man was spotted in Chicago and, naturally, when he was dying of it twenty months later. But at no point did any of the enterprising reporters bother to find out precisely what it was. Had they done so, they would have learned that the melanoma that had cost Bader-Johnson his left eye ten months *before* his exposure had been, in effect, his death warrant. A melanoma is a tumor of high malignancy that metastasizes rapidly and widely. Usually the cancer reappears within a few years in the liver. In a man his age, it almost invariably does. It is fatal.

Did Bader-Johnson know, after his eye operation but before his fateful trip to Chicago, that his life was being cut short?

It is not an easy question to ask, it is harder to answer. His physician, Dr. Bevilacqua, told me that his patient understood prior to his eye operation that "it was an almost absolute certainty" that the tumor was malignant. The malignancy was confirmed afterwards by several pathologists. "Following this diagnosis of which he was told," Bevilacqua explained, "[Fritz] was then instructed by me to appear every three to six months for liver and blood studies because of the possibility of future metastasis to the liver. He very diligently underwent all of these examinations. . . ."

Bader-Johnson knew. What neither he nor anyone else could know was when. How this ominous knowledge affected him, determined the course of his actions, shaped his response to the momentous events in his immediate future, can only be conjectured. He did not mention it. In May 1966, when the radioactive liver "skan" and subsequent biopsy confirmed the inevitable, Bader-Johnson accepted it with impressive stoicism.

"First I notified his brothers in Akron, then I told Nancy, then I asked him to come to see me," Bevilacqua remembered. "His first words were: 'Give it to me straight. Don't pull any punches.' I told him, and he shuddered. He didn't cry, and that was surprising. I have never known anyone who didn't cry at that moment. Even I cried when I told him he would die. But he just said: 'I want you to promise me two things. When it comes obvious that I'm about to die, don't be a hero and keep me alive for a few extra days. Let me go out easy. And secondly, when I start looking bad, get me to the hospital. I don't want the kids seeing me very sick.' "

When the appropriate moment came, Bevilacqua kept his promise. Meanwhile, the news of Bader-Johnson's terminal illness was released to the press. Nancy Johnson, whose marriage to Fritz was annulled after his previous identity had become known, immediately insisted that her former husband give up his room at the YMCA and return to the home they had shared during their brief marriage.* His many friends began making the arrangements for a benefit dance the following month in a downtown hotel. The affair raised several thousand dollars for the couple, and even the mayor of Omaha participated.

In Akron, Mrs. Bader had her attorney approach the New York Life Insurance Company to have her "legally resurrected" husband's policy reinstated. She offered to pay the accumulated premiums on the $7,000 policy from 1957, when her husband had disappeared. But New York Life, with assets of approximately $2.9 billion, refused—despite the fact

---

* After her marriage to Johnson was dissolved, Nancy had secured employment as a reservations clerk with United Air Lines. On September 4, 1967, she married Gene Bos, a divorced salesman from Atlanta, Ga.

that the unpaid premiums could be deducted from the pending death claim, which would no longer involve double indemnity. The company's official position was that the Bader policy had lapsed, that the policy belonged not to Mrs. Bader, the beneficiary, but to a man who now claimed no knowledge of ever being Bader.

That Mrs. Bader needed the insurance money more than ever seems obvious. After her husband had been relocated in 1965, Fidelity & Deposit Company of Maryland had repaid New York Life and then informed Mrs. Bader that it still possessed the deed to her home, as well as the original bank mortgage note, which Mrs. Bader insisted she had satisfied out of the insurance proceeds. Fidelity announced that thenceforth she would have to make regular mortgage payments to that company. When she did not, Fidelity foreclosed and demanded that the home of Mrs. Bader, soon again to become a widow with four children, be sold at a sheriff's sale.

The combination of Fidelity's action and New York Life's inaction left Mrs. Bader little choice. On August 3, 1966, she filed suit against New York Life in the Common Pleas Court of Summit County, Ohio, to have her dying husband's life insurance reinstated in full force.

Forty-one days later he died.

"In his last ten days of life," Bevilacqua, his friend and physician, later wrote, "he was under constant surveillance twenty-four hours a day. He was under heavy doses of sedation and he was quite toxic from the advancement of his liver disease. During this period there were many moments of hallucinations and irrational conversation as we often see in medicine with the heavy sedation and toxicity. Let me say that at no time did Mr. Johnson make any reference to his previous existence in Akron, Ohio. All of the remarks were geared to his life in the orphanage and with people he had known here in Omaha."

XV

The Escape Mechanism

Why?

Why do they do it?

Why do some men and women, faced with the same pressures and responsibilities as the rest of us, similarly obligated to justify their harmless triumphs and explain their meaningless defeats, vulnerable to equal doses of despair, why do these people succumb, turn about, and disappear?

The question contains its own hypothetical imperative.

One approach involves an understanding of what the psychiatrists call *emotional homeostasis*. In theory it is quite simple. Homeostasis is the relative stability or the tendency toward equilibrium between the various independent parts or subsystems of an organism. Emotional homeostasis essentially means personality balance.

The personality is ever shifting. It is under constant assault from outside influences and stress; internally it is steadily bombarded by impulses that originate below the level of personal awareness. These impulses are reactions to our environment. Many would be considered socially unacceptable. When we block them, energy is generated, which we must expend in other ways. If appropriate outlets cannot be found, anxiety is created. In short, emotional homeostasis is maintained so long as we are able to reconcile our impulses to our environmental demands.

The mechanics of this process of adaptation are called, appropriately enough, the adaptive mechanisms. The three basic ones are *evaluation, inhibition,* and *facilitation*. Each is almost self-explanatory. Evaluation, or what the Freudians describe as "reality testing," is the way we decide what is happening around us and what is expected of us under the given circumstances. Inhibition controls antisocial responses. Facilitation is the process by which we modify these unacceptable impulses so that they can be expressed in more respectable forms.

It works something like this:

As you are strolling down a carnival midway, you notice (evaluation) that Samantha the Snake Queen (external stress) is gazing at you in a most suggestive manner. You consider turning (impulse) toward her trailer, but your wife tugs your sleeve (inhibition) and points out a particularly lovely flower arrangement in the Methodist Church Ladies' Auxiliary booth. Moments later you part with a quarter for the dubious privilege of throwing (facilitation) frayed baseballs at cleverly weighted wooden bottles. As depressing as it all may sound, emotional homeostasis has been achieved—momentarily.

Now let us add the ingredient of tension to the same scene. For some time the pressure has been mounting. The office work has not been going well. Your spouse seems to be taking you for granted; the children have become openly insolent. Unpaid bills are accumulating. The appliances, according to the manufacturers' plans, are breaking down on schedule. The hot-water tank leaks, the fresh paint on the house is peeling, the new car rattles even when parked. The railroad has petitioned the state for permission to abolish your commuter train. The manager of the liquor store has informed your mother-in-law that he has canceled your credit. The local newspaper has discontinued your favorite cartoon, "Mary Worth." Not surprisingly, you have exhausted the adaptive capacity you normally hold in reserve for emergency stress. This time, as you walk that carnival midway, one of your adaptive mechanisms has malfunctioned. You are, although you probably are not aware of it, in danger.

For reasons the psychiatrists frankly do not understand, all three of the adaptors are not equally affected when emotional homeostasis disintegrates. Usually only one adaptor falters. In fact, within certain limits, it is quite feasible for the other two to go on functioning adequately.

Suppose the evaluation mechanism has broken down. You perceive, as before, the provocative gesture of the Snake Queen. But because you are unable to evaluate the situation correctly, you fail to notice that her sensuous invitation is not actually intended for you. Samantha is looking at the man behind you, Bartholomew the Human Hammer, who happens to be her jealous husband.

This is not as perilous a position as it might appear. Few people can continuously analyze their total circumstances with much consistency or clarity. Most of us must settle for a functional fix on events, especially at the crucial moments; then, with native wisdom, we try to avoid any desperate acts and trust our instincts to sustain us until bedtime. Unless we are moved to action, the failure of evaluation usually just means that we are further out of touch with the actual situation.

In a sense, the collapse of the facilitation adaptor is even less dramatic. When it breaks down, nothing happens. Which is a real problem. You go on "reading" environment, and unacceptable behavior is still successfully inhibited. But without facilitation, there is no displacement activity. Consequently, the sense of anxiety—emotional energy generated by the suppression (conscious) and the repression (unconscious) of antisocial impulses—builds and builds and builds.

The failure of the inhibiting adaptor, however, can result in serious and—in the case of Samantha and Bartholomew— immediate consequences. Antisocial commands penetrate the area of consciousness, and the personality finds itself too weak

to resist. Impulse is converted into performance. In spite of
the knowledge that Bartholomew is fashioning a club from a
section of railroad track, you find yourself striding toward the
Snake Queen. Or you take a swing, verbally or physically, at
your boss. Or you tell the overweight president of the
Women's Club what you really thought of her latest inane
speech. Or you kick the chair you just stumbled over.

Or you disappear.

Flight, the polarity of fight, is one of man's most important
biological instincts. It assumes a million forms. Most are
quite harmless and of temporary duration. Through repetition from childhood, these diversionary activities attain the
status of habit. They become almost involuntary exercises,
whose purpose is to gain a few moments' relief from the op-
pressive ultimatums of reality. Whatever form it assumes—a
daydream or a hobby, recreation, alcohol, religion, or some
less subtle narcotic—the therapeutic effect is much the same:
briefly we escape and are refreshed. At the same time, we
replenish the reserve reservoir of emotional strength that we
need for periods of unusual stress.

For instance, every so often a shoelace snaps.

Ordinarily this is a calamity of minute magnitude. You
shrug, knot the parted string in the most expedient manner,
and make a mental note to buy a replacement. At other
times, such a catastrophe forces a man to his knees in blind
rage. Why? Because the offending shoelace summarizes
months of accumulated procrastination, unfinished projects,
untended tasks, unwritten letters, unpaid bills, undecided
decisions. One moment you were bending over tying your
shoe; the next, your life is out of control, and you grope for
the lock with a ring of unfamiliar keys.

When this happens, there is only one viable course of action. You quickly retreat to fundamentals. You compile a list
of all the things you have been putting off. Then you start
slowly, first with the easiest ones, such as the shoelace. Carefully and cautiously, you restore order, from the ground up,

gradually increasing the scope and complexity of your involvement, until you again begin to assert some authority over your own affairs.

By analogy, this protective procedure is the way the personality responds when one of its adaptive mechanisms falters. It regroups, rushes reinforcements to the weakened zone, and prepares to do battle for a much smaller plot of ground. It simplifies, yes; but mainly it drastically reduces the circumference of environment. This concept is crucial to any comprehension of the voluntary absentee, who resides in all of us.

In the first chapter, a query was directed at Wakefield, the "dead man" in the East Side Manhattan tavern, who had inexplicably abandoned his wife and family and a secure, well-paying job with his father-in-law. For what? we demanded. A menial job in a strange city, without friends and under a spurious name, cramped in a solitary room full of secondhand furniture?

Wakefield had been an accountant, and he did not lose his skill when he changed his name. What he did lose was the opportunity to exercise it. He could not apply for a similar job without showing his credentials, without listing his education, without producing references. To do so would have brought the investigators to his new doorstep by return mail. Therefore he was reduced to finding semiskilled work, the low pay for which dictated a considerably reduced scale of living.

This explanation would be sufficient if we were justified in considering Wakefield and his colleagues as merely fugitives, men and women running *from* something. What psychiatry suggests, however, is that these people are also refugees, fleeing *toward* something else. That something else assumes varied forms, forms as varied as the role of a foreman in a New York City sweatshop or a bartender in Omaha or a laborer in Key West or a pigment grinder in Illinois or a tile setter in Kansas City or a commercial fisherman in Madeira

Beach, Fla. But the variety of these alternatives, in this context, only emphasizes their comparative simplicity when contrasted with what the person had been doing before he or she disappeared.

The absentee who, like Wakefield and Bader and all the rest, changes his name and becomes a menial worker has assuredly increased his chances for anonymity, as well as the possibilities for employment. He may even be personally convinced that this was his sole motive for the maneuver. Nevertheless, it appears equally certain that the actions of these absentees represent a collective response to powerful psychological demands for adaptation. Inhibition has collapsed, the resulting anxiety can no longer be facilitated, the personality has been overwhelmed by environment. From the unconscious comes a severe injunction: simplify or perish.

Does the choice seem overly dramatized?

Not really. Not when voluntary identity conversion, at least in this extreme form, is viewed as a type of suicide. A symbolic type, to be sure. But the symbolism merely alters the fact of loss, without diminishing it. The removal of self through the renunciation of name and status and vocation is only slightly less drastic and final than the physical destruction of self. Death permeates the very act of disappearance. It is strongest in situations where the absentee actually feigned his demise, as Bader-Johnson did, or left an ambiguous "suicide" note, as Wakefield did. "Life had lost much of its charm for me," author Ted Robinson, Jr., explicitly explained, "and I had tentatively decided to have nothing more to do with it, but I thought I ought to enter into a sort of trial separation first." With or without articulation, the absentee voluntarily abandons and thereby pronounces dead a portion of his life; if his "trial separation" continues for any length of time, society reciprocates in kind with a legal declaration of presumed death.

What is being "destroyed" in each instance, of course, is not the individual but the particular environment that proved too powerful (which is to say, uninhabitable) for that individual. The absentee accomplishes this otherwise impossible transformation by seeking out a less complex environment and reestablishing himself as a less complicated person. Mobility in a success-oriented society is a decidedly one-way proposition; and that way, or at least the appearance of that way, is upward. Obviously there is little point in laboring the uncomprehending pressure exerted to this end by family and friends. The doctor's son who announces that he would prefer to become an auto mechanic has censured himself. In this sense, we are all the children of physicians, compelled by the intuition that the lower our origins, the greater the necessity to increase our status, one way or another. Exceptions to the rule are sometimes tolerated, never condoned.

The central question remains: What is the source of this unresolved anxiety?

Theoretically the question would logically be directed at those who have experienced it. In practice this proves extremely difficult. Most of them are still missing. Those who have returned or have been located cannot be approached for a variety of reasons, usually legal. The few who will talk—that is, the handful who consented to be interviewed—proved unable or unwilling to generalize. This was disappointing but not especially surprising. There is really no reason for the voluntary absentee to be more articulate or less reluctant to discuss his motivations than those who have not disappeared.

This does not mean that he is mute. The absentee has acted. In that all action is an affirmative statement of belief or disbelief, he has already spoken. He has said something both desperate and dramatic, and if we are prevented from picking up the individual voice, perhaps a partial answer to the question may be sounded from their collective experience. But only perhaps. A statistical profile of any group, regardless of the precision of conception and execution, can calculate only a small fraction of personal worth. The group here assembled—Wakefield and 166 other adults—suffers an additional and unavoidable disadvantage: the information about them was collected by their pursuers. In pursuit, the emphasis is not on motivation but on more functional data that might lead to the recovery of the missing person.

Two characteristics unite these people. First the available evidence indicates that everyone of them vanished of his or her accord. Second, each is still missing. This was not so much a requirement for inclusion as it was a research necessity. The amount of information that accumulates during the course of an investigation is in direct proportion to the length, breadth, and difficulty of the search. Suffice it that the more circumstantial the disappearance, the greater the determination of the claims detective and the heavier the dossier.

The second point requires qualification. Technically, nineteen of the men and two of the women are still missing only to their relatives. The investigators have successfully located sixteen of them, including Wakefield; the other five contacted the insurance companies of their own volition; in every one of these cases the person's current whereabouts has been kept confidential by the companies. An additional eight are known to have died subsequent to their disappearances; their death certificates, replete with aliases, are on file in connection with claims made against their insurance policies. Of the remaining 138, only two involve what the insurance officials consider "a strong presumption of death." Neither of these cases contained the element of death simulation at the moment of disappearance.

Naturally, the limited availability of this type of information has shaped the statistical results. This situation was as uncontrollable as it is regrettable. Otherwise, only two requirements governed the selection of examples. The family income at the time of disappearance must have exceeded $6,500. The figure was arbitrarily chosen. It was intended primarily as an indicator of middle-class status. By itself the amount is meaningless; in combination with life insurance and other documented evidence of possession and position, it establishes an income base for financial reference.

The other requirement was that the disappearance date after 1945. Originally this cutoff was an attempt to minimize the disruptive social effects of such factors as the world war just ended and the Depression that had preceded it. On reflection, however, it now seems absurd to pretend that the past quarter century might be considered some sort of homogeneous experience, except that the warfare and the economic reverses have been on a smaller scale. The post-World War II epoch is simply nearest in time and somewhat clearer in memory.

Only five women are included in the group. This is not meant to suggest the actual proportion by sex in disappearance cases, although men do predominate by a vast margin; rather it represents the percentage experience of the insurance industry. All the participants are white. The reason for this should be apparent by this time to every literate American.

MARITAL STATUS

Every person in this group was or had been married. Seven of the men and one woman had been married twice; one other man had divorced and remarried the same woman. Two of these men were among the twelve described as "separated" from their wives at the time of disappearance. One hundred and forty-three of these missing persons were parents, although in two instances the men had had children by their first wives but not by their second. Only one family with more than five children was involved. The records indicate that in at least thirty-four cases, or approximately twenty-four percent of the parent category, the family was either expecting another child or included an infant less than a year old.

Age

The range, at the time of disappearance, was from 27 to 66. The median age was 41; the average, 42.9. The breakdown, with ages calculated to the closest birthday, was as follows:

AGE	NUMBER	PERCENTAGE
27–29	5	2.9
30–39	47	28.1
40–49	84	50.3
50–59	23	13.8
60–66	8	4.8

The ages of the women were 29, 32, 35, 38, and 42. The largest concentration, 117 (seventy percent), was between the ages of 38 and 51.

Education

College level, 124; high school, 19; not indicated, 24. What percentage of the "college level" group actually completed the course of study is impossible to determine. In some cases, the person was included because his vocation (e.g., engineer) clearly implied college training; in other instances, the person was placed in this category because of a mention that the investigators had contacted a university alumni association during their search. Similarly, most of the "not indicated" group, on the basis of reasonable assumptions of the educational requirements for the types of jobs they held, belong with the high-school graduates. Three of the five women were college graduates; no information was available on the other two. Only six men (a chemist, three lawyers, a doctor, and a high-school guidance counselor) were known to have completed advanced degrees.

Military Service

At least 128 of the 162 men served in the armed forces. Nine of these incurred limited disabilities that were considered "service-connected"; four of them and seven others apparently were wounded in combat. Otherwise, it is extremely difficult to tell from the records much about the type of duration of their military experience. It would seem likely that the majority of them, to judge from the concentration of age groupings, were in uniform during the Second World War and/or the Korean War.

OCCUPATIONS

Seventy-one, or approximately forty-four percent, of the men may be described as salaried. Thirty-seven were self-employed, mostly in entrepreneurial situations. The remaining fifty-four worked on either a commission or a salary-plus-commission basis. Only one of the women was employed at the time of her disappearance. Because of the unevenness of the documentation (some company records had not been updated since the policyholder applied for insurance) and, to a lesser extent, because of the tendency in large corporations to assign embroidered job titles and defy functional interpretation, the subdivision of the salaried and commission groups into management and nonmanagement becomes more intuitive than mathematical. Nevertheless it would appear that about a third of these men could conceivably be considered "middle management," in that they seem to have exercised some control and authority over other employees. What influence, if any, they may have had in the shaping of company or institutional policies is not evident.

The wide variety of skills and professions and vocations pursued by these men is already manifest in the examples cited previously in this book. The largest subcategory in the salaried group is accountants, 9; in the self-employed group, the high-risk construction industry (contractors, builders, developers, etc.) leads with 7; among the commission types, interestingly enough it is insurance salesmen, 14, with real estate a close second with 11, of whom 4 also sold insurance. Seven of the other 33 in the commission group had previously attempted to sell one or both, which is indicative of both the high personnel turnover in commission-sales work and also the tremendous job mobility that characterizes the industry in general. This mobility was observable, if immeasurable, in almost every instance, regardless of category or salary range, in which a vocational biography was available.

FINANCES

The basic source of this information was insurance applications, which demanded an approximation of current income from the prospective policyholder. This automatically dated the information. In only seven instances did the investigative reports mention the income of the missing person at the time of his departure. As a result, the majority of the income figures represent reasonable estimates* of what a particular job *might* have paid at a particular point in time, making suitable—though perhaps unrealistic—adjustments for experience. Obviously, no consideration of investments or other outside income was possible. In situations where the disappearance occurred prior to 1957, the estimated income has been modified to reflect more closely the current dollar values:

$6,500–10,000	22 percent
$10,000–15,000	56 percent
$15,000–25,000	18 percent
Over $25,000	4 percent

Similar problems were encountered in attempting to fix the percentages of home owners and renters. Unless the insurance policies involved mortgage riders, the investigators were seldom concerned with housing arrangements. The suburban predominance among these absentees, however, would imply a high percentage of mortgagees.

---

* As a salaried employee, I admit to a tendency to err optimistically on behalf of the wage earner, an inflationary mistake that most employers, especially those employers who were themselves once employees, seldom make except when computing their own worth.

RELIGION

Protestant, 74; Roman Catholic, 28; Jewish, 16; Other, 4; Unknown, 49. This compilation was also complicated by the lack of concern for such information on the part of the investigators. Many affiliations were based on such assumptions as church weddings, the use of clerics as character references, memberships in patently church-oriented organizations, and, in a few instances, the ethnic implications of the person's name. With the exception of two men, one of whom had been a Pentecostal lay preacher in his spare time, the men and women in this group evidenced little active interest in organized religion. This observation is reinforced in part by the apparent nonaffiliation of twenty-nine percent.

HEALTH

Major operations had been performed on thirteen of the men during the eighteen months prior to their disappearances. In addition, three of these men and four others had medical histories involving various cardiac problems. One of this latter group and a second man with a terminal kidney ailment (hyperphroma) are the two cases previously mentioned in which, because of their ages and the length of time elapsed, a strong presumption of death exists in the opinion of the investigators. Partial disabilities were reported in twenty-six instances, nine of which were the result of injuries suffered in the armed forces. While "erratic behavior" was cited in seventeen cases, the probability of serious mental illness was raised in only three. On numerous occasions, the investigators were informed by the wives that their husbands had complained frequently of headaches in the period just before they vanished. Although most of the people in the group drank, alcoholism was suggested as a possible cause in only twelve instances, again mainly on the testimony of the abandoned spouses.

Sex

Two of the five missing women are the objects of company investigations because they are known to have disappeared with policyholders. These are the only four persons in the group with verifiable extramarital "love interests." In the first case, the couple was last observed riding in the woman's car. In the other, the woman, a divorcée, quit her job and confided to her roommate that she intended to join a man whose mysterious disappearance had been on the front page of the local newspaper for four days. The probability of a sexual motivation was raised in twenty-seven other cases (twenty-six men, one woman), although in most of these instances no supporting evidence was supplied; forty-nine wives emphatically rejected it as a possible cause. Two wives hinted at a homosexual conflict.

Method of Departure

One hundred and three of these people apparently went away without saying anything to their families. (The chief claims investigator of one of the largest companies is skeptical of this statistic on the ground that many wives attempt to hold back such information from the investigators, often in the belief that they thereby strengthen their chances of obtaining death benefits from the insurance companies.) Fifty-six indicated their intentions, either verbally (seven were described as having left as an immediate result of a marital disagreement) or in writing; in eighteen of these cases, the potential of suicide was strongly implied. The element of "specific peril" or simulated death was presented in only three cases; two involved water accidents of a suspicious nature; the other involved a man reportedly lost on a hunting trip. The last five cases were marred by conflicting versions of the circumstances under which the missing person vanished.

DISTRIBUTION

For some reason, it has always been assumed that most absentees vanish in the springtime. The majority of the people in this group, by the timing of their departures, disagreed. The largest concentration (71.3 percent) occurred during the fall and winter. September, not April, was by far the cruelest month of all, and June, rather than December, was the kindest:

Month	Number	Percentage
January	13	7.8
February	8	4.8
March	14	8.4
April	12	7.2
May	7	4.2
June	4	2.3
July	9	5.4
August	16	9.5
September	34	20.4
October	23	13.7
November	18	10.8
December	9	5.4

Any geographic breakdown must necessarily reflect the business patterns of the companies that served as statistical sources. Yet demographically, the following percentages do not appear unrealistic: New England, 16; Middle Atlantic, 25; Southeast, 11; Middle West, 13; Southwest, 7; and Pacific Coast, 28. More significant, however, is the urban-suburban-rural distribution. If it is permissible to lump all isolated small towns with a population in excess of 10,000 together with those communities situated within thirty-five miles of a major metropolitan center under the heading of "suburban," then less than three percent of this sampling can be considered rural. Of the remainder, the suburbanites hold a commanding sixty-one percent to thirty-six percent advantage over their urban colleagues.

At first glance, these statistics appear rather inconclusive. They tell, for instance, the marital status of the absentees but little about the marriages themselves; they reveal income but not financial condition; they hint at health but disclose nothing concerning well-being. Numbers shed no light on a man's threshold of pain or his tolerance of debt. Moreover, it is impossible to extrapolate—in the stylish terms of contemporary motivation research—how many grew up in broken homes, how many were breast-fed rather than bottle-weaned, how many may or may not have envied their fathers' penises, how many came from rich or poor or small or large families, how many were dominated by mothers or rejected by fathers, how many sucked their thumbs, how many were improperly toilet-trained, how many were enuretics, how many were brutalized by incompetent first-grade teachers. Whatever the value of such information, it is unobtainable under these circumstances and therefore irrelevant.

What is obtainable and relevant is the composite portrait of the absentee that can be drawn from these figures. He is in his forty-third year. He lives, presumably when he is not commuting, in a suburban home with his wife, his two or three children, and a mortgage. He has had some college training. His vocation is sales-oriented, and it is probable that part of his income, in the $10,000 to $15,000 bracket, results from commissions. He has switched jobs three to five times since entering the workforce. He is a veteran. Although he was raised in association with one of the major religious denominations, he is not an active or dedicated participant in church activities. His health is about normal for a man of his age. When he disappeared shortly after Labor Day, he did so abruptly and without explanation. He went alone.

The weakness of such faceless statistical exercises is undoubtedly aggravated in this instance by the acknowledged imprecision of the research. What justifies the inclusion of a generalized profile here is the extremity of human conduct that is involved. Up to this point, we have approached these desperate acts through personal examples, a tactic that necessarily stressed the aberrations of personal behavior and subordinated the shared characteristics. Thus, each person appeared to be reacting drastically to peculiar, alien circumstances. But when we lump these singular people together and mathematically dilute their separateness, a different and potentially disturbing picture emerges:

The "average" absentee is very average.

Disturbing? Frankly, that depends on how strongly each of us needs to deny the impulse to flight. Most of the time this need is quite powerful. To consider it is to consider, by extension, what we would flee, namely, our present circumstances. This is hardly a comforting proposition. In moments of partial candor, we freely admit that our value structures are mainly instinctual. Despair occasionally drives us to confess, in the privacy of our cubicles of doubt, that compromise often outweighs commitment in our lives. We have had to make do, accepting what appeared at the time as the lesser threat to unarticulated principles. What we sense at these isolated moments is the real danger of scrutinizing ourselves, our condition, our prospects. The danger is, of course, that intensive self-examination might well find the individual seriously wanting, and without substantial hope of improvement or even change.

But just how introspective is the average absentee? And how could we possibly tell? Where is the evidence that these men and women have at any time considered their circumstances, past and present and future? What proof is offered to suggest that such people are ever consciously concerned about, much less aware of, the reality of their situations? Or especially tempted to brood about it to the point of extreme action?

Again, no one can know for certain. The absentee will not reply, although his silence becomes more understandable when and if we pose similar queries to ourselves. Nevertheless, these unusual people, who are so much like the rest of us, have provided an important clue. This clue derives from their collective statistical experience. This clue contains potential meaning and insight for those left behind.

These men and women disappeared when they were a certain age.

XVI

The Terrible Nines

Frank I. Cobb was the editor of the New York *World*. As the premier editorial writer of his generation, he was articulate and very perceptive. "I shall soon be 40 years old," he wrote his publisher in the summer of 1909, "and that is the most depressing thing of all. Forty is ten years older than 39, although I believe you hold to the theory that everybody is a damned fool until he is 40, and not necessarily very intelligent after that."

With one slashing stroke of psychological arithmetic, Cobb defined the crisis of the decades. "Forty is ten years older than 39," he reasoned, although in his momentary anguish he expressed it backwards: thirty-nine is ten years younger than forty. It certainly seemed that way to the editor as he contemplated his approaching birthday.

The thought bears examination. What is it that compresses a decade into a year? Why should one birthday in ten carry special meaning and weight? Why, in this case, forty? Does this number signify somehow the end of youth, the diminution of promise, the advent of middle age, the preliminary acknowledgment of death? Cannot similar assertions be made for twenty and thirty and fifty and sixty?

An answer involves the nature of personal decades, which have become chronological measurements of individual progress. We sense the unreality of this procedure, but we have little choice. Society long ago decided that age was the most convenient system for mass evaluation, first of a person's privileges and responsibilities, later of his growth and accomplishment. At a certain age, for instance, we are adjudged sufficiently mature to operate a motor vehicle; at another, to vote and to drink. Certain political offices are restricted by age requirements; Selective Service is circumscribed by them. Insurance premiums are calculated by age brackets; numerous jobs—despite the pious disclaimers of many employers—are denied applicants beyond specified birthdays. We are expected to retire according to the calendar; most benefit and welfare programs adhere rigorously to age rules.

Our current understanding of the extreme variations of individual maturation leads us to view such arbitrary age requirements with condescending amusement—after we have exceeded them, that is. Yet in the process, we have been conditioned to assess ourselves and others in equally irrational terms. Our internal gauges are set, not by what year it happens to be but by what year *we* happen to be. Consciously or not, we continually equate the achievements of those around us against their ages. We know intuitively that an impressive degree of success for a man of twenty-seven might be considered mediocre for someone at forty-three. Compulsively, we compare and contrast ourselves with anyone else our own age and of similar background. "The passion to get ahead," Eric Hoffer correctly observed, "is sometimes born of the fear lest we be left behind."

The most conclusive test of one's relative standing, however, consists of periodic personal inventories, the drawing up of private balance sheets of debits and credits, strengths and weaknesses, successes and failures. This is no easy task. In all honesty, this is often a decidedly unpleasant task. Not because we are such unpleasant folk but because, as people, we have an urgent need to establish higher standards for ourselves, to be far more rigid in the application of these standards, and to be much more critical of the results. It is only human, therefore, that we usually postpone as long as possible any self-examination of motives and accomplishment.

Most of the time, this is not very difficult to do. In the normal course of affairs, more immediate obligations constantly interfere and distract our attention. Procrastination is readily rationalized. But such introspective moments cannot be put off indefinitely. At fairly regular intervals, we call upon ourselves for progress reports. We do so almost involuntarily and with a decided sense of foreboding. But the impulse cannot be ignored. Time alone has mandated it.

That mandate is herein described as the Terrible Nines.

The adult Nines—twenty-nine, thirty-nine, forty-nine, and, probably to a lesser extent, fifty-nine and sixty-nine—represent considerably more than just the end of personal decades; they are emotional watersheds that, like death in the family, propel a person toward the front of the generations. As such, they contain undeniable tension. Externally the symptoms are few and difficult to detect. The people traversing these traumatic periods offer little surface evidence of inner turmoil; indeed, they may often be inclined to joke publicly about not growing any older, as one of the nation's most popular comedians has done for the more than three decades since his thirty-ninth birthday. Nevertheless, these people have been conscious for some time of the quiet terror that gradually takes possession of their psyche as they approach each new decade.

This terror, this interrupted cry, is an intensely personal experience. It consists of unfocused anxiety, and it assumes many, many guises, just as it provokes an infinite variety of individual responses. It is extremely difficult to describe, almost impossible to share. But it is awesomely real, and everyone who has passed through one or more of the Terrible Nines has experienced it in some form and will not forget it, which is not quite the same as remembering it.

If decade crisis is in fact a common and devastating human hurdle, then this age factor should be an observable phe-

nomenon among such aberrant behavior groups as voluntary
absentees. And it emphatically is. In the previous chapter,
the ages of the 167 missing persons under study were divided
by decades; the results showed that half of the group were in
their forties and that about seventy percent of the people
were between thirty-eight and fifty-one years of age. This
established a concentration, without providing any particular
insight to motivation or timing. When, however, the same
statistics are rearranged around decades—allowing two years
for the tension to accumulate and two more years for reaction—a different and more significant pattern emerges:

Age	Number	Percentage
28–31	14	8.3
38–41	51	30.5
48–51	29	17.4
58–61	8	4.8

The Terrible Nines, it appears, are a demonstrable factor
in 102 of the cases, or sixty-one percent. Such a percentage is
too large to be considered coincidental; it clearly constitutes
a marked trend, a trend that is, moreover, closely approxi-
mated beyond the survey group in the examples used else-
where in this book. (To name a few, Lawrence Bader was
thirty; William Cary, thirty-eight; Ted Robinson, Jr., forty;
Thomas Buntin, twenty-eight; C. Verne Holmberg, thirty-
eight; William Waldron, forty; Norman Briggs, twenty-
eight; Charles Beth, forty-one; Charles Waterman, thirty;
and Lewis Hano, who disappeared twice, was thirty-eight *and*
forty-one.)

Statistically and psychologically, the worst Nine is the one
that brought Editor Cobb to the edge of despair: thirty-nine.
This age bracket, thirty-eight to forty-one, accounted for half
of the absentees who disappeared about the time of a decade
change. Almost a third of the entire survey group vanished
during these four crucial and disturbing years. Part of the
explanation might seem obvious from a casual analysis of the
decade involved. The forties are usually considered the so-

called meridian years, the apogee of adult prowess and achievement. What ascends, of course, must still descend, so that these same years also mark an individual point of no return. All sorts of life commitments, formed in the twenties and nurtured during the thirties, now harden into habit or, worse, lethargic molds. The challenges of a new, vigorous generation—especially on the job mart, where vocational mobility is drastically stunted after the age of forty—and felt precisely at that moment when personal security and tenure begins to assume important dimensions.

In this sense, the forties could accurately be considered a kind of twilight period between youth and seniority. The body is dying; for more than a decade, it has been dying at a faster rate than it has been renewed. What causes concern is not so much the frequency of minor ailments as the realization that physical abuse can no longer be tolerated. The body's resiliency has been seriously diminished; gone is the capacity to go carelessly to pot and then snap back with a crash diet of exercise. Physical or mental exertion requires longer periods of rest and recuperation. Familiar names start appearing among the newspaper obituaries, and occasionally the reader wonders to himself about the content and the length of his own death notice.

This is the pivotal decade, the decade for self-evaluation, for anxiety, for escapism, for accommodation, for disappearances. Forty-eight percent of the survey group vanished either at the beginning or the end of this decennium. When we add the remaining thirty-seven absentees in their forties, the full impact of decade crisis becomes clear. This raises the total number to 139 and the percentage to a startling 83.2, meaning that:

Four out of five voluntary absentees are either two years from a decade birthday or in their fifth decade or both.

At this point a careful qualification is required. A person's age has at best an indirect influence on behavior. No one does something *because* he is a certain age. Rather, because he *is* a certain age, latent tendencies are unleashed, resident doubts are exacerbated, and the person is forced to confront and resolve situations and realities that he has been attempting to avoid.

While this is clearly indicated in the statistical evidence deposited by 167 absentees, it is best demonstrated by the experience of those of us who have not disappeared. When we examine this experience objectively, we find ample illustrations of how we have instinctively confirmed or altered or reversed our life patterns during one or all of the adult Nines. In retrospect, we are provided with abundant examples of the truly important "life decisions" that we have made during these same periods—decisions about what kind of work we shall do and where, decisions about the type of goals we shall pursue and how far, decisions about our style of living, decisions about the dimensions of our expectations, even decisions about whom we do or do not wish to be married to.

None of these decisions happened on a particular weekend; there was no agenda for the questions; it was not necessarily a conscious event. The individual approaching a new decade is aware instead of a peculiar restlessness, but it usually goes unspoken, with the possible exception of an occasional silent exclamation: "My God, I'm almost thirty!" (or forty or fifty or sixty). Later, he or she may wonder from time to time what really occurred, may ask quietly how it all came about, why things worked out the way they did. There is no point in trying to remember some sort of systematic cross-examination of self. There was none. Still, at some time during the forty-eight months surrounding the decade birthday, important decisions were made, significant changes were effected.

The process is more discernible from a distance in time. One day, for example, I was trying to explain the concept of the Terrible Nines to a friend who was in the act of leaving the Episcopal Church for what he persisted in calling "civilian life." Having been educated as a sociologist, he had difficulty grasping the idea. A more direct approach seemed called for:

"Quitting the ministry is a serious step. How old are you?"

"I just turned fifty-two."

"How long ago did you make this decision?"

"I guess it's been about two years in the making."

"Now, tell me, can you recall what happened to you when you were thirty-nine?"

He thought for a moment. "I was in Korea."

"What were you doing there?"

"Well, the year before was when I had all that trouble with the bishop. You remember what that was all about. So I decided to get out of parish life, and I joined the Army as a chaplain and asked for an assignment in the Far East."

"One more question. You once told me that right after the Second World War you were some sort of executive assistant to the president of a large corporation. You said you had a promising future in business. How old were you when you threw that over and decided to become a priest?"

"I was twenty-nine."

The example of a man who changed the direction of his life at twenty-nine, the shape of his life at thirty-eight, and the form of his life at fifty-two may appear somewhat extreme, if not contrived. Yet his biographical detours are not that exceptional. Most of us have gone through remarkably similar experiences. We have encountered, each in our own way, decade crisis; we have known the excruciating anxiety that marks such periods in our lives; we have facilitated (though perhaps not as dramatically as the former priest) by making vital adjustments in our life styles. What distinguishes us from the people who facilitate by vanishing, then, is essentially the manner of resolution.

But resolution of what? In the case of voluntary absentees, we have been informed over and over again by the police and other self-appointed experts that people disappear in order to escape from bad marriages, debt, and unsuccessful job situations. This traditional notion was rejected in Chapter I as too simplistic. Rather, it was suggested that the absentee was abandoning much more than a spouse, a credit rating, and a job; what he was abandoning was, in reality, a way of life. More specifically, by the act of disappearance he was renouncing life as a card-carrying member of the broad middle class of American society.

This expanded explanation seemed indicated by the fact that the absentee was rejecting not only his status in society but also, and more significantly, society's proffered alternatives to marital, financial, and vocational problems. By discarding these alternative "solutions," the absentee strongly implies that such transparent difficulties are merely symptoms, not causes, of a more profound discontent. Hence, the conventional responses—divorce, economic retrenchment, a new or different job—are looked upon as stopgap measures at best that treat superficially and do not penetrate to the core of the problem. Thus it does not appear unreasonable to conclude that what the absentee is dissatisfied with is his general existence and not his particular situation.

Specific situations may be altered, they may be rearranged, they may even be improved; but the situation remains. A person's existence is more complicated. Existence involves basic challenges to a person's very being: it calls personal values into question; it strikes hard at the definition of life. By the extremity of his act, the absentee has admitted that he has considered these fundamental questions in some form and that the answers provided were not sufficient, at least for him. By the timing of his extreme act, he has confirmed the bitter conclusion that the realities of middle age will not and cannot sustain the limitless bright promise of youth. By the direction of his extreme act, he has demonstrated that he has somehow evaluated the price of action, the cost of inaction, and the worth of personal gain and loss—and then decided that American middle-class status did not justify the effort. The decision cannot be emphasized too strongly, since we are talking and have been talking about identity.

This conclusion is supported, more intuitively than empirically perhaps, by the examples of the voluntary absentees, their backgrounds and activities, their education and intelligence, the environmental situations they have abandoned, the scheduling of their disappearances, the mechanics of the adaptive process, and the circumstances to which they have instinctively gravitated. Yet it is not difficult to anticipate vigorous disagreement from two types of dissenters.

The first consists of the rationalists, those confident but mistaken intellectuals who cling to the theory that man is primarily a reasonable being whose dominion of intellect extends to his own life. Each individual act, therefore, is the direct result of conscious decision, just as each person, to a considerable extent, is the deliberate master of his own fate. Hence, the very illogic of an antisocial action like disappearance, coupled with the lack of concrete evidence of thoughtful premeditation, leads them to discard the possibility that flight could involve philosophic rejection.

The second and far larger group of dissenters is characterized better by pragmatic necessity than by logic. These people would frankly prefer to believe that it is practically impossible to disappear at all. Such an ostrichlike posture relieves them of any obligation to examine their own commitments and presumably permits them to concentrate on improving, rather than altering, their circumstances. Confronted with the evidence that no one is really "locked" into place, they counter with the sweeping assertion that all voluntary absentees are mentally disturbed cowards, men and women incapable of coping with the routine pressures of contemporary society. This was, for instance, the reflex reaction of that insurance-company official when he received the news that Fritz Johnson had been identified as the missing Lawrence Bader. A "modern-day schizophrenic" was his unsolicited prognosis of Bader-Johnson, and it is a denigrating opinion shared, though frequently with far less charity, by the relatives and associates and pursuers of many other absentees. To them and to everyone else who would deny the commonly held impulse to flight, the suggestion that voluntary absentees might be, in the main, rather "average" people must be considered annoying.

What will undoubtedly prove more annoying, however, is the corollary contention that these disappearances are in some way connected to fundamental flaws in the content and quality of life in these United States today. This is hardly a subject casually raised, and only a fool would venture a quick reply. To reply at all is to contemplate individual worth—and that can be a potentially devastating experience, whether the examiner is a kitchenware salesman in Ohio or an executive in New York or a lawyer in Virginia or an accountant in California or a teacher in Pennsylvania or a product manager in Illinois or a builder in Texas or a physician in New Jersey. Each is transparently a tiny cog in a vast, interconnected system that is under withering attack from every direction.

Pick up any newspaper or magazine, go to a movie, turn on the television, and the chances are excellent that someone has unburdened himself or herself of another searing criticism of the apathetic, tasteless, money-grubbing, accumulating, lip-licking middle class. The world is disintegrating, but Mr. Suburbanite (and his urban equivalent), his grimy white collar loosened, is sprawled, drink in hand, before the boob tube, watching a re-rerun of "Gunsmoke." He has returned on crowded, dirty, undependable transportation to his jerry-built home in a monotonous development from one more unproductive day at a superfluous job, to face again the unending chore of raising extra money to buy unneeded, poorly made accessories for his bored wife and spoiled children. Predictably, all of the laborsaving appliances he has purchased on credit are breaking down.

This dismal portrait does not vary much, whether its source is a pimply-faced revolutionary on the so-called New Left or an articulate, embittered black militant or an aging, disgruntled immigrant radical sponging on his American heiress wife. The theme is alienation, and it all began—to

hear them tell it—with the industrial revolution and enclosure, which drove our bucolic ancestors away from the
glorious land and beloved nature into the polluted cities and
onto dreary assembly lines. Technology increased produc-
tivity, thereby expanding the market and creating a need for
more and more consumers and then a demand for anticipated
revenue or credit spending. Wages were increased, commerce-
oriented public education was instituted, work schedules
were reduced, job functions were divided and diluted, which
produced more new positions—all to the purpose of enlarging
the numbers of customers, endowing them with acquisitive
appetites, and committing them to a philosophy of bourgeois
success.

The price tag for this incredible commercial transformation, according to these contemporary Cassandras, is beyond
reckoning. In the process of reconstituting a primarily urban
civilization, man has despoiled the countryside, recklessly
exploited the earth's resources, poisoned its environment,
and dehumanized himself. By establishing wealth and pos-
sessions as the hallmarks of achievement, he has ruthlessly
destroyed all the genuine accomplishments of human community. The material has overwhelmed the spiritual. Science
and technology, elevated along with business to the level of
religion, have demolished the mansion of God and erected in
its stead an automated temple where man, classified now in
binary terms, is permitted to worship the new cybernetic
credo: "DO NOT FOLD, BEND, OR SPINDLE."

It is thus easy to understand, these critics conclude with
predictable monotony, why members of the middle class lead
empty, sterile lives on a treadmill of debt and planned ob-
solescence, hypocritically spouting by rote to their bewil-
dered offspring the remnants of the Protestant ethic: work,
save, improve. What function could such oppressed automa-
tons serve, unless it be to prepare another generation for
another tedious round of marital discord, vocational disillu-
sionment, and capricious consumption, consumption, con-

290 "If I had it to do over again . . ."

sumption? No wonder their children rebel, and no wonder their parents cannot comprehend.

Hardly any purpose would be served here by adding anything to this self-defeating dialogue of disaffection, beyond the general observation that there is no lack of derogatory "evidence" in support of such pessimism. Indeed, at times it would appear that half the population is engaged in gathering statistics to prove the unworthiness of the other half. To a considerable extent they have succeeded. Figures are readily available for everything imaginable: divorce, alcoholism, drug addiction, white-collar crime, credit expenditures, building starts, used-car sales, population growth, mental illness, unmarried mothers, cardiac arrests, venereal disease, new bishops, and cavities. Like the average height of the American male, all these assorted social malefactions seem on the increase (with the possible exception of cavities, which probably just goes to prove that no society can be all bad). Obviously, such statistics require a minimum of manipulation and a maximum of repetition to convert them into damning demonstrations of, as the saying goes, the deterioration of the fabric of American life.

Not that there is much point in trying to argue with the government's computers. We are literally surrounded by and bombarded with visible testimony to the quality and quantity of our society; our senses perceive all the information necessary. We do not need to be informed, for instance, by the United States Department of Labor that white-collar employment now exceeds blue-collar, that the clerks outnumber the producers; one glance at that department's office staff in Washington or the accounting section of any insurance company suffices. The portentous calculations of the demographers add nothing to our knowledge of urban-suburban sprawl, gleaned from our car windows as we inch along high-speed turnpikes. Nor can the Census Bureau surprise us with anything that we have not already learned in a crowded subway or shopping center or national park campsite.

The tone and texture of our daily lives does not lend itself so readily to numerical analysis, and yet it is equally accessible. An evening of televised commercial messages, irritatingly disguised as "pauses for station identification" and all of them universal affronts to common sense, reveals more than we need to know about our society's discovery that it is more profitable to introduce "new" products than to improve old ones. Affluence and waste are adequately symbolized by those expensive "busy boxes" that blink purposelessly on and on until the batteries expire and cannot be restored. Facts and figures could not begin to describe the defeat and frustration that mar the temper of middle-class marriage and home life. The complete story is written unwittingly, at unguarded moments, across the face of the homeward commuter, just as it is spelled out by the frenetic efforts of so many housewives to become involved in "meaningful engagement" with the momentous issues of the day.

Well, why deny it? Most of us, the vast majority, are underemployed at relatively insignificant tasks, the function of which eludes us and the value of which is negligible. We married strangers, as quickly as possible, and have subsequently grown in different directions or not at all. We have packed our surroundings with merchandise of dubious worth, and adopted unexciting modes of living that suffer chiefly from being neither degrading nor elevating. Mediocrity has enveloped every aspect of society and indicts us daily—not because we tolerate it, which we do, but because we have become almost immune to it. Unlike Wallace Stevens' old sailor, drunk and asleep in his boots with his Technicolor fantasies, we dream of the commonplace, in black and white. We spend annually more on alcoholic beverages and tobacco than on education. We subscribe to the *Reader's Digest.*

But assuming that the worst that can be said specifically about the morals, manners, and mores of the American middle class is absolutely true, which it is assuredly not, what then might be the flaws in this sweeping, disparaging criticism? Numerous possibilities come to mind, though one seems paramount: the lack of perspective.

To say, and many have, that the great mass of people in this country today lead mean, narrow, selfish, mediocre lives

292 "If I had it to do over again . . ."

is to seriously imply that the vast majority of men and
women in this or any other society formerly led lives that
were not mean and narrow and selfish and mediocre. To
submit for intelligent consideration the notion that, at some
indeterminate time in the immediate past, the bulk of the
population was more happily married or more gainfully employed is as indefensible as that fatuous myth about the
noble savage. And to insist that the conversion of society
from agricultural to industrial to consumer-oriented has
somehow created for the first time in history a race of egoistic
collectors of wealth and material goods is to ignore the insightful contributions of sociohistorical research for the past
century.

The past simply cannot be compared to the present, and to
attempt such evaluation of today in terms of imagined yester-
days is to risk exposure as an idiot or an idealist or both.
There is really only one generalization that may be made
confidently about the past, and that is that it was different.
One of the significant differences, it would seem, was the
middle class itself. Just a few decades ago, it truly constituted
a class in the middle. It was dwarfed by the low-income, blue-
collar group; it was openly patronized by a self-ordained
landed aristocracy; its complexion was strongly entrepreneurial and managerial. For most of America, the middle class
was a cherished and attainable goal, the main installment on
this nation's promise of opportunity. The middle class recognized its vital role and responded with zest and certainty. It
set the tempo for the country, prescribed attitudes and priorities, waved the flag, and gathered every Thursday for a
starchy lunch at a local hotel. As a cohesive class, it possessed
a decided tendency toward boosterism and a habit of closing
ranks to cover any excesses on the part of the membership.
But its achievements were many, and the measure of its belief
in itself was that the middle class retained its pervasive and
infectious sense of optimism even after the stock market
crashed.

That optimism was not entirely misplaced. It was based on

unswerving devotion to a democratic politic and a (relatively) free-enterprise system that would expand and perpetuate itself through the built-in expedient of raising the living standards and expectations of its various parts. With some notable exceptions that will undoubtedly be rectified or, more likely, alleviated by the end of the century, the mechanism has worked to an astounding degree. Today it is apparent that almost eighty percent of the population has made it at least into the lower echelons of the middle class. The disparity between the top and the bottom of the middle class is enormous, to be sure. But this distance is primarily an educational and financial measurement; philosophically, such differences are actually minute. The middle-class mentality, with its positive reverence for property and propriety, has triumphed. In the process, we have in this country effectively wiped out all but a few minor (though expensive) vestiges of class distinction.

The blurring of class lines is hardly the same as having a classless society, which, if not impractical in concept, is certainly boring in prospect. What is instead indicated is the transformation of a mercantile class that was truly "in the middle" into a massive, dominant class that remains in the middle only to the extent that it bridges the huge chasm from extreme poverty to tremendous wealth. Politically, this transformation might be viewed as an impressive demonstration of social mobility; socially, as the result of the leveling processes of democracy; economically, as a justification of sorts of laissez-faire capitalism. But psychologically, the disappearance of the sense and appearance of class distinction may be described as the loss of a very important identity crutch, one of the conscious devices used by man to determine, if not who he is, then at least who he is not.

Ultimately, inevitably, logically, it all revolves around identity. Every question that man directs at himself, his accomplishments, his direction, his goals, his convictions, is part of a continuous effort to affirm personal identity. What have I done? What am I doing? Where have I been? Where am I going? How successful or unsuccessful am I? What do I want? How do I get it? Why do I want it? Why should I want it? What does it mean? These queries and a hundred like them dissolve into one essential inquiry: Who am I?

In the sense that individual identity is the sum total of personal belief, there can be no more important inquiry. We are what we think we are, what we do, and how well the world thinks we do it, and our entire lives could accurately be defined as an unending pursuit of that vital knowledge. Identity is the root factor in all human equations, whether we are probing the nature of social sterility or conformity or marital discord or anxiety or traditional values or the repeated failure of middle age to sustain the promising ideals of youth. It is an intensely subjective experience, yes. But do we really, at this moment in history, have a viable alternative?

Identity is easier to describe than to analyze. The first clue we are offered is that identity has little to do with name. Unless a hereditary significance is attached or some well-known achievement is implied, a name no longer has any relationship—as it was originally intended to—to function or ancestry. Hence we instinctively augment our names, upon introduction, with vocational or corporate or geographical situations. We do so because we sense our opponent's need to know *whom* he is meeting; in all but a few instances, the name alone is of little aid. Moreover, we participate in these annoying identity contests in the vague hope that our response will elicit more information from the other person. As games go, this is surely a trifling one; simultaneously, it is one of the most crucial games a man is required to play, since his own opinion of himself is dependent to a startling degree on society's opinion of him.

This collective judgment by society accounts for the more tenuous half of personal identity, the half that we may as well call status. Status is what we are about daily. It consists of the operational activities of life, which change sometimes from hour to hour and invariably from year to year. Status represents the visible, external, conscious aspects of identity—the type of work we do, our progress and achievements on the job, our social standing and prospects, where we live, how we live, whom we married, the company we keep, the activities we are involved with, the causes we support, the views we espouse. Typically, we are not so much whom we know as we are whom we are known by. Our individual circumstances, then, are direct and constant reminders of our special identity. As a result, the strength of our identity depends to a considerable degree upon our confidence in these circumstances.

The other half of identity could be loosely described as faith. Faith is the bedrock of identity, and it is composed of all the absolutes in our lives. What makes this instinctual aspect of identity so important is the stabilizing effect it can have on a faltering personality during periods of serious fluctuation in status. Fortunately or unfortunately, man has never been endowed with many absolutes, most of which tend to be inherited rather than revealed. Commonly we assign names like God and Country and Institution and Race (which is what Yale used to mean) to these absolutes, and it is tempting to approach them in those forms. But in a larger sense, they are each extensions of man's historic self-love, of his continuing efforts to justify his existence—and thus reaffirm his fundamental identity—by proving his uniqueness. By and large, it has proved and is proving a losing effort, for much the same reason that, as Mark Twain observed, "We have not the reverent feeling for the rainbow that the savage has, because we know how it is made. We have lost as much as we have gained by prying into that matter."

Briefly, man's ego has suffered three mighty blows in the past four centuries. The first was struck by Copernicus, with his confounding theory that the earth was not the center of the universe but a dust mote in some celestial infinity. It would not be much of an exaggeration to suggest that theology has never quite recovered from this spatial rabbit punch. Darwin administered the second one, in Freud's opinion and phraseology, by robbing "man of his peculiar privilege of having been specially created, and relegated him to a descent from the animal world." Freud then proceeded to reason, somewhat immodestly but probably correctly, that his own revelatory investigations into the unconscious and subsequent discovery that man was not, in effect, "even the master of his own house" constituted a third shock of devastating proportions.

Some physicists, of course, will want to dispute whether Copernicus or Galileo or even Ptolemy should be properly credited with realigning the cosmos. It does not matter. Somebody did it, and man, no longer unique, would not again be as assured of the meaningful division of heaven and earth and his place in both. That his current existence is largely a genetic accident and that he is ruled to a considerable extent by hereditary instincts he does not understand are of secondary importance compared to his irreparable loss of divinity, of special identity. Thus, in theory and general outline, the consuming impact of such ego-shattering experiences on human mythology cannot be overestimated.

No myth has suffered more by all this than religion. In a constantly changing world, religion has made and continues to make the diminishing error of emulating the immutability of the Creator. God may indeed be immutable, despite, as Anatole France complained, the conflicting testimony of the Old and New Testaments, but religion is manifestly not so, and its obstinate pretense adds daily to its growing irrelevance. The real loser, however, is not the tax-exempt church, which will probably survive for its architecture and music, but man, who suddenly finds himself deprived of his major and traditional source of guilt.

Guilt is more important to mental health than we sometimes realize. Without a personal concept of sin and the implied elements of expiation and redemption and damnation and salvation, what the hell is the whole point to life? Earlier generations did not have the answer either, but they possessed an unshakable alternative, and that was religion. For them, God or Jehovah or Yahweh was not so much a refuge as He was an absolute assurance. One of the things that He assured them of, beside their unique situation in His firmament, was something after death which would explain and perhaps justify all the bewildering, painful mysteries of this cruel world. Hence, the vicissitudes of daily existence—hardship and disease and famine and success—could not disturb this faith, which was a fundamental part of their identity.

That modern man lacks such specific assurances would seem undeniable. One by one, the instinctive elements of our individual identities—those articles of faith upon which man has unconsciously relied for centuries to remind him of his place and to assure him of his position—have deteriorated and disintegrated. These vital items of absolute knowledge have not been replaced by the forces that invalidated them. The role of science, in this instance, has been to explain and expose, not to substitute; what man has lost from prying into the matter of matter, he has lost, period. In the process and as a result, man has been required more and more to reconstruct his personal identity almost entirely in terms of his conscious status, which, in this country today, means primarily his membership in the amorphous middle class.

The peril in such a procedure is implicit. Status, by definition, is a relative value judgment. It is subject to whim and to fashion, vulnerable to external events and to age. We understand that what is meritorious at one stage of our lives to be and to do and to have and to expect will be considered below average, even condemnable, at another. We sense at an early age that much of what we hold dear then will more than likely seem shallow and insignificant later on, even though we anticipate that afterwards we will marvel at our naïveté and deplore our lack of conviction at the crucial junctures. The risk of depending upon such transparent and transitory indications of character is immense. We know that. We also comprehend that, with few if any absolutes to fall back on, there is no longer much of a personal choice. We are either satisfied with what we are—or else.

Did Larry Bader, for example, arrive at a similar conclusion sometime prior to his sudden disappearance on May 15, 1957? Did he take some sort of personal survey of his immediate circumstances and prospects at the age of thirty and discover, to his dismay, that his life had become, in Wilson Follett's plaintive metaphor, "unbearably like a promissory note that is perpetually renewed"? Did he become convinced, as the diarist was, that he had allowed himself to be enmeshed in basically meaningless activity? Did he hear at the end, as Sherwood Anderson heard, the mocking laughter within himself, and did he finally determine, as did Anderson, to go out of a door in search of a stronger identity?

It is really not difficult to evoke a certain empathy for Bader at that decisive moment. Not when we reconsider his plight in outline. As the youngest son of a successful dentist, he had been raised in a comfortable, carefree middle-class environment, encouraged to pursue pleasurable interests. He was not a good student, but his academic problems consisted mainly of a pronounced lack of motivation, not a narrowness of intellect; he was much too involved in more exciting activities. By the time he reached his junior year in high school, the Second World War was in progress. As soon as he turned eighteen, he dropped out and joined up, but the shooting ended before he could get overseas.

Back home in Akron, the nineteen-year-old "veteran" completed high school and matriculated at the local university. He did so more or less intuitively; such a course was expected by his kind of family. He quickly flunked out, again not because he could not do the work but because he was too busy doing more interesting things. It must have been a lark. Working by day in the family restaurant or selling something or other off a truck; at night and on weekends, dates with pretty girls, parties, outings, hunting and fishing trips. Finally, one girl in particular, who had become a woman and who then became his wife and the mother of their children.

A man wants to provide, has been conditioned to provide, for his family. The new job, a grueling sales assignment peddling kitchenware on commission, a job that placed on him the burden of filing his income tax, promised the additional finances that would be needed to pay for the new babies. And the new car. And the new house. And the new . . . well, the rest of the necessities of routine life in the middle class.

It happens so gradually, so naturally, so effortlessly, that even a few years after the fact we have trouble reconstructing any simple chain of events. One thing led to another, and another, and another, until one morning we awake to find that we have entered a new decade, that we are engaged in work that does not really interest us, that the family is expecting another child, that we have accumulated a large mortgage and more creditors than debtors, that our lives have unaccountably assumed shapes we never imagined and directions we never intended.

It is enough to make a person wonder, frankly and out loud, just how did it all come about, how in the world did he or she become that particular person, and, more importantly, whether this is the kind of person that this man or that woman wants to be. The questions contain a paramount necessity. For man will still make any sacrifice, including his life if needed, in defense of identity—provided he is convinced that that identity is worth saving. When he is not, he is quite capable of doing something desperate, such as departing in search of a different, more viable identity. Often, depending to a great extent on how young and flexible the person is, this can be done within the limits of our society's accepted guidelines. He can do this, with the active acquiescence of his family, by altering his vocation, his style of living, his purpose, and, most of all, his special status in the community.

Society obviously prefers it that way, for society is a meticulous, self-conscious organism, with a fetish for knowing constantly its exact size and composition. At regular intervals, it counts heads. Between, it keeps careful watch on the comings and goings of its diverse parts, of births and immigrations and migrations and emigrations and deaths. Nevertheless, the bureaucracy is not infallible, and from time to time, at unexpected places, people casting thin shadows slip unnoticed through the coroner's filing system.

These vanished people are the voluntary absent.

For decades they obeyed the rules and regulations, trying, with varying degrees of success, to do what they felt was expected of them. Initially their inculcated expectations were high and gilded with bright promise. They did what they were told, and told themselves that it would all work out all right in the end. But as time passed, their optimism gave way to despair, their identity was challenged, their confidence badly crippled. At this anxious moment—their departure point—these men and women, who are so much like the rest of us, faced the modern dilemma of continuing to exist with a sense of helplessness in an indifferent world lacking transcendent meaning.

"Maybe I will," they replied, as Lawrence J. Bader did that final fateful day, "and maybe I won't."

Suddenly they were gone.

Acknowledgments

We live in an incredibly free society—a vast and impersonal system in which individual flight is demonstrably feasible. We move about and alter the shape of our lives virtually unimpeded by any government, and the reassuring proof of this consists partly of these singular people who—*primarily because our society has placed a historic premium on personal privacy*—can and do disappear, change their names, and achieve fragmentary fulfillment of that universal wish "to do it all over again. . . ."

This reassuring reality, however, posed a constant dilemma. In order to show that people could disappear in our society, it was necessary to overcome partially the protective mechanisms and procedures that made such mobility possible. The extent to which I succeeded in this is primarily the result of the efforts of a small group of men who accepted my purpose, who shared my anxious curiosity about the phenomenon, and who became willing accomplices in trust. Their contributions were crucial.

Here a distinction must be made. For the tenacious researcher, there exists no shortage of factual material. "Facts," however, are either accurate or inaccurate and maintain only a marginal relationship with truth. I could not have relied on much of this information had it not been for the confidential background data supplied by my anonymous colleagues, the majority of whom are employed by insurance companies. For their vocational protection, these men must stay nameless and, I hasten to add, blameless. I shall repay my overwhelming debt to them in a less conspicuous way.

301

Not that I could begin to acknowledge adequately by name those whose encouraging assistance exceeded my demands and surpassed my expectations. Most authors conclude with a recognition of their wife's patience and understanding support. The nature of my alienated subject and the peculiar implications of its potential applications impel me to *begin* with Martha, who has endured and, I earnestly pray, will. Invaluable aid is herewith appreciated from numerous editorial, business, and government contacts across the country. My special gratitude is extended to Robert W. Waldron of the Institute of Life Insurance; Robert Giles, assistant to the executive editor of the Akron *Beacon Journal*; Valerie Vondermuhll of Time-Life Editorial Services; Ronald J. Semple, managing editor of the Billings (Mont.) *Gazette*; Captain Joseph Lynch and Lieutenant William Morkan of the New York City Missing Persons Bureau; Charles J. Wellner, editor of the Lockport (N.Y.) *Union Sun & Journal*; Lieutenant W. H. Porter of the California Highway Patrol; Edward O'Dea, managing editor of the *Daily Hampshire Gazette* in Northampton, Mass.; William E. Keller of the Illinois State Historical Library in Springfield; Howard Tedder of the Trenton (N.J.) *Times*; and Police Chief Don R. Derning of Winnetka, Ill.

I would also like to thank Charles B. Robinson; U.S. Representative Cornelius E. Gallagher (D.-N.J.); Helen Waverly Adessa; Eugene and Elna Reiss; Roberta T. Waldman; New Jersey Assemblyman David Friedland; Robert N. Sanders; N.J. Superior Court Judge T. James Tumulty; Lorraine Stewart Fiske; Drs. Dickson Dunlap and Lee C. Bevilacqua; Joan B. Brown; and my friend and colleague, E. M. Halliday, whose generous review improved this manuscript.

R.S.G.

Notes and Sources

Hundreds of newspapermen, magazine writers, and book authors have indirectly assisted me in the research and preparation of this volume. The bulk of the factual material has been extracted from their scattered reports, the most important of which are listed by publication and date.

Chapter I

The biographical material on Wakefield, including his real and assumed names, was furnished by the insurance company that located him, and was then changed by prearrangement to disguise completely both of the man's identities. The Hano case, however, consists of a combination of newspaper stories about his two disappearances and the investigation conducted by the Dallas Police Department. That Texas agency is understandably sensitive about its dealings with the press and officially refuses to discuss the case; nevertheless, if it will recheck its own information in the Hano file, No. OT-29101, it will find several serious errors of fact. Hawthorne's short story, "Wakefield," which is recommended reading for anyone interested in the metaphysical aspects of voluntary absenteeism, can be found in any edition of his book, *Twice-Told Tales*.

Other sources:

The New York Times, February 28, 1956.
New York *Daily News*, January 18, 1956.
New York *Mirror*, January 18, 1956.

Chapter II

The tremendous outburst of publicity about the Bader-Johnson case, while invaluable to the research of this book, created numerous problems involving the accuracy of the information. Whenever possible, the author has attempted to recheck the apparent contradictions in the various news reports. In other instances, these discrepancies have been resolved on the basis of the general reliability of one source over another.

Other sources:

New York *Sunday News,* February 21, 1965.
Life, March 5, 1965.
Newsweek, February 22, 1965.
Chicago *Tribune,* February 7, 1965.
United Press International, February 13, 1965.
Akron *Beacon Journal,* May 18, 1957; February 8, 11, 12, 13, and 15, 1965.
Omaha *World-Herald,* August 11 and December 8, 1963; February 12, 1965.
Omaha *Sun,* October 12, 1962.

Chapter III

Too many books have already been written on "celebrity missing persons" such as Judge Crater, Dorothy Arnold, *et al.* One of the more interesting surveys is *They Never Came Back,* by Allen Churchill (New York: Doubleday, 1960). The government statistics were supplied by the agencies named, either in material furnished to the Special House Subcommittee on Invasion of Privacy or in correspondence with the author.

Other sources:

Akron *Beacon Journal,* February 19, 1965.
Collier's, November 21, 1925.
Daniel M. Eisenberg, as told to John Nicholas Beffel, *I Find the Missing* (New York: Farrar & Rinehart, Inc., 1938).
Life, April 14, 1952.
Reader's Digest, May 1961.

Charlotte (N.C.) *News,* February 11, 1965.
Salt Lake City *Times,* July 8, 1966.
The Wall Street Journal, October 10, 1966.
New York *World Journal Tribune,* January 19, 1967.

Chapter IV

San Francisco *Chronicle,* July 10, 13, and 15, 1966.
Jacksonville (Ill.) *Journal,* April 15, 17, and 18, 1959; April 6, 1960.
Northampton, Mass., *Daily Hampshire Gazette,* April 15, 16, and 17, 1959.
New York *Daily News,* October 5, 1963.
Lockport (N.Y.) *Union Sun & Journal,* June 9, 1941; September 1, 1946; March 29, 1948; February 1, 1954; and October 5, 1963.
Saturday Evening Post, March 4, 1950.
Jersey Journal, July 31 and August 8, 1961.
Monterey (Calif.) *Peninsula Herald,* October 8, 1956.
Boston *Globe,* July 13, 1966.
San Francisco *Examiner,* July 6, 8, and 14, 1966.
Los Angeles *Times,* August 1, 1966.
San Jose *Mercury,* July 8, 10, and 11, 1966.
San Jose *News,* July 7 and 13, 1966.
Tucson *Citizen,* August 12, 1966.
Tucson *Star,* August 24, 1966.

Chapter V

To reveal how this unusual personal document came to my attention or to describe the outcome of its author's three-year hiatus from the work force would seriously compromise the anonymity of the man whose current whereabouts and activities are still unknown to many of his former friends and associates.

Chapter VI

Ted Robinson, Jr., "How to Disappear," *Harper's,* March 1952.
The New York Times, July 21, 1966.
Cleveland *Plain Dealer,* September 21, 1946.

Esquire, October 1942.

New York *Daily News,* February 15, 1962.

Syracuse *Herald-Journal,* February 15, 1962.

New York *World-Telegram,* February 16, 1962.

Detroit *Free Press,* February 16, 1962.

Syracuse *Post-Standard,* June 28, 1958.

The Associated Press, February 15, 1962.

San Francisco *Chronicle,* February 15, 1962.

Chapter VII

Syracuse *Herald-Journal,* February 15, 1962.

Al Hirshberg, "The Long Search of Laurie Van Buren," *Good Housekeeping,* July 1963.

Pittsburgh *Post-Gazette,* October 20, 1960.

Pittsburgh *Press,* July 9, 1963.

The New York Times, March 10, 1965.

Time, December 7, 1953.

Omaha *Sun* feature, 1962.

Robert Crichton, *The Great Impostor* (New York: Random House, 1959).

Chapter VIII

The identity of the anonymous writer of "To a Daughter, One Year Lost" was not disclosed by the *Atlantic,* nor is it published for the first time here. Rather, it was revealed in *Barbara: The Unconscious Autobiography of a Child Genius,* edited by Harold Grier McCurdy, in collaboration with Helen Follett (Chapel Hill: University of North Carolina Press, 1966).

Other Sources:

Akron *Beacon Journal,* March 5, 1965.

Gadsden (Ala.) *Times,* September 26, 1966.

Mansfield (Ohio) *News Journal,* July 3 and October 16, 1966.

Life, April 14, 1952.

Atlantic, May 1941.

Chapter IX

The information concerning the operation of commercial credit bureaus was taken largely from the printed testimony of the hearings conducted by the Special House Subcommittee on Invasion of Privacy on March 12, 13, and 14, 1968. For readers who wish to explore an even more frightening threat to the privacy of every American, I recommend the subcommittee's July 1966 report on the Bureau of the Budget's proposal to establish a computerized National Data Center.

Other sources:

The New York Times, July 10, 1959, and September 6, 1963.

Asbury Park (N.J.) *Press,* August 20, 1966.

Trenton (N.J.) *Times,* September 11 and December 18, 1966; May 24, 1967.

Point Pleasant (N.J.) *Leader,* August 25, 1966.

St. Petersburg (Fla.) *Times,* August 23, 1966.

New York *Post,* August 24, 1966.

Myron Brenton, *The Privacy Invaders* (New York: Coward-McCann, 1964).

Vance Packard, *The Naked Society* (New York: David McKay, 1964).

Chapter X

Akron *Beacon Journal,* February 12, 1965.

New York *Daily News,* February 21 and March 9, 1965; January 6, 1967.

New York *Herald Tribune,* November 7, 1953.

Time, December 7, 1953.

Nashville *Tennessean,* November 5 and 26, 1953.

United Press, November 27, 1953; September 27, 1954.

The New York Times, April 28, 1956; March 10, 1965; January 6, 1967; May 31, 1967.

The Associated Press, January 6, 1967.

Troy (N.Y.) *Record,* July 19, 21, and 23, 1960; May 2, 1962; July 23, 1966.

Chapter XI

The compilation of various state requirements for presumptive declarations of death was made in 1950 by a New York attorney, Franz Fraenkel, for his booklet, *Missing Persons* (Dobbs Ferry, N.Y.: Oceana Publications, Legal Almanac Series No. 18, 1950).

Unless the legal requirement is qualified by a more recent date, it therefore may not reflect subsequent statutory revisions.

Other sources:

> Akron *Beacon Journal,* February 14, 1965.
> New York *Daily News,* February 21, 1965.
> W. Calvin Wells, Jr., "When the Insured Disappears," *Mississippi Law Journal,* Vol. 35.
> William P. Hindman, Jr., "The Presumption Against Suicide in Disappearance Cases," *The Insurance Law Journal,* No. 514, November 1965.
> *The New York Times,* September 29, 1959.
> *Jacqueline Barber* v. *John Hancock Insurance Co.,* 61 Civil 219, U.S. District Court, Southern District of New York.
> Newark (N.J.) *Star Ledger,* July 2, 1967.

Chapter XII

The descriptions of the electrochemical composition of the human mind and the discussion of memory disorders are based primarily on material from *Modern Clinical Psychiatry,* by Arthur Noyes and Laurence Kolb (Philadelphia: W. B. Saunders Co., 1958) ; "That Odd Chemical Complex, The Human Mind," by Isaac Asimov, *The New York Times Magazine,* July 3, 1966; and "Inside the Molecules of the Mind," by Lawrence Lessing, *Fortune,* July 1966.

Other sources:

> Omaha *Evening World-Herald,* February 12 and March 5, 1965.
> New York *Post,* May 13, 1966.
> Chicago *Tribune,* February 8, 9, and 10, 1965.
> Akron *Beacon Journal,* February 13 and 19, 1965.
> *Life,* March 5, 1965.
> New York *Daily News,* February 21 and 23, 1965.
> New York *Herald Tribune,* February 9, 1965.
> United Press International, February 12, 1965.
> *Collier's,* November 21, 1925.
> Kansas City *Times,* August 10 and 11, 1951; November 25, 1954; and March 17, 1955.

Kansas City *Morning Times,* August 13, 1951.
Kansas City *Evening Star,* August 13, 1951.
Columbia *Missourian,* March 26, 1953.

Chapter XIII

The copyrighted interview with Mrs. Bader was conducted by the Akron *Beacon Journal*'s city editor, Bruce McIntyre, who maintained an active and perceptive interest in the Bader-Johnson story from start to finish. I would also like to cite the excellent reportage of two other *Beacon Journal* writers, Larry Fields and David Meeker, and the comprehensive coverage provided by Christine Kirk of the New York *Daily News* and David Smothers of United Press International.

Other sources:

Life, March 5, 1965.
The New York Times, March 9 and 10, 1965.
Akron *Beacon Journal,* February 14, March 25, and September 1, 1965; and February 19, 1966.
Troy (N.Y.) *Record,* July 23, 1960; March 12 and July 5, 1965; and July 23, 1966.
United Press International, February 13, 1965.
Fidelity & Deposit Co. of Maryland v. *Mary Lou Bader,* from pretrial briefs filed with the Summit County (Ohio) Common Pleas Court (pending).

Chapter XIV

Sherwood Anderson may not have bothered to record his experiences as a voluntary absentee, but few authors can begin to match the insightful intensity which the author brings to his discussion of the shared impulse to flight in *Sherwood Anderson's Memoirs: A Critical Edition,* by Ray Lewis White (Chapel Hill: University of North Carolina Press, 1969).

Other sources:

Omaha *Morning World-Herald,* September 17 and 20, 1966.
Omaha *Evening World-Herald,* February 12, September 16, 17, 22, and 29, October 11, 1966.

Sherwood Anderson, *Dark Laughter* (New York: Boni & Liveright, 1925).

Irving Howe, *Sherwood Anderson,* The American Men of Letters Series (New York: William Sloane Associates, 1951).

The Cleveland *Leader,* December 2, 1912.

Sherwood Anderson, *A Story Teller's Story* (New York: Grove Press, 1958). Copyright renewed 1951 by Eleanor Copehaver Anderson.

Sherwood Anderson, *Sherwood Anderson's Memoirs* (New York: Harcourt, Brace and Company, 1942). A new edition entitled *Sherwood Anderson's Memoirs: A Critical Edition* was published in 1969 by The University of North Carolina Press.

Life, March 5, 1965.

The New York Times, May 21 and September 17, 1966.

Akron *Beacon Journal,* September 4, 16, and 17, 1966.

Lawrence (Mass.) *Eagle-Tribune,* September 17, 1966.

Mary Lou Bader v. *New York Life,* Summit County (Ohio) Common Pleas Court, filed August 3, 1966 (pending).

Fidelity & Deposit Co. of Maryland v. *Mary Lou Bader,* Summit County (Ohio) Common Pleas Court, filed June 7, 1966 (pending).

Chapter XV

The principal sources for the statistical profile were the investigative files of life-insurance claims departments. In many instances, the author was granted supervised access to the material; otherwise, depersonalized data were obtained from the case folders by questioning a company representative. Less than fifteen percent of the cases were supplied by the police and three private detective agencies, who were generally more enthusiastic about cooperating than the insurance industry but far less helpful.

Index